Working with Relational Trauma in Schools

also in the Guides to Working with Relational Trauma Using DDP series

Working with Relational Trauma in Social Care and Child Protection
Andrew Lister, Alison Keith and Kim S. Golding
Foreword by Dan Hughes
ISBN 978 1 78775 274 0
eISBN 978 1 78775 275 7

also by Kim S. Golding

Everyday Parenting with Security and Love
Using PACE to Provide Foundations for Attachment
Kim S. Golding
Illustrated by Alex Barrett
Foreword by Dan Hughes
ISBN 978 1 78592 115 5
eISBN 978 1 78450 384 0

Observing Children with Attachment Difficulties in Preschool Settings
A Tool for Identifying and Supporting Emotional and Social Difficulties
Kim S. Golding, Jane Fain, Ann Frost, Sian Templeton and Eleanor Durrant
ISBN 978 1 84905 337 2
eISBN 978 0 85700 676 9

Observing Children with Attachment Difficulties in School
A Tool for Identifying and Supporting Emotional and
Social Difficulties in Children Aged 5–11
Kim S. Golding, Jane Fain, Ann Frost, Cathy Mills, Helen Worrall,
Netty Roberts, Eleanor Durrant and Sian Templeton
ISBN 978 1 84905 336 5
eISBN 978 0 85700 675 2

Observing Adolescents with Attachment Difficulties in Educational Settings
A Tool for Identifying and Supporting Emotional and
Social Difficulties in Young People Aged 11–16
Kim S. Golding, Mary T. Turner, Helen Worrall, Jennifer Roberts and Ann E. Cadman
ISBN 978 1 84905 617 5
eISBN 978 1 78450 174 7

A Tiny Spark of Hope
Healing Childhood Trauma in Adulthood
Kim S. Golding and Alexia Jones
ISBN 978 1 78775 431 7
eISBN 978 1 78775 432 4

Working with Relational Trauma in Schools

AN EDUCATOR'S GUIDE TO USING DYADIC DEVELOPMENTAL PRACTICE

Kim S. Golding, Sian Phillips
and Louise Michelle Bombèr

Jessica Kingsley Publishers
London and Philadelphia

First published in Great Britain in 2021 by Jessica Kingsley Publishers
An Hachette Company

2

A CIP catalogue record for this title is available from the
British Library and the Library of Congress

ISBN 978 1 78775 219 1
eISBN 978 1 78775 220 7

Printed and bound in Great Britain by Clays Ltd

Jessica Kingsley Publishers' policy is to use papers that are natural, renewable and recyclable products and made from wood grown in sustainable forests. The logging and manufacturing processes are expected to conform to the environmental regulations of the country of origin.

Jessica Kingsley Publishers
Carmelite House
50 Victoria Embankment
London EC4Y 0DZ

www.jkp.com

Dedicated to all the brave young people
who turn up for school not knowing if they
will actually be truly met and known.

Contents

Series Editor's Foreword

KIM S. GOLDING

This book is part of a series exploring the application of Dyadic Developmental Psychotherapy (DDP), parenting and practice in different settings and with different populations. Written by experienced DDP clinicians, these books provide an up-to-date exploration of how DDP is being applied, and look to the future to see what might be possible as we continue to discover how DDP can facilitate open and engaged, emotionally connected relationships, supporting children and young people with experience of developmental trauma to heal and grow emotionally.

In this volume, I am joined by Sian Phillips and Louise Michelle Bombèr to explore DDP within education. We consider why a relational model of intervention like DDP is useful for the teams supporting individual pupils in education settings. We reflect on how this can assist educators to help pupils with experience of developmental trauma (referred to as vulnerable pupils) get the support they need to grow and develop emotionally, socially and educationally. We drew our inspiration from my book *Everyday Parenting with Security and Love* (Golding, 2017). This is informed by Sian and Louise's practical experience in supporting schools to provide attachment-aware and trauma-informed and responsive environments within which all pupils will thrive and vulnerable pupils will get the support they need.

We explore how the same DDP principles that can successfully inform parenting can be readily adapted to the teaching and support of pupils at all levels of their schooling. This rests on an understanding of the theories of attachment and intersubjectivity and the growing field of neuroscience, which emphasize the central role that relationship has in helping pupils feel safe and supported enough to engage in education.

Relational support involves the educators remaining open and engaged to the pupils so that they can emotionally connect with them using the attitude of PACE (playfulness, acceptance, curiosity and empathy).

From this relational base, and with adults' support, pupils can be helped to attain emotional regulation and to make sense of their experience. This provides a foundation from which behaviour support can be provided, helping the pupils reach the calm and curious states needed for learning. The book ends by exploring the importance of self-understanding and support for the educators, helping them to have the emotional resilience to take the often long and slow roads that vulnerable pupils need.

A word about culture

We are white privileged women living in England and Canada. This book will be infused with the values that we have internalized from our cultures. We respect, however, that these may be different within other cultures and anticipate that each of you will have different cultural experiences and values. We do believe that the power of connection is universal among human beings. Much of what we are writing will be helpful to educators of all cultures. We invite you to reflect on your own cultural beliefs and values; how they fit with the importance of relationships and how they are communicated.

Acknowledgements

I am so pleased to have been able to start this series of Dyadic Developmental Practice guides with a focus on education. School can be a transforming experience for children, and it is deeply sad when this opportunity is missed. I want to acknowledge all the teachers and support staff I have worked with over the years. They have taught me much about supporting children in school and helped me to understand the challenges of trying to implement a DDP approach in educational environments. As well as being the series editor, I have had the privilege of being a co-author on this guide. It has been a pleasure to work alongside Louise and Sian, whose knowledge and wisdom have enhanced this book greatly. I want also to mention Sarah Fernihough and her team at Nurture Learning. They are doing great work providing a different educational opportunity for pupils struggling in mainstream schooling. It has been a privilege to guide and witness this example of DDP in action. Thanks are due, as ever, to my family who always support me in my writing without begrudging me the time this takes. A special acknowledgement to my daughter, Lily, whose own journey through education was so difficult. I witnessed first-hand the detrimental impact of an education system that does not understand why you are struggling or what you need. Her struggles have increased my passion to get schooling right for children.

Kim S. Golding

Thank you to all the teachers, educational assistants, principals and supporting professionals who work tirelessly and creatively to support some of our most vulnerable students. It has been so exciting to see the power of DDP in the classroom and to see how students begin to trust that the classroom can be a safe place and form new possibilities for relationships. Thank you to my colleagues who have worked with me over the last ten years in Kingston, Ontario, as we wrestled with what embedding DDP into educational practice looked like. I am honoured to have learned alongside you. DDP is a relational model and I am blessed to have a large DDP family who create the safety for me to continue to learn and grow. Kim and Louise, thank you for being part of that network! To Chris, Alastair and Megan, thank you for being my secure base. No matter where I am in the world, I am always excited to come home.

Sian Phillips

Thank you to the DDP Institute who allowed me to be the first certified DDP practitioner to use my work in schools as part of my practicum. I am so grateful to Dan Hughes, who has inspired and influenced all my work in therapy and education and in the wider community since 2000, when I discovered his work while learning the ropes on the Attachment Team in Brighton. I will never forget the time I was sitting in one of his audiences in Brighton and I was stunned as he recommended my first publication regarding education. I'm glad I was brave enough to declare myself! That first connection opened up another layer of opportunity to integrate DDP into my advocacy work in schools, on behalf of children who are hurting. A big thank you to Kim Golding for her continual professional support and her incredible dedication in ensuring a wider understanding of DDP. I am so glad I met you! There is strength in togetherness. And finally, thanks to the education team at TouchBase, who are passionate about ensuring that all those who have experienced relational trauma and loss have every opportunity at school to settle to learn. Every child we 'meet' teaches us so much about how they learn best.

Louise Michelle Bombèr

Introduction

KIM S. GOLDING

Introduction to the Dyadic Developmental Psychotherapy (DDP) model of intervention

As a relatively new clinical psychologist, I remember sitting with a young man who had come to see me for 'therapy'. He was 15 years of age and lived in a children's home. His 'worker' had brought him to me and would return to collect him after an hour. I was not at all sure what I was going to do for that hour. This young man, I will call him Mark, was polite but wary. He feigned disinterest but I suspect this was to cover the sense of threat he was experiencing. He sat in the chair opposite me and gave monosyllabic answers to my questions. I was not sure what he was expecting from me, nor was I sure what he would like to achieve by attending a series of appointments. I remember that the only time I felt engaged with Mark in that session was when we played 'noughts and crosses'. He seemed to come alive as he tried his best to beat me. As he left, I felt particularly unskilled for my job. I suspected I could build a relationship with him but could not foresee us progressing to this given the allocated time we had. Even if I could argue for more time, I was not sure what therapy he would benefit from. Cognitive behavioural therapy did not seem to offer many options for young people like Mark.

Nearly ten years later, with a little more experience under my belt, I was involved in setting up a service for supporting foster and residential carers. I was feeling more confident than I did when working with Mark. I enjoyed supporting parents with their parenting and felt I had the skills to do this. I had worked with a range of parents, including parents at risk of losing their children to the care system. I remember visiting a foster carer, Betty. She was a grandmother who had been offering short-term placements for many years. She was caring for a highly troubled young lady with a history of sexual and physical abuse. Sherry was 14 years old and had been moving from foster placement to foster placement since coming into care a few years previously. We discussed the behaviours she was displaying, and I found it hard to make sense of these. I suggested a range of behavioural strategies that I thought might help. Betty was kind to me, but I could see in her eyes that she doubted these ideas would be useful. I knew about attachment theory and maternal bonding and had worked with parents previously to help them bond with their children, allowing the child to form a more secure attachment to them. These children were eager for this attachment and responded well to the changes the parents made. Sherry was different – she did not appear interested in a relationship with Betty and was actively rejecting of any attempts Betty made to offer this. I wasn't surprised, as Sherry had never successfully attached to any foster carer, but I was at a loss as to how to make life different for her. Last I heard of Sherry she was selling *The Big Issue* in a local city having recently left an abusive relationship.

If I was to make a difference for young people like Mark and Sherry, and for parents caring for children in or adopted from care, like Betty, I needed something else. It was at this time that I was fortunate to meet and start working with Dan Hughes, a clinical psychologist living and working in the USA. His model of Dyadic Developmental Psychotherapy gave me what I was looking for (Hughes, 2007, 2009, 2011; Hughes, Golding and Hudson, 2019). It provided a different way of working with children, young people and their parents. The ongoing development of DDP has additionally provided ways of working within school environments, social care settings and supervisory and management relationships.

In this book, DDP will be explored as a relationship-based intervention model that can be applied at many levels, including children, young people and their families, parents, schools and the networks and environments surrounding these. In this introduction, I present an overview of what DDP is, both as therapy and as a practice model. This provides a foundation for an exploration of the application of DDP in education settings.

What is DDP?

Developed more than 20 years ago, DDP is a model of intervention for children who have experienced relational trauma (also called developmental trauma) early in life, many of whom are growing up in care or adopted from care. The model is grounded in relationship theory, neuroscience and an understanding of the impact of relational trauma on a child's development and functioning (Hughes *et al.*, 2019).

DDP is based on the assumptions that children need healthy, reciprocal relationships in order to thrive, but that some have learned to avoid these relationships because of their previous traumatic experience.

DDP interventions offer children the opportunity for the new relational experiences necessary for healthy development. Children are invited into reciprocal relationships modelled on healthy parent–child relationships. The children's reluctance to take these invitations is met with acceptance and empathy. Curiosity helps these children to discover who they are and to experience open and engaged relationships that are interested in them and all they experience. Playfulness offers new experiences within which children can feel joy in these relationships. Through this attitude of PACE (playfulness, acceptance, curiosity and empathy), children are offered the safety needed to manage some gentle challenge. They are challenged to experience a different way of being. The children are helped to feel safe when open and engaged to the relationship, a move away from the defensive ways of being that have become so much a part of who they are. As social engagement increases, and vulnerability decreases, opportunities for emotional growth arise.

> DDP enables children who have experienced relational trauma to feel safe, often for the first time in their lives – safe to be sad and safe to seek and experience reciprocal joy. In DDP, children learn too that they may develop their unique sense of autonomy while at the same time maintaining a close relationship with someone who will keep them safe and assist them in their development. (Hughes *et al.*, 2019, p.6)

Children who have experienced relational trauma in the form of abuse, neglect, loss and exposure to frightening environments without parental protection are often left in states of shame and terror. This in turn distorts the developing self-identity and expectations of others. They need different relationships within which they can learn about themselves and others, not distorted by past experiences. This reduces shame and terror and opens the child to relationships which offer comfort and joy. The children receive healthy developmental experience within which emotional states are identified, regulated and expressed.

Reflective capacities to understand self and other, not distorted by past learning, increase. Children discover that they can seek comfort, resolve conflicts and engage in relationship repair without the gnawing fear of abandonment and loss that they have been anticipating for so long.

The development of DDP

DDP is a therapy model which has its roots in a range of theoretical and clinical knowledge. The model developed from eclectic beginnings, drawing from what we know about healthy therapist–client relationships and healthy parent–child relationships. The increase in neuroscientific understanding has also contributed, with additional knowledge about the impact of abusive and neglectful parent relationships on children. DDP is therefore an integrative psychotherapy, giving it flexibility and strength.

Healthy therapist–client relationships

Clinical inspiration was drawn by Dan Hughes from clinicians and researchers working primarily with adults, for example the work of Milton Erickson, Carl Rogers and Diana Fosha (Hughes, 2007). He adapted these to provide a relationship-focused therapy for children and families. This included careful consideration of healthy parent–child relationships. Erickson's stance of accepting and utilizing his client's presence to achieve therapeutic change; Rogers's person-centred therapy with the therapeutic stance of unconditional positive regard (acceptance), congruence (genuineness) and warmth (empathy); and Fosha's attention to developing coherent autobiographical narrative by integrating affect and cognition are all echoed in the DDP principles guiding the interventions.

Healthy parent–child relationships

Theoretical understanding of healthy parent–child relationships was drawn from the work of John Bowlby, Colwyn Trevarthen, Daniel Stern, Dan Siegel and Allan Schore (Hughes, 2007). Dan Hughes integrated understanding of attachment relationship experience articulated by John Bowlby (1988/1989) with intersubjective relationship experience articulated by Colwyn Trevarthen (2001).

Attachment theory focuses on the parents' role in helping children to feel safe and to regulate strong emotions (including those associated with experiencing trauma). These attachment connections offer a secure base for exploration and learning about self, others and the world.

Intersubjectivity theory provides a detailed understanding of the reciprocal relationship experience children need with their parents. Within this relationship, children develop a sense of who they, and their parents, are.

Within DDP, these theories are applied to interventions which can recreate this experience, attending to both the attachment and intersubjective needs of the child.

Alongside this, several other researchers have influenced the development of DDP:

- The work of Stern on understanding attunement and the importance of affect matching the vitality of the child's expression (Stern, 2000).
- Schore's insights on the integration of right and left hemispheric brain functioning for communication, with the telling of the story seen as important as the content of the story for developing a successful relationship (Schore, 2012).
- Siegel's attention to integration and coherence of brain functioning assisted through the child experiencing inter-subjective engagement with the adult's brain (Siegel, 1999).

These have all influenced how DDP-trained therapists are guided towards a relational approach to working with child and parent. The therapist provides the child with a healing and integrative relational experience based on meeting attachment and intersubjective needs, supporting integrated brain functioning and healthy neurodevelopment. Working with the parents separately and involving the parents in the therapy sessions ensures that this relational experience includes these attachment figures. This also ensures that the same experience is provided outside the therapy room.

Abusive and neglectful parent–child relationships

As DDP has continued to develop there has been a corresponding growth in understanding neuroscience which has further strengthened the DDP model.

Many studies have demonstrated the interpersonal nature of the human nervous system. Research by Daniel Siegel (1999), Allan Schore (2012), Stephen Porges (2017), Ed Tronick (2007) and others is guiding our understanding of the role and importance of relationship in human development. This has provided increased insights into what goes wrong in abusive and neglectful parent–child relationships. With the work of these researchers we understand much more about the impact of challenging parenting on children. This can provide a road map showing us what children need to recover from and the harmful impact of this experience.

A more detailed discussion of this theoretical body of knowledge and its influence on the practice of DDP can be found in Appendix 2.

Dyadic Developmental Psychotherapy

The DDP model integrates understanding of what works in therapist–client relationships with an understanding of healthy and unhealthy parent–child relationships. A goal of therapy is to help the child to become open to relationship experience again, overcoming the trauma of early frightening relationships. The therapist provides here and now intersubjective experiences with the child and facilitates these between the child and parents. This provides emotional co-regulation and increases sense of safety. In this way, the child can develop a more secure attachment with the parent. This secure base provides room for exploration. Therapist, parents and child explore the child's current experience and better understand the defences that have enabled that child to survive difficult past experiences. Defences are described by Stephen Porges as heroic, in honour of the role they have played in the child's life (Porges, 2017). Trauma narratives of fear and terror are thus understood, and from these, new narratives of hope and healing are co-created.

Dyadic Developmental Parenting

The importance of involving parents in the therapy as well as supporting them through a DDP-informed approach to parenting has always been a central part of the DDP model. This recognizes that if the child cannot seek some security of attachment to his current parents, he will remain stuck in the past, relying on defences that served him well but have reached their sell-by date. Increased safety and security provide the fertile soil needed for developmental and emotional growth, as the child discovers a way of being beyond his defences. This relies on the parent providing parenting which offers healing through emotional connection as well as guidance and discipline (Golding, 2017). The attitude of PACE (Playfulness which expresses joy in the relationship; Acceptance of the child's inner world; Curiosity about the meaning underneath the behaviour; and Empathy for the child's emotional state) is central within DDP. PACE is a parenting attitude, a way of being that facilitates emotional connection between parent and child (Golding and Hughes, 2012; Hughes, 2009). PACE increases security for the child, reducing shame and opening new possibilities for the self and for relationships with others.

Parenting children with experience of developmental trauma can be a challenge. Parents are touched by the child's trauma, sometimes colliding with their own past traumatic experiences. They are hurt by the child's need to control and the rejection of the nurture they are offering. They are exhausted by the sometimes-overwhelming emotional demands made on them. They are worried by a bewildering array of difficulties and symptoms displayed by the child, and the search for answers as to what is wrong and how it can be put right. And of course, they still have the range of practical and emotional parenting tasks that all children require of their parents. Asking them to additionally join the therapist to play a pivotal role in the child's therapy, and to support this by a style of parenting that can be very different from how they were raised, is a lot to ask. For this reason, DDP interventions involve a high level of support for the parents. This support provides the parents with someone who can:

- guide them as to the best time to introduce therapy to the child and help them to understand what is happening in therapy, and how to carry out their role in this
- guide them in their parenting of the child, helping them to understand the DDP model and to apply this to their unique child
- provide emotional support when this feels too hard and overwhelming
- encourage them to seek social support and to engage in self-care

- recognize for them when they have moved into blocked care, temporarily losing their capacity to provide empathic, attuned caregiving because of physiological changes in the brain linked to the impact of the child (Hughes and Baylin, 2012). The therapist provides relational support which helps the parent to move out of blocked care again
- help them to understand the impact the child is having on them, knowing what the triggers are and how to manage these. This involves jointly understanding the parents' attachment and past relationship experience
- advocate for them and their child while also helping them to find their voice in the network surrounding the child and family.

DDP is therefore a model of parenting support, used alongside therapy when this is felt to be appropriate for the child.

Dyadic Developmental Practice: The development of DDP as a practice model

DDP has as its aim the healing of relational (developmental) trauma for children who have been exposed to abusive, neglectful and frightening parenting. With this healing, children can benefit from healthy parenting that supports neurodevelopment and emotional well-being. This parenting can be described as therapeutic. It needs to be good enough to provide a healthy environment for the child to grow up in. It also needs to provide conditions within which children can benefit from different healthy relationship experiences, facilitating healing from trauma. While challenges might remain because of neurodevelopmental difficulties resulting from environmental experience combined with genetic influences, if children are provided with good enough therapeutic parenting this will give them the best chance in life to grow emotionally and cognitively and thus to fulfil their potential.

This type of parenting will have the best chance of succeeding if it is supported by networks also informed by the DDP principles. Trauma tends to have an organizing influence on systems. They become defensive in their activities and responses. To avoid this, the systems need to become informed about the trauma of the people they are supporting (Bloom, 2013). Trauma-informed organizations are less defensive and more able to support individuals at all levels of the organization to stay open and engaged to each other and their clients. Open and engaged states promote healthy growth, exploration and learning.

The DDP model provides a set of principles that can be used by all staff, supervisors and managers, supported by DDP-trained practitioners, to facilitate these open and engaged states within organizations. Dyadic Developmental Practice describes a model where the DDP principles are being applied at all levels (see Figure I.1).

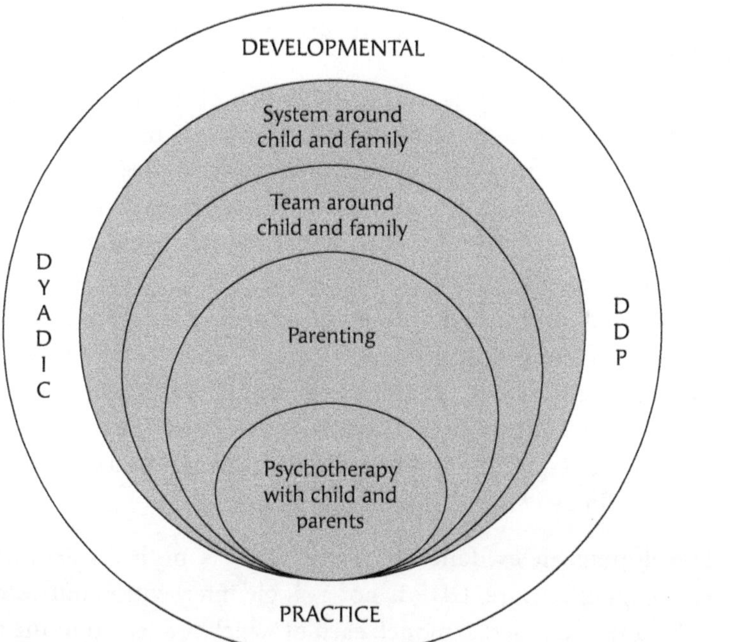

Figure I.1: The DDP Practice Model

This model illustrates how the DDP principles can be applied to increase safety for the child in all aspects of their life. This includes home, school, the community, professional relationships (e.g. social care, health, educational and community practitioners), and the organizations that provide these practitioners.

Trauma-informed education (TIE)

For those working in the UK, Louise Michelle Bombèr, along with UK practitioners from the Theraplay and DDP community, has recommended a developmental pathway for training educators who are supporting children with experience of developmental trauma. TIE practitioners have completed the recommended training which includes a seven-day foundational course facilitated by TouchBase in attachment-aware and trauma-responsive practice followed by Theraplay level one and then DDP level one training. Further information and a list of the TIE practitioners who have completed these trainings can be found online.[1]

Evidence base for DDP

The DDP community is active in developing an evidence base, supporting single case studies, evaluation with outcome measures, waiting-list comparison studies and qualitative studies. A research base is growing, with qualitative and quantitative research demonstrating the efficacy of the DDP model as a therapy, as a parenting approach and as applied in school environments. This has been published in peer-reviewed journals and research is ongoing (Hughes *et al.*, 2019). Practitioners are being offered support to develop an evaluative approach to their work. Trainee and student doctoral and masters research is also supported. Additionally, pilot and feasibility work has been carried out and funding secured for a randomized controlled trial (Turner-Halliday *et al.*, 2014).

> Developing an evidence-base for DDP is both an exciting and challenging venture. DDP is not a single intervention but comprises a therapy and practice model, each of which is adapted to the unique needs and circumstances of individual children and their families. In addition, DDP has applications in supporting education staff in schools and the professional social care and health networks surrounding the families. Developing an evidence base for the efficacy of Dyadic Developmental Psychotherapy, Parenting and Practice will require a wide range of evidence using a range of research designs. (Hughes *et al.*, 2019, p.302)

1 https://traumainformededucation.org.uk

Over the last 20 years, DDP has grown and become established as a helpful intervention for children with experience of developmental trauma. It has face validity because of its grounding in research from a range of relation-focused theories. In addition, robust processes are in place to train, certify and supervise DDP practitioners guided by the DDP Institute, with local support in the UK from DDP Connects UK.[2]

We hope that this book will help many of you to adopt the DDP model in your school or educational setting.

This in turn will lead to us all building further knowledge of how DDP can be successfully applied in a range of settings with a range of children and their families who have been touched by developmental trauma. Together we can bring healthy relationships into the support and parenting of our children for the benefit of all.

2 https://ddpnetwork.org

CHAPTER 1

Blocked Trust and its Impact on Vulnerable Pupils in School

In this chapter, we will explore blocked trust. The development of blocked trust leads to a range of difficulties that impact on the functioning of vulnerable pupils in school. These will be explored later and include fear of intersubjective connections and relationships; overwhelming experiences of shame; and compromised attachment patterns of relating that lead to the expression and hiding of different emotional needs. This chapter and the next one build on the relationship theories and understanding of developmental trauma outlined in the introduction and Appendix 1.

Blocked trust

Developmental trauma involving abuse, neglect and exposure to frightening experiences has pervasive impacts that continue to influence the pupils as they move through school. The early nature of this traumatic experience means that it informs the development of the child's nervous system. The child arrives at school prepared for danger at the biological as well as the behavioural level.

At the time when the developmentally traumatized child is learning about himself in relation to others, he is absorbing experience which suggests that others are unreliable and frightening, leading to doubts about his lovability or other people's availability. This leads to the development of templates, called internal working models, about self and others. These inform the expectations that the child develops as he matures. Developmental trauma leads to predictions that others will be unavailable, disinterested and frightening. The child will be on high alert for signs that confirm these expectations. This influences the way that these pupils relate to educators from the very beginning of their school experience. They do not trust in the good intentions of the adults nor expect that they will have interest in them. As explained in Appendix 1, the pupil's trust in others has been blocked because of their early experience.

A lack of unconditional love early in life therefore leads to the development of expectations that other people will also only have a conditional interest in them. The pupil relates to the educators based on this prediction. Different pupils respond in different ways; they may be withdrawn, self-reliant and/or coercive. None of these pupils can relax, confident that the educator will give them what they need as they need it.

Going to school: Moving out into the world

The maturing child is getting many new experiences supported by her parents – going to a soft play area, visiting a beach, attending a toddler group and being enrolled in nursery – and later school provides the child with increasingly challenging experiences of moving out into the world. This includes learning to separate from parents. The child who has developed trust and security at home will manage these challenges, confidently going out into the world and returning to the parents or close caregivers when in need of support. These children can feel confident in the care of other adults because they have internalized the expectation that adults will support them when needed. With cognitive maturity, the child becomes more sophisticated in this. He learns that some adults are better at supporting him than others or that some adults are good for some things while others are better for other things. The child makes choices about who to turn to for what. The secure start in life provides the child with confidence to relate to other adults. This provides important experience, which in turn influences his developing maturity. Relating to peers is also part of this experience, and the secure child can approach peer relationships with a similar confidence, these too becoming more sophisticated with maturity.

Blocked trust has a pervasive impact on these relationships. It is safer to anticipate danger than to wait and see. The defensive nervous system is ready at all times for the expected threat. Danger is predicted, becoming a self-fulfilling prophecy, as the child interprets the actions of others in line with earlier developed beliefs. A neutral face is seen as threatening, innocuous sounds are perceived as dangerous, and normal boundaries and limits are witnessed as evidence that these relationships too are conditional and that the adult will hurt or abandon them eventually.

The way that pupils respond can help us to understand when they are experiencing threat. Louise remembers one 16-year-old pupil who told her: 'I kept my eye on her [teacher] the whole time as she freaked me out. I had no idea what she was up to.' The teacher in question was just going about her day-to-day tasks, but for this pupil even ordinary tasks and neutral expressions on the teacher's face were confusing to her. She perceived them as threatening.

Under feelings of threat pupils will communicate with others defensively. Consider the list of statements below:

'I don't need you!'

'What are you looking at?'

'Leave me alone...'

'I was fine before you came along...'

'No, I'm not doing that.'

'What was that?'

In each of these, the pupils are communicating that they are feeling threatened, and their communications sound angry or oppositional or, as in the last one, hypersensitive and jumpy.

The early development which has allowed the children to adapt to a dangerous world has led to a nervous system that is over-sensitive to signs of danger. Predicting danger when it is actually safe is a preferred option to predicting safety when it is really dangerous. The nervous system is wired for these preferences. The pupil comes into the new school environment ill-equipped to find comfort, experience joy or curiously learn from the adults around her. The focus remains on protecting herself from anticipated danger. This can be disturbing for those supporting the pupil. Being perceived as dangerous when you are providing safety can be a deeply uncomfortable experience. This can lead to a range of experiences of anger, frustration and hopelessness, as well as feelings of failure with that pupil. Notice how these feelings are expressed in these teacher statements:

'I didn't come into education to be treated like this.'

'I'm not sure we are the right school for Chloe but then I don't know where she should be.'

'I've had enough.'

'What is the point? I try and support Billy but she just doesn't want to be helped!'

'I don't think I'm the right person for Liza. She makes it very clear that I just make things worse.'

Thus, the pupil's blocked trust impacts on the adult. This leads to changed responses from the adult as they experience anxiety, a sense of failure and sometimes even fear of a very threatening pupil. The educators' responses in turn reinforce the blocked trust that developed elsewhere but continues to be prevalent in these different environments.

The challenge of educating pupils with blocked trust

The implication of this for educators is very clear. A certain standard of behaviour is expected in school, often with expectations that are in line with the pupil's chronological age. Behavioural policies are designed to help pupils to fall in line with these expectations. The pupil with blocked trust is likely to meet these expectations very differently from the more secure pupil. When pupils believe in their own badness and have a strong need to control the behaviours of others, they are less likely to behave in ways that meet the behavioural standards set by the adults. However these standards are enforced, whether through rewards, praise or consequences, the pupils will interpret this as further evidence that they are not good enough and that they are not unconditionally accepted. This leads to increased stress and fear activating the already primed nervous system and a range of fight, flight or shut-down behaviours become likely. It is not that the pupils cannot conform to the boundaries being set for them, it is more that these very boundaries remind them that they are in an unsafe world. Their need to stay in control is reinforced.

The education staff will witness much hypervigilance from the pupils. For example, they won't be able to sit still, and they will need to check out the environment. They seem to need and do ask for a lot of space. They feel hemmed in very quickly, especially when asked to sit down in a classroom. Corridors can be a particular source of stress.

These are unpredictable places within schools, with many different entrances and exits. Corridors can go on and on, especially in the larger educational settings. This is not an area of school generally patrolled by adults, so it is not unusual for a pupil to find herself alone without a safe adult to support her if she begins to feel anxious or scared. In secondary school, corridors are often places of commotion as large numbers of pupils move from class to class. This includes pushing, shoving, pupils slamming into each other, fights starting and bags being thrown. It can feel as if these pupils are security guards of the school, as they have to know what is going on and even try to control the situations. In all of these behaviours, the preoccupation for the pupils is less about how they should behave and more about how can they can keep themselves safe.

In addition, vulnerable pupils will have stunted emotional growth. Emotional growth needs an environment of safety and security. When safety and security are not experienced, energy is diverted from emotional growth into defence and protection. This means that these children will be emotionally younger than their peers whatever their cognitive capacity. This presents a further challenge to teams supporting the pupils, as these pupils are so often organized into groups consistent with their chronological age. Expectations for the majority of the group will be met less well by pupils with developmental traumas in their backgrounds.

Working in partnership with parents, educators need to help pupils to recover from blocked trust. This is done through continually demonstrating and making explicit that the pupil is unconditionally accepted. To do this, the adult needs to attune to the internal experience of the pupil, find empathy for this experience and help the pupil to know that his feelings are understood.

This can be tricky for several reasons. As we will explore later, it is not always easy to know what a pupil is feeling or thinking, especially when he has learned to hide this from others. Often the pupil does not know himself, so he can't help the adult out! Education staff need to be mindreaders, making guesses about how the pupil might be feeling, often noticing small non-verbal cues from the pupil about whether the guess fits or not.

Often the adult is trying to do this while also feeling stressed and uncertain. Any of us can feel triggered into strong defensive emotion, especially when the child is expressing his strong feelings with very personal statements such as 'I hate you', 'You are a fat cow' or 'I hope you get cancer'. When a staff member feels unsafe, just like a pupil, insight becomes limited and polarized. Events are viewed as right or wrong. A pupil is seen as good or bad. Staff members can become very rigid in their management of behaviour at these times, rather than flexible in their approaches. This is when the sentiment 'one size fits all' is most likely to be applied. The focus narrows down to responding to the behaviour while the wider context is overlooked (Bombèr and Hughes, 2013).

If the staff member can feel safe and confident with the pupil, she will be more able to look beneath the behaviour, to understand the context within which it has arisen. Efforts to do this will also help the pupil to feel safer. He may now be able to offer his own suggestions about what he was feeling or thinking. Educators now need to accept this experience, to remember that feelings are neither right nor wrong, they just are. When staff members feel calm, regulated and supported themselves they can open their minds to another. Now they can be 'mind-minded' in their approaches, wondering together with the pupil about what he might be thinking or feeling.

It is worth pausing and thinking about this as it is a critical part of understanding how to support these pupils. We all have an inner life which we are more or less in touch with. Our inner life is full of feelings, thoughts and beliefs. Children need help to notice and make sense of their inner life. Importantly, they need to know that it is okay to have even difficult and negative feelings and thoughts. We have all had strong angry feelings at times and may have a passing thought: 'I could kill you right now.' Of course, we have no intention of acting on this thought, it is just a sign of how strongly we are feeling. We keep the thought to ourselves, take care of our strong feelings and then go on to manage the relationship with the person who has made us angry.

Children are less able to do this. They have the strong feeling and express the thought. Thus, they might shout angrily: 'I am going to kill you!' They need us to help them to manage this strong emotion, not to become judgemental about what they are saying. Accept the statement as a symbol of the strong feeling and connect with this emotional experience. A staff member might say to the pupil: 'You are feeling so angry right now. I expect you are angry because… If that is how you are feeling I am not surprised that you are feeling so cross.' Notice that the staff member is not saying to the pupil that the feelings and thoughts are right, nor that they are wrong. This is just how it feels right now. This acceptance and understanding, which is conveyed with empathy, will soothe the pupil. The angry feelings will reduce in a way that would not happen if the staff member tries to tell him that he should not talk about killing people. This is connection with the internal experience of the pupil. This connection is what helps the pupil to feel safer, and over time to start to trust in the adult's good intentions and to believe that he is acceptable to them – that he is accepted unconditionally.

Acceptance in this way is not always an easy thing to convey as a teacher or within the larger school system. School boards can operate from a 'zero-tolerance' policy. A child who threatens 'I will kill you! I wish you were dead! I am going to cut you into pieces and feed you to your dog!' or intimidates the other children through verbal and physical aggression, fuelled by his survival system, is quickly suspended. Sometimes a risk assessment is required before the child can return to school, resulting in long periods away from the classroom. Responses are often quick and based in fear of what the child 'might do' or protective of the emotional safety of staff and other pupils. Such responses do not address the child's underlying fear or the inner experiences that led to the aggression.

Educators sometimes fear that acceptance condones the behaviour and if a rapid and punishing response is not given that the child will continue to behave in this way. Punishment and incentives to influence their pupils are what most teachers are taught in teacher training. Pupils who trust relationships can manage rewards and punishments. Pupils who have learned to survive relational trauma cannot yet learn in this way and require us to help them manage their strong feelings and thoughts without acting on them.

Cole at nine years old was living with his elderly grandparents. His father was in jail for assault of his mother. His mother sometimes visited but struggled with her own mental health and addictions and would be absent from his life for long periods of time. Cole had witnessed his parents' angry and frightening outbursts from the time he was an infant. Neither parent was able to pay attention to Cole's inner experiences of terror, shame and sadness. Neither felt safe enough to pay attention to their child's need for safety. His attempts to get his needs met were typically responded to with anger or disinterest. Cole had to learn how to manage his big feelings himself.

He then brought his expectancy that adults were frightening and unavailable to school. His nervous system was primed for fight and flight behaviour. He received numerous suspensions for aggressive behaviour.

Cole's teacher recognized that repeated suspensions were making no difference, that in fact they seemed to make things worse for Cole. When he returned from a three-day suspension, he would walk into the classroom ready for another fight. He would refuse to hang up his backpack, say something mean to another child, wander around the classroom, doing anything but his work. His hypervigilance for more trouble prevented him from relaxing, even for a minute. He could not respond to the teacher's attempts to engage with him or settle him to learn. The staff in this school had had some recent training with PACE and agreed to try responding differently to Cole's behaviour.

First, they kept in mind that his behaviour was a reflection of his inner experience. His fight and flight responses, which were certainly big and scary, were strategies for survival. His team worked hard to keep in mind the image of a boy who had been badly frightened and was doing his best to manage. The acceptance was of his inner experience. When Cole started to get angry, his teacher would move closer to him making sure that her tone of voice and facial expressions were not angry or fearful. Conversations started to sound like this:

> 'Cole, I see you are worried about something. Do you know how I know? When you are worried or unsure, your anger comes so quickly to help you out. Right now, I think you want to yell at me and throw something and break it! Your brain is saying this is a good way to manage my hard, scary feelings – just throw something! Just do it! You have been managing your big feelings in this way for so long and I don't think we, as teachers, have understood that behind your anger are scared or worried feelings. I'm sorry we didn't notice. It's so tiring to manage big feelings all by yourself. It's so hard trying to protect yourself with anger. I'm going to really try harder to help you with your feelings. You probably aren't too keen on that [said with a smile and acceptance of his reluctance] but I am one stubborn lady. In fact, if we put your stubborn and my stubborn together, I think we could conquer the world!'

Initially, Cole was surprised. He expected his anger to be met with anger and rejection. He was suspicious of his teacher's intentions and would respond with his own anger. However, her acceptance soothed him at a level that he hadn't felt before. Initially he was determined not to show his teacher that he liked it. With repetition of the unconditional acceptance of his inner world, however, he began to settle in the classroom. There were times when his behaviour was too aggressive to manage in school and the decision was for him to go home. This decision was also communicated with PACE and as a way to help him rather than as a punishment.

> 'Cole, your behaviours are just so, so big today – bigger than you know what to do with – and they are getting you into all kinds of trouble! You have enough trouble in your life kiddo and you don't need any more. I have called Grandma and asked her to come and get you. I have asked her to do something nice with you this afternoon so that you can feel better and be ready to come back tomorrow. Don't think you get to play video games all afternoon! I have suggested going to the park or playing something together. Tomorrow maybe we can spend some time figuring out what is making it so hard for you today. I'd like to figure out what's on your mind. Deal?'

It is important to notice that acceptance does not excuse behaviour. If the pupil has hit the staff member, the hitting remains wrong. Once the staff member has connected with the feelings, she can then support the behaviour so that the pupil learns to deal with strong feelings and thoughts without acting on them. This is what discipline literally means – it is an act of teaching someone, giving them knowledge. In our discipline, we are teaching pupils how to behave. We will explore this further later in this book.

Of course, as we mentioned earlier, educators also have their own internal experience, their own thoughts and feelings which can become triggered by the pupil's behaviour. This makes it hard to use PACE in this way. When a staff member hears the pupil telling her that he will kill her, she will feel angry with him. The staff member might have some additional worries. She might have a sense that she is failing the pupil. She might believe that if she can't curb the pupil's aggressive tendencies, he might become violent in the future. A staff member's own internal experience, which again is neither right nor wrong but just is, might provoke a less helpful response to the pupil. When a staff member has her own defensive reactions to the pupil, she is less able to accept his internal experience. This is normal and understandable. One of the challenges of supporting these pupils is to notice your own worries and beliefs and to put these to one side while you focus on what the pupil is experiencing. Only then will your angry or frustrated feelings subside, and you can focus on understanding what is going on for the pupil. Once you understand why the pupil is feeling so angry with you, it is easier to support the pupil and to find a way forward in helping him to express his anger in more acceptable ways.

A staff member can feel frustrated that she has not been able to stay open to accepting the pupil's feelings. Perhaps she has given a consequence to the pupil or sent the pupil away from her without understanding what has been going on with him. The pupil is left experiencing shame and feeling unsupported. Feeling not good enough, the pupil finds that his feelings become bigger rather than smaller. The staff member is only human, and her own feelings can make it hard to continue with acceptance for the pupil. Fortunately, there is a way out of this situation. If the staff member can notice that she is being defensive, and have compassion and acceptance for herself, she is then able to make it right again. This is called relationship or rupture repair. The staff member lets the pupil know that she acted hastily and that she had not fully understood what was going on for him. She would like to understand this now and then they can together decide what should happen next.

Cole's teacher was not always able to respond in the way she liked. Sometimes she was having a bad day or other pupils' needs were more pressing. She recognized that she would be irritable at these times and that shame was beneath that irritability. She learned to give herself some time to calm her own mind, whether this was five minutes or the rest of the school day. She then made sure to connect with Cole and repair the relationship.

> 'Cole, I am not happy with the way I talked to you just now. I was angry that you pushed Michael. I know that me being angry makes you worry that I don't like you any more. No wonder you got angry right back! You might have thought: "Here it comes, I am going to get kicked out of class and here is another adult who is going to leave me! I'll get rid of her before she gets rid of me!" Instead of taking time to wonder with you about what's going on I jumped to "Cut it out!" I forgot that when you are struggling it's because there is something on your mind and I need to help you figure it out, not just tell you to cut it out! I'm sorry. I have some time now to figure this out.'

In this way, the teacher conveys that her relationship with him is important and therefore she will make the relationship okay again. Pushing is not right but feeling angry is acceptable. The pupil learns that none of this is because he is a bad child. Strong feelings are okay, and adults can help you to figure out how to manage these and to express them safely. He is accepted 'no matter what'. Consequences become something that the pupil is supported with. Grudgingly, perhaps, the pupil may then be able to accept the consequence for his behaviour, knowing that he is acceptable to his teacher or support worker. His behaviour will be supported, and he is worthy of the staff member's attention.

The staff member's response might be very different to what he expects. Importantly, it does not fit with his sense of self. Pupils can be deeply uncomfortable with a supportive staff member who appears to be interested in them. They instinctively want to put some distance between them. Like Cole, they may behave in an unpleasant or angry way in order to create this distance. They might try and provoke the staff member into anger in turn, in order to feel more comfortable themselves. Sometimes a pupil may experience some closeness to a staff member who has expressed understanding towards him. This can be frightening if the pupil does not feel deserving of closeness. Behaviour can be used to demonstrate that he is not deserving, spoiling the relationship before he can get too used to it. All of this can be very challenging for the team supporting him. It can also be hurtful when the staff member feels he is getting somewhere with a pupil who appears to just throw it back in her face. Staying open to the pupil through what can be a long testing period is one of the challenges of supporting vulnerable pupils in school.

Recovering capacity for comfort, curiosity and joy

Children who have grown up in developmentally traumatizing environments need opportunities to recover their capacity for comfort, curiosity and joy. Parents are central in providing these opportunities. It is the ongoing parenting that allows children to start to feel safer and to build trust in the parents. This then allows their nervous systems to change and start to organize around this newly found sense of safety. They can become less alert for danger and therefore more open to social engagement. They become open and engaged to the parents, open to their comfort, and also open to curiosity. In addition, the child can be joyfully engaged with his parents. Cole unfortunately did not have parents who could provide him with these opportunities. He needed to learn how to manage a world without comfort, joy or curiosity. His grandparents tried their best and loved their grandson, but his mistrust of adults and their limited health and own lack of experience with nurturing made it difficult for them to help Cole feel safe.

There are ways that education staff can support this recovery by providing complementary experiences in school. When parents and education staff work together to provide healing environments for the child to live and work in, recovery is likely. Even when the child is not receiving optimal parenting, the educator should not underestimate the difference that he can make to the pupil. A pupil spends many hours in school, and next to parents and close family members, educators provide some of the closest relationships that pupils will experience in their childhoods. The experiences teams supporting the pupils provide can be influential in how far pupils can recover from early experience and adapt to the safety being provided for them.

Comfort

Children need to recover the capacity for sadness. Feeling sad is a vulnerable feeling, but when a child experiences sadness, he also becomes open to comfort.

If a child anticipates pain instead of comfort, he will try to remain disconnected from the feelings of sadness. He disconnects from the person who is a potential source of comfort because he fears she is more likely to be the source of pain.

Sadness is the hardest emotion to experience for vulnerable pupils. They are afraid to feel sad, because they anticipate no comfort. They resist the educator's empathy, fearing the emotional experience that this empathy will awaken. They try to hide from their own emotional experience of fear and sadness – emotions that make them feel so vulnerable. Often these feelings get covered in a blanket of anger and rage – emotions that make the pupil feel less vulnerable and help to keep the sadness buried within.

Educators help pupils to experience their empathy, demonstrating their availability to help them with the emotional experience that this evokes. The pupils feel safe to be sad and to need comfort.

As we mentioned, Cole was initially very suspicious of his teacher's empathy. He didn't understand it and believed it was a trick, that she was just pretending to be nice. With her team's support, she learned to accept and have empathy for his reticence. She would say things like, 'Cole, it's so hard for you to trust that I want to help you with your big feelings. You have worked so hard to manage all by yourself. How tiring that is.' Then she would give him his space. There was no expectation that he talked to or approached her. Later she might put a note on his desk, saying she hoped he was feeling better. Her noticing and naming of his experiences communicated that he was *not* alone.

It can be a challenge to find time for this within a school day. The task of teaching is all consuming, and being available for an individual pupil can be lost. These quality moments are so important for the successful education of children. Working as a team of educational staff, including teachers and key support staff, it is vital to prioritize these moments. Staff can be present, attentive, attuned and responsive as they are mindfully aware of what is going on for the pupil. Educators can do this in the knowledge that as the pupils are able to experience comfort and feel soothed, the world of learning will open up to them.

Curiosity

Recovering the capacity for curiosity easily fits with the purpose of schooling. After all, without curiosity, how can a pupil learn? As children begin to experience some safety and security with their parents, they become able to relax in their own curiosity. School, however, presents a different set of challenges. The sense of failure that new learning can engender, working alongside and relating to peers, spending many hours away from the parents and the inevitable changes in routine and structure that arise can all lead to a pupil experiencing less safety at school than at home. This can reawaken the defensive nervous system, increasing the likelihood of defensive responding. This reduces the possibility of curiosity. Even a pupil who appears settled and well behaved in school but who doesn't experience safety can be responding defensively. Appearing settled and showing compulsive good behaviour can be another form of control to manage the responses of the adults. The effort that this takes will limit curiosity and reduce the energy for learning.

Ten-year-old Nadia is one such pupil who had learned to survive by recognizing what made adults happy. In school she was compliant, was the first to offer to do something for the teacher, kept her desk neat and never seemed to make a fuss. Initially her teacher had no concerns for her pupil. She believed Nadia would sail through Year 5. However, she began to notice that Nadia wasn't completing her work. She erased things frequently and took a long time to get anything done. If her teacher asked if she needed help, Nadia would refuse and say she was fine. Any attempts to talk with her about her work or even non-work-related things were met with a polite smile. Her teacher would report that it just seemed difficult to have a conversation with Nadia. She couldn't put her finger on why. Like Cole, Nadia was creating distance in relationships. It wasn't with anger and aggression but with steely resistance to being known. She kept the focus of conversation on others, stayed busy by being helpful and avoided her teacher's attempts to help.

The effort that this self-protection takes leaves the pupils very tired by the end of the school day. Parents will often report meltdowns and challenging behaviour from the child once home. This is a clue that the pupil is not as settled and comfortable in school as she appears. The effort of the day is released in one big response once home again.

Attending to the pupil's safety in school is important whether or not the pupil is displaying a lack of safety. When it is known that the pupil has experienced developmental trauma it is better to assume that the pupil does not feel safe and to put effort into explicitly demonstrating how school is a safe place. Louise and Sian, among others, provide many practical ideas for increasing a pupil's sense of safety in school within their written work. These include attachment figures in school, safety tours of the school, attention to where the pupil is sitting in the classroom, finding ways to make school feel smaller, and opportunities for regulation and soothing at regular intervals. These can all help to calm a defensive nervous system (Bombèr, 2007, 2011, 2016, 2020; Bombèr and Hughes, 2013; Forbes, 2012; Howard, 2013; Jennings, 2018; Phillips, Melim and Hughes, 2020; Tranter, Carson and Boland, 2018). The pupil will then be able to respond to an open and engaged staff member, finding her own curiosity in response to the staff member's curiosity.

Nadia's teacher started to gently wonder what made it hard for Nadia to accept help from her. There was no expectation that Nadia knew the answer to that. Her teacher would make some guesses: 'I wonder if you feel that I won't like you if you tell me you don't understand; that I will think you are dumb?' She would then provide empathy for how hard that would be if Nadia did think that. Her acceptance, empathy and gentle curiosity created the safety for Nadia to change her focus from protection to wondering about herself and her world.

Joy

Joy in learning and in peer relationships are big parts of the school experience. How sad when stress and anxiety make these activities a joyless experience. You always know when you have a joyful connection with another because each of your positive feelings is amplified by the experience of the other. Just remember a time when you have ended up in helpless laughter over something that is really not that funny. It just happened to have tickled one of you, who shares his amusement. You become amused in turn and the amusement becomes amplified into helpless laughter. This is the power of the relationship. The sense of fun and happiness is relational. If we can help pupils to discover, or rediscover, relational joy, their school experience will be transformed and their relationship with learning altered for the better. Small moments and low-key activities can offer opportunities to dip into these feelings. The pupil will manage these because they are light and momentary. As he gets used to experiencing fun and joy, the small moments can become bigger and more extended.

It was easy to see that Jackson had had a hard life. At age 15, he exuded his disdain for people, saw nothing positive about himself and wore a permanent scowl. Yet he came to school each day. His woodwork teacher felt tremendous compassion for this young man who seemed so world weary. Jackson was polite but rejected any attempts to get to know him. His teacher was determined to find a way to help Jackson discover that he was liked and enjoyed. He began to bring in funny cartoons and drop them on his desk with a note that said, 'I thought you might find this funny!' For many days, Jackson didn't show any interest, but after about a month his teacher noticed a softening when he came to class and that he would look for what was on his desk with some interest rather than indifference. He then started to drop by Jackson's desk to share a YouTube video with him. It became harder for Jackson to resist his teacher's infectious laughter and enjoyment of the cartoons and videos and he began to smile. By the end of the year, Jackson was more engaged in learning and occasionally would bring in a cartoon for his teacher.

Educating a tiger, opossum or chameleon

Jon Baylin and Dan Hughes (2016) describe the differences in the way that children can respond to the experience of blocked trust. Not all children respond in the same way, and Baylin and Hughes have helpfully expressed this through comparison with different animals. Analogies which we are borrowing from them are discussed here.

The first type of pupil is a *tiger*. Education staff always know when they are trying to educate a tiger, as the pupil is obvious about how mistrust feels – responding with anger and aggression. Cole, in our earlier example, is a tiger. If the staff member is drawn into these cycles of negative, aggressive reactions, both are left experiencing mistrust. Taming the tiger means supporting the pupil with strong feelings of anger. The pupil is accepted, this is how he is feeling. As anger is accepted, the pupil has less need to display anger through aggressive behaviours.

Anger and vulnerability will alternate, as the pupil explores being more open to the relationships, allowing the education staff to support her within the school. A pupil newly experiencing fun, joy and learning can feel very vulnerable. She has let her guard down, which means not attending to signs of danger in the environment. Initially, this is likely to be in small moments, and often followed by a retreat back to anger, which can feel less risky. If the adults can stay open and accepting of both when the pupil is angry, and when she is allowing herself to engage in what feels like more vulnerable experiences, the pupil will be able to spend more time within the more positive times.

The *opossum* will keep a very low profile. Unlike the tigers, these pupils will try to appear small and silent as they attempt to stay out of sight and out of mind. They do not want to draw attention to themselves. The educator reaches out but finds the pupil not there. Education staff can feel rejected and a sense of failure as they try to reach these shut-away pupils. They find it hard to stay engaged with these pupils when they are receiving so little back.

Again, acceptance is the key. The education staff remain close to the pupil, accepting his need to withdraw from the relationship. Gentle presence provides the pupil with an experience of the adult remaining open even when the pupil needs to stay closed and shut off. The adult is then also present when the pupil makes tentative moves to be more open to the relationship. The adult remains steady as the child moves backwards and forwards between being open and being shut down. As the pupil experiences acceptance for both these parts, trust will build and the pupil will withdraw less often.

The *chameleon* is the third animal. Chameleons are expert at blending in, and these pupils have this ability also. They will constantly assess the mood of those around them and try to adapt their behaviour to this mood. Nadia is a chameleon. Pupils like Nadia suppress their own needs as they attempt to accommodate to the needs and moods of the adults. They are superficially social, but without any substance to the connections they are forming. These pupils can be lost in schools where other pupils are taking up so much of the emotional energy.

Parents of chameleons can describe a falseness about these children which makes any connections they have with them feel manipulative and unreal. This can also be experienced in school, especially for the adults who are making a special effort to get to know and support the pupil. As with tigers and opossums, adults need to stay present and steady whatever the chameleon is expressing. Their openness to their pupils and the acceptance that these pupils need to present this 'fitting in' self just now will build trust. Pupils may tentatively test out how acceptable their authentic self is. As adults accept the pupils in all their parts, the chameleon tendencies will reduce.

Open and engaged teaching

When environments change, the pupil is likely to remain defensive and less open to social engagement. New learning does not happen easily. If a pupil anticipates that he is going to be hurt, rejected or ignored, he will behave defensively. If the team supporting him can help him to feel safe, over time he will move across to the open and engaged state and be ready for learning. Creating that safety depends so much on adults staying regulated and in their social engagement system.

When we are in a relationship we tend to move into the same state as the other person. If a pupil is defensive, it can pull the adult into becoming defensive in turn. If, however, the adult can remain open and engaged, a level of safety will build up, mistrust becomes trust, and the pupil will be able to match the adult and become open and engaged in turn.

Such experience can reset the sensitivity of the stress system so that pupils are less likely to react to innocuous events as if they are dangerous. However, this is not an easy or quick process. The pupils are hyper-focused on threat or potential threat, and much less able to attend to signs of safety. Facial expressions provide a good example of this. Studies have shown that children who have experienced abuse will detect anger in faces and voices faster than children who have not experienced abuse. They also cannot withdraw this attention to notice other things (Pollak, 2003, cited in Baylin and Hughes, 2016). Thus, children will miss signs of safety in their environment, a phenomenon that Baylin and Hughes (2016) have called 'safety blindness'. The task of the educators is to calm the pupils' defensive reactions through their own open and engaged state, providing the regulatory support needed. As they are doing this, they will be cracking the door open on the pupils' blocked attachment system; the pupils learn to anticipate safety and support from their educators. It then becomes easier to activate the exploratory system, aiding engagement with activities and learning.

For Cole and Nadia, their teachers noticed their pupil's defence system, accepted its value and remained curious about the child underneath the defence. Their ability to stay regulated, to repair the relationship when there was a rupture and the warmth in their voice and faces were only possible when they were in their open and engaged state. The teachers' persistence in offering the opportunity for being understood helped these two pupils develop new expectancies and unblock their lack of trust.

Conclusion

Blocked trust emerges when children experience only conditional relationships early in life. They learn that they are not lovable for themselves and that others are likely to be available to meet their needs based only on certain conditions. This impacts on the developing nervous system. The children become attuned to potential signs of physical or psychological danger in the environment. They are biased to perceive danger even in benign situations. They quickly move to defensive responding. Pupils in school will be more attentive to these signs than to the learning task. In addition, they will anticipate that others will be a source of threat. They will not be able to use the support on offer. For example:

Seven-year-old Ben fell over in the playground and hurt himself very badly. Instead of seeking proximity with an adult he continued with his game, as if totally oblivious. The lunchtime supervisor approached him to offer help, but Ben just screwed up his face at her and went off laughing. He retorted 'I don't need anything from no one!' as he walked away. The supervisor, feeling dejected, muttered, 'I was only trying to help.'

A consequence of blocked trust is that pupils are deprived of opportunities for comfort and joy in relationships, preoccupied as they are with monitoring safety and danger. In addition, a defensive state means that they are not open and engaged to others, nor can they engage in the curiosity necessary for learning.

Educators need to pay attention to blocked trust before they are likely to experience success with these vulnerable pupils. An open and engaged stance which can soothe over-reactive nervous systems is an important starting point for helping the pupils benefit from and thrive in school. When Ben falls over in the playground stating 'I don't need anything from no one!', an open and engaged response might be: 'You are letting me know loud and clear that you really don't trust grown-ups. They have let you down in the past. I get that. C'mon, we do need to get this sorted so we can keep that leg strong for these games you play. Let's go...' Ben is likely to comply, even if reluctantly, to such an engaging response.

CHAPTER 2

Relationship Difficulties that Develop from Blocked Trust

Fear of intersubjectivity

Children who are in a state of blocked trust develop a fear of intersubjective relationships with close caregivers. In this chapter, we will explore this fear and the way that it can generalize to a fear of adults outside the family. For those unfamiliar with the theory of intersubjectivity, including primary and secondary intersubjective experiences, this is described in Appendix 2.

Children need emotional connection in order to survive. When this connection comes with an experience of loss, pain or fear, they learn to fear connection. As soon as children can do without connection, they will find ways to exist disconnected from others. We see this most clearly in the controlling behaviours that even very young children can develop. They use the close relationships around them but with a resistance to being influenced by others.

This is a significant difficulty for pupils in school. They have learned to manage relationships through controlling behaviours but at the cost of developing reciprocity. The give and take in a reciprocal relationship is what helps us to co-operate. It is central to healthy relationships. Pupils who move through school without having learned to reciprocate will be at a considerable disadvantage.

When pupils fear letting others have influence over them, they will not enter into reciprocal relationships, even if they know how to. They will struggle to take guidance and support from teaching staff. They will find peer relationships difficult. They will be denied the benefits of intersubjective experiences. Experience is enhanced and learning increased when we can do this intersubjectively with others.

When pupils fear being open to influence, they deny themselves such intersubjective experiences.

The impact of a fear of intersubjectivity on learning

The early intersubjective experiences that children receive within their families are part of the foundation for their development. As a social species, humans need a particularly strong foundation of relationship experience. The way that they can manage and navigate relationships will in large part determine their later success whether in maintaining strong friendships and intimate partnerships, in the world of work or of course in their own parenting adventures. Being able to connect with others is the foundation for success as a human.

School provides pupils with important opportunities to discover a wider range of relationships, influenced by the early experience within their families. From the parallel play of the toddler through to the sophisticated friendships and intimacy of the adolescent, young people are learning the give and take of reciprocal relationships. With adult support which gradually reduces through childhood, children learn how to interact, co-operate, resolve disagreements, seek friendships, live alongside peers, and generally find their place within the highly social human race. When the initial foundation for developing this relationship success is shaky, all of this will be much harder. Like a house without good foundations, relationships will be less stable, shakier and more troublesome. These pupils will need more support from teams around them if they are going to be able to discover a different relationship experience within school, allowing them to discover healthier, intersubjective ways of relating. Small teams from within the larger pool of education and support staff can work together to be an individual pupil's support team. Louise calls these 'Team Pupil' (inserting pupil's name) in recognition of their unique role to that pupil (these teams are further explored in book four of her *Attachment Aware School Series*, Bombèr, 2016).

Simply offering alternative ways for relating will not be enough. These pupils need relational experiences with their educators before they will be open to the teaching. As we explored above, vulnerable pupils have learned to fear relationships. This means that they will resist the adult's attempts to help them. The pupils who need the most support are also likely to be the pupils who resist the support being offered.

Unless the teams supporting these pupils can undo some of the learned patterns of controlling relationships the pupils have arrived at school with, they will find it hard to help them discover a new world of interactions.

This will also impact on learning. Acquiring knowledge rests on curiosity and learning. Sharing this curiosity and learning within intersubjective relationships enhances education at all levels. Discovering together provides a learning experience that enhances the education and lasts. Being open to the experiences of others while learning provides us with a deeper, richer learning experience. Pupils who have more success in school, and afterwards, will be the ones who have experienced these intersubjective learning experiences.

Educating children who fear intersubjective connections

Opening up the intersubjective world of learning is therefore an important part of teaching pupils. Children have their first experience of intersubjective connections within their families. Healthy experience enhances the children's readiness for the world of school, allowing them to connect with the education staff and to relate comfortably with their peers. The educator's job is to support the pupils to use their capacity for connection with others both to aid learning and to foster good relating. Education staff need to help the pupils to overcome their mistrust so that they can be helped to develop the capacity for relationship that they did not develop in their earliest experience. This will be harder to do for the vulnerable pupils, because this world is not one that they want to enter. Their fear, combined with a limited capacity for such relationships, adds to the difficulty of educating vulnerable pupils. This may feel anxiety provoking to some educators, who feel that helping pupils overcome mistrust is the job of a therapist. They may feel ill-equipped to work at this psychological level or worried that they will make the child's experience worse somehow. Overcoming mistrust within their day-to-day environments of home and school is, however, what these children need.

Safe connections will help pupils risk new ways of relating, and learn to allow adults to help them with this. Teachers and other educational staff can become such important attachment figures. As children become more comfortable within relationships and start to experience primary intersubjectivity – the adults' enjoyment, delight and interest in them – safety will increase further. This will help to soothe and regulate their over-sensitive nervous systems, allowing them to move from defensive ways of engaging with others towards true social engagement. Only now will the world of learning start to open to them; secondary intersubjectivity – having a different knowledge of themselves or the world, because it is discovered with another – becomes a possibility. The pupil will finally be ready for school and education. Trying to educate a pupil who experiences the world as dangerous and who is defensive towards others is like trying to collect water in a sieve. Learning experiences are provided but will not have a lasting impact.

Connecting with all pupils is an important part of helping them to be successful in school. The challenge for the teams supporting vulnerable pupils is that these connections must be built when connections are feared. Helping pupils to reduce their need for control so that they can experience intersubjective interactions is a slow, painful task.

Brandon entered school as a raging four-year-old. He could not follow routines, he bit any child who got in his way, he spent most of his time under a desk or running along the corridors and could swear like a trucker. At the age of three, his step-father had died tragically in a car accident. His mother, who already struggled with mental health issues, withdrew further and Brandon was often left to forage for food in neighbours' bins. He wandered the streets without supervision until taken into care at the age of three-and-a-half. He spent a year in foster care and then returned to his mother's care. By his first year in school, Brandon had learned that adults don't stick around and that he had better rely on himself.

Brandon found it impossible to relax. He was highly reactive, alternating between fight and flight behaviours. He could not make use of his teacher's compassion or opportunities for socialization. He spent more time out of the classroom than in it, decreasing further the opportunity for intersubjectivity – primary or secondary. Any attempts to address Brandon's behaviour were met with an escalation of that behaviour. Any attempts to connect with him were met with rejection. Both the teacher and teaching assistant felt stuck.

Often children who are so difficult are given modified days. However, the team knew that to send Brandon home would mean long hours on his own, which was the opposite of what they wanted for him. They started by taking any academic expectation off the table. He was not ready to learn. They built him a den at the back of the room that had a blanket over it so that he could hide but still be part of the classroom. They would place some Lego and snacks each morning in the den. Their goal was to have him be part of the classroom for 30 minutes a day. When he couldn't be in the classroom, there was a team of adults who would spend time with him.

Like many children with developmental trauma, when pressure is off learning and adults are spending time doing what the children want to do, behavioural difficulties are fewer. He had dens all over the school. When he had had enough of relationships or if the adult was busy, Brandon would be encouraged to listen to music or books on tape in one of his dens. The team treated him more like an 18-month-old child. If he could relax enough to sleep, that was celebrated. Every day, the adults in the school greeted him with delight. Every day, they showed interest in his day and asked him how he was feeling or what he was thinking. Big behaviours were met with acceptance for his anger, but limits and consequences for aggression. Limits were reparative – when he was ready, he would help clean up the room or he would accompany a staff member to do an errand for his teacher or he would make cookies for his classmates who had been inconvenienced by his outbursts. There were many times where the educators felt that they couldn't help Brandon.

Three years later, Brandon could stay in the classroom for most of the day. He was beginning to say sorry to people he hurt, and he was asking to learn how to read. It was a long and painful process, but the reward was equally huge.

Educating pupils who are not open to connection within the relationship can have a negative impact on the educators. Having open and engaged relationships with pupils is part of what teaching is all about. When educators are met with rejection, it can have a painful impact and can lead to a sense of failure or uneasiness with pupils.

The pupils' negative responses to offers of connection from an educator will be very similar to their responses to parents offering the same. Some pupils might respond with rejection and hostility and this is experienced as very personal and hurtful. The pupil might or might not show an interest in the teaching task, but he won't want the teacher to help him with this. Alternatively, a pupil might be very clingy but whatever the staff member does she will not soothe or be comforted. She will not move her focus from the staff member to the teaching task.

This triggers a sense of uselessness; the staff member can feel deskilled as a consequence of not being able to help the pupil focus on learning. In these situations, the staff member can be left with a range of worries, fears or beliefs: 'Am I a bad teacher?' 'Maybe I can't do this.' 'Maybe this is the wrong school/class.' 'Maybe I am not the teacher this pupil needs.'

To protect themselves from these painful feelings, staff members may withdraw from the intersubjective relationship also. They try to manage the pupils without connecting with them. They too become more controlling as they try to avoid the pain of offering reciprocity and receiving hurt or inadequacy in return. We see both pupil and educator turning their backs on intersubjective relationships and turning away from each other in the process. This can confirm a process that a pupil is experiencing at home with parents who continue to provide unhealthy parenting. It can also mirror a process which alternative parents, such as foster or adoptive parents, are experiencing. As the adults withdraw from painful connections with the child, it confirms the beliefs the child already holds about relationships and the need for control rather than connection. Without realizing it we can confirm existing beliefs these pupils might hold about relating with others.

Sometimes educators will respond to such disconnection by falling back on familiar behavioural approaches. They try to praise and reward the pupil into being different; they use consequences to try and show the pupil what he should do. Behavioural teaching without intersubjective connections becomes a battle of wills as each tries to control the other. As a pupil experiences this, their own defences strengthen so that control becomes stronger. The staff member often feels useless and ineffectual but communicates this to the pupil in a way that makes the pupil feel naughty and not good enough. The pupil makes sense of these experiences as she has her previous experiences. It confirms her view of herself as bad, useless and ineffectual. This increases her insecurity and makes challenging behaviours more likely. The staff member, too, is making sense of his experiences from within the relationship. The pupil is not responding to him with improved behaviour. This communicates to him a sense of failure and the pair become even more disconnected.

Mrs Jenning was an experienced educator. She had entered teaching because she was passionate about learning and believed that good education was a foundation for a good life. Mrs Jenning had noticed that she was feeling more tired and grumpy than usual. She had less energy for the things she enjoyed outside work and would wake up on Monday morning with a sense of dread rather than the excitement she used to feel. She was aware that she didn't like one of her pupils. Increasingly, the two of them would find themselves in power struggles where Mrs Jenning lost her temper and sent him to the principal. Although she would feel justified in the moment, as soon as her anger receded, she would feel shame. It wasn't how she wanted to be, yet she didn't seem to be able to control her behaviour. She felt that the other pupils were evaluating her negatively and that if this pupil was not in her class everyone's life would be better.

Mrs Jenning was not able to be in her open and engaged stance. The constant demands and lack of reciprocity with her pupil were impacting on how she could understand and be with him. The pupil needed her to make sense of and empathize with his internal emotional experience more than he needed behaviour controlled. Unfortunately, his angry and rejecting behaviour was pulling Mrs Jenning out of her socially engaged stance and into her pupil's world. They were locked in a mutually escalating pattern of pain and mistrust.

As we will explore later in the book when a pupil experiences safe connection, she is more open to behavioural support. Without this she will experience her behaviour being managed by the other – as the adult being mean. The pupil has little belief that the adult has good intentions towards her. It also confirms her sense of herself as bad, a belief which was bred from her early relationships but is now reinforced by these later interactions.

It is hard for educators to take these steps without someone offering them the same support as they need to provide to the pupil. Mrs Jenning also needed someone to accept and empathize with her strong feelings of failure and regret. To have known that these make sense to someone else who was not judging her for it would be very supportive. The intersubjective connections she could safely make with others would help her to remain open and engaged to the pupil, and to move back to this at times when this was inevitably lost. It is this type of support that can lead to resilience. All education staff need their own key adult who can support them by checking in on them (Bombèr, 2016). Support helps educators to continue trying despite their fears and doubts.

Mrs Jenning found some support from her senior colleagues. She was met with acceptance and empathy for how hard it was to teach a child who was so well defended. Together they were curious about what it was about this pupil, at this time, that was causing Mrs Jenning to lose her confidence. As she experienced the principal's unconditional regard for her abilities and motivations, Mrs Jenning began to feel more hopeful and to be more compassionate to herself. Her sense of humour returned, and she was able to return to a more open and engaged stance with her pupil.

If the educators can find ways to stay connected to the pupils, then they can help the pupils to become more open to relationship. As intersubjectivity becomes possible, the pupils experience a relationship within which they can learn. They become open to behavioural support. They become interested in learning tasks.

Understanding shame

Closely linked to blocked trust and fear of intersubjective experiences are pupils' experiences of shame. The fears that we have been exploring are explicitly fears about relationships. Underlying these fears is a more personal fear – the fear of not being good enough. In order to make sense of this fear we need to understand the emotion of shame and what happens when pupils are not helped to manage shameful experiences. This can lead to a range of challenging behaviours which make these pupils difficult to live with and impossible to teach. As we try and manage these behaviours, we can unwittingly reinforce the shame that created them in the first place. This is a further difficulty stemming from developmental trauma – the need to understand and support pupils experiencing shame.

Educating pupils living in shame

There are many ways that school environments can strengthen the shame-based sense of identities that pupils bring with them. We have already seen how vulnerable pupils can find learning and peer relationships difficult. Evidence that they are no good, not liked and failing is never far away.

Learning from mistakes is a part of the school experience. Healthy pupils can tolerate that mistakes are just mistakes and have no bearing on their self-worth. Pupils who have experienced developmental trauma tend to get stuck in shame, with a fundamental sense that there is something wrong or disgusting about them when they make mistakes. Shame makes us want to hide, reducing the opportunity for connection and learning. Shame can also lead to over-reactive responses in an attempt to create distance from the shame.

Seven-year-old Adnan struggled to make mistakes. He had grown up with a highly critical father and had a strong need to please people as a consequence. Sometimes, however, he would have huge emotional outbursts which appeared to come from nowhere or were triggered by very small things. These outbursts were commonly triggered when Adnan experienced shame in response to one of the teachers. For example, when his teacher gently pointed out a mistake in his number work, Adnan became angry and distressed with himself, taking this out on the classroom furniture! On another occasion, Adnan was distracted and failed to line up for assembly with the rest of the class. He had been preoccupied since he had arrived at school, following a difficult evening with his father. The teacher had failed to notice that he was not fully attending to what was going on around him. When she suddenly realized that he was still sitting in the book corner her face registered some disapproval. Adnan noticed and his anger was as sudden as it was intense. He swore at the teacher and hid underneath the desk. Adnan's angry responses were confusing to those who were observing or involved in the incident. These were out of character with his otherwise compliant behaviours. Often, the staff did not pick up on the triggers, nor was it easy to recognize the shame that Adnan was experiencing at these times. A generally compliant child had suddenly become a monster!

The Shield against Shame is a defence when shame is overwhelming (see Figure 2.1); behaviours are used as a distraction or diversion from the sense of badness the pupil is experiencing. However, these behaviours get them into trouble in school. Lying, minimizing and blaming others are perceived as the pupil not taking responsibility for their behaviour. When these fail, and the pupil rages, educators and peers are overwhelmed by the pupil's dysregulated emotion.

Far from not taking responsibility, these pupils are feeling very responsible. Rather than perceiving themselves as making a mistake following a bad choice, they believe that it is evidence that they are bad to their core. They cannot feel remorse and reach out to others to make amends; they are too overwhelmed about themselves to be able to look outwards. When educators try to discipline the pupil, this adds to the sense of shame; the pupil is even more caught up with his own sense of badness and even less able to reach out to others. The pupil becomes caught in a cycle of shame–defend–shame. The development of shame is described in more detail in Appendix 2.

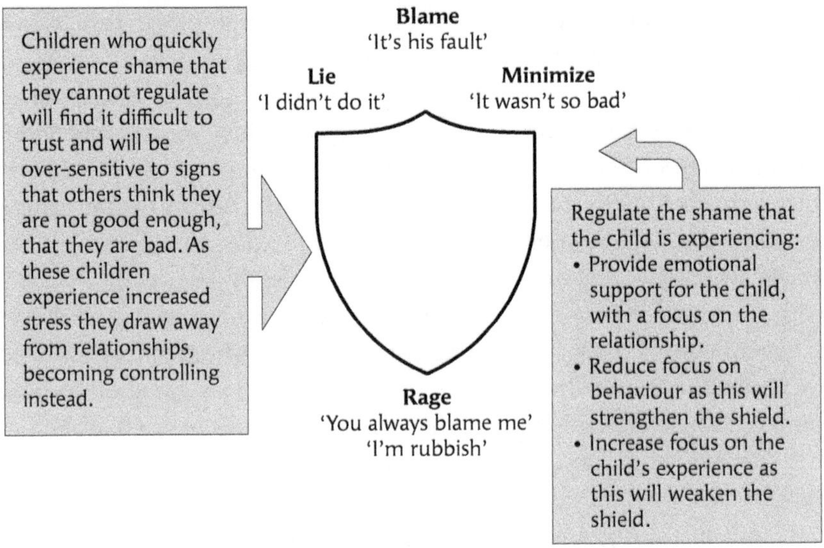

Figure 2.1: The Shield against Shame

Behavioural management strategies are utilized by adults in attempts to reduce shame-based behaviours and increase the capacity to demonstrate remorse and make amends. Unfortunately, this just serves to increase the sense of shame and the shield is reinforced.

The behaviours that defend against shame are typically highly disruptive within the school. They impact on the other pupils and divert education staff from the act of teaching. The educator has an understandable need to help the pupil to stop so that the class can become focused on the learning tasks. In addition, behaviours such as lying, blaming, minimizing and raging are all visible to others within the schools as well as visitors from outside. They can be viewed as a sign of the educator not doing a good job. The educator needs to do something to show that she is working towards improving the pupil's behaviour. It can be very easy for teachers to get caught up in the criticisms of those witnessing the difficulties. They end up piling on top of this their own recriminations: 'I am a useless teacher', 'Why did I ever think I could teach this pupil?', 'Someone else would do better.' Shame intensifies and the educator can end up becoming increasingly punitive as a consequence, for example engaging in relational withdrawal such as time out, isolation, seclusion and exclusion. Both pupil and teacher become locked in protecting themselves from shame but reinforcing it in the process.

Instead of stopping to understand what is going on for the pupil – identifying the emotional experience underneath the behaviour – the focus becomes on what the educator is doing about the behaviour. As each behavioural strategy fails, others are tried. This is with good motivations. They want the pupil to behave, not only because it will reflect better on themselves, but also because they know the pupil will ultimately be happier too. Without understanding, acceptance of and empathy for the shame and fear that underlie each person's behaviour, good intentions will ultimately be ineffective.

The pupils need adults who help them to regulate the shame they are experiencing. As the shame reduces, the pupils become open to behavioural support. This helps them to take responsibility for their behaviour, to experience remorse and to make amends. The pupils learn that things can go wrong, but this is recoverable. They are good, and relationships are stronger than the worst that they can do. They are worthy of unconditional support. They now want to find a way forward and to work with the adult to make things right again.

As we will explore in the next chapter, regulation and behavioural support needs to start with connection with the pupil's internal experiences. The adult understands and accepts the fear, shame and complex range of emotional experiences that can be connected to behaviours. This is communicated to the pupil via the empathy that the adult experiences, alongside understanding. The key to this acceptance and empathy is curiosity. If the adult can hold on to her curiosity, to wonder about the experiences of the pupil, she will understand the pupil more deeply and acceptance and empathy will follow. An adult can't be both curious and defensive at the same time. As we move into defensive behaviours, curiosity will reduce. Holding on to curiosity, or moving back to curiosity when it is lost, is central to providing the connection that these pupils need.

As Mrs Jenning experienced acceptance and empathy from her peers, she was able to regain her curiosity about her pupil's experiences. She began to recognize his anxiety, worries and fears that fuelled his controlling behaviour and could have compassion for him. Reminding herself to wonder about his inner experiences allowed her acceptance and empathy to flow naturally. Because she could now approach and interact with him with less fear, he was able to be more open to her influence. Over time, Mrs Jenning was able to collaborate with her pupil and they could figure out together how they might help him with his fears as well as meet her expectations for him around learning.

The prioritizing of connection and exploration of emotional experiences before offering behavioural support allows pupils to experience an attuned relationship. They learn that relationships can always be repaired, and that they are accepted unconditionally.

Understanding hidden and expressed attachment needs

Attachment difficulties are commonly found in children who have experienced developmental traumas. This is not surprising as the very nature of this type of trauma is that children cannot feel safe with their attachment figures. It is the parents who offer the children security, but it is also the parents who are the source of trauma, whether through neglect, illness, abuse, separation or loss. All the difficulties we have explored have relationship problems at their heart. This is equally true when we explore problems with early attachments and the way that these lead to patterns of relating which children bring into school with them.

When attachment patterns move into school environments

Appendix 2 explores the way that attachment patterns develop. This describes the role of the parent in the formation of the patterns and in encouraging different, healthier patterns to develop. These attachment experiences will also have an impact on the pupil in school.

Pupils' early attachment experience with their immediate caregivers is stored within the nervous system in the form of an internal working model. This is a template which helps the person to understand current experience and make predictions about this based on past experience. Attachment experience has an important role in guiding pupils in how to manage later close relationships, such as those with educators, mentors and friends. Rather than having to learn afresh with each new situation they encounter, their memory of past experience can provide them with a short cut. This can give important information about whether their nervous systems need to be prepared for defence or engagement. This allows them to make more rapid judgements about what to do in the situation. Over time, these internal working models can and do change and adapt to new circumstances as long as the vulnerable pupils get different, healthier relationship experiences.

Educators can have a powerful influence on the pupil's emotional experience of relationships. If they behave in ways that are different from the pupil's past experience, the pupil's nervous system gets new information which revises the internal working model. For example, rather than 'all close adults are dangerous', an internal working model might adapt to 'some close adults are dangerous, others are kind'. Notice that the new experience does not overwrite the old experience. Once children have experience of dangerous caregivers, they will always know that close adults can be dangerous. The difference is that they are also learning that there are other possibilities.

Educators, as close adults in pupils' lives, have an important role in providing alternative, different experiences of relationships that can make a difference to how children will manage relationships as they mature. Pupils enrolled in the Belong programme that Sian runs in Canada for children with developmental trauma enter the programme with clear mistrust of adults. They are typically enrolled in the programme for two years. Consistent feedback from teachers when they return to their home school is that the children now know how to ask for help. Their internal working model has adapted from 'no adult is reliable' to 'teachers can be relied upon to offer help when needed'. They become better at discriminating who they will approach and who they will avoid rather than being hijacked by an internal working model and nervous system that dictate that everyone should be avoided (Phillips, Melim and Hughes, 2020).

There is a challenge to providing alternative relationship experience, however. Mary Dozier (2003) studied what happened to attachment patterns of relating when toddlers moved into their foster and adoptive homes. She found that the adult's capacity to stay open and engaged and curious was essential to alter the child's internal working model. When adults were not aware of their own attachment patterns or internal working model, they could unwittingly respond to the toddlers in ways that reinforced their mistrust. Some parents would behave as if the children did not need them when the children demonstrated avoidant attachment patterns, or they would become frustrated, and sometimes angry, when the children demonstrated ambivalent-resistant attachment patterns and resisted comfort. Attachment patterns for children are a strategy to maintain connection to adults for survival while managing the expectation that adults will harm or let them down. 'Tigers' learn to show adults that they couldn't care less about pleasing them. 'Opossums' learn to de-activate their need for comfort and communicate that they have no need of adults. 'Chameleons' express that adult needs outweigh their own in their attempt to avoid harm. All three types of children have learned to hide their need for connection, comfort and joy. This is confusing, and parents can end up responding to the miscuing, trying to meet the needs that are expressed but overlooking the hidden needs.

It is likely that education staff can also be pulled into these attachment dances. Without recognizing the hidden needs, they are much more likely to respond behaviourally and in misattuned ways. That misattunement proves to the child that they are right to be protective. When defence meets defence, old patterns are more likely to continue.

If a teacher is responding defensively, her pupil's demands for attention when the headteacher is in the classroom may be responded to with frustration. The teacher may believe that the pupil 'always' disrupts the class, is deliberately trying to show her up in front of the headteacher and may feel shame and inadequacy at her failure to control this pupil. Her frustration will be shown on her face, in her tone of voice and in her attempts to control the child. This may mirror the experiences the child had with his parents and limit the opportunity to change the internal working model. However, if the teacher can remain open and engaged, maintaining her curious stance about the sudden increase in demanding behaviour, she can offer a different experience of relationships with adults. With acceptance and empathy, she may say, 'I really notice how you worry when something is different in our room. It is hard for you and I'm sorry I didn't notice that before. Stay close to me when this happens, and if I know ahead of time, I will let you know so you are not surprised.' The child will experience this attuned response in a way that challenges his expectancy that adults will not care or will be irritated. With repetition, his internal working model can adapt.

Education staff are not the primary attachment figures for pupils, but they can become additional attachment figures. They are safe adults who can help pupils to feel secure. This is an experience that pupils can benefit from if they have had good enough attachment experience, and if they are mature enough to leave their attachment figures for a number of hours each day. For younger pupils, and pupils who have had poor attachment experience, the lack of an attachment figure is more problematic, leaving the pupil feeling anxious and unsafe. This is why there is a greater ratio of adults to pupils for the younger pupils. The adults need to be educators and also emotional supporters, providing a secondary attachment experience while pupils are away from their primary attachment figures.

Vulnerable pupils will continue to have difficulties without the presence of a safe attachment figure throughout their schooling. It is recommended that these pupils are given a key adult to provide them with the additional emotional support that they need – a substitute or additional attachment figure (see Bombèr, 2007).

> For pupils with disrupted attachment histories, the provision of an attachment figure in school, *in addition to* the primary attachment figure at home, can make all the difference. These pupils need countless, repetitive, positive and healthy relationship experiences in order to literally 're-wire' those parts of the brain that have organized themselves to survive the overwhelming traumatic stress the child experienced in their early lives. What was once an adaptive response to a traumatizing environment…now needs challenging in the safe context of the classroom. This is necessary for the pupil to function fully in school, to make the most of all the educative opportunities on offer to him, rather than for him to remain undiscovered behind his habitual defences. (Bombèr and Hughes, 2013, p.10, emphasis original)

These pupils find it hard to manage without an attachment figure present. They struggle to share adult support with other pupils. They also need more help managing peer relationships and coping with increasing expectations for independence as they move through school.

Recognizing how attachment patterns are enacted within school environments is helpful so that these key adults can give the pupils the emotional support that they need. Vulnerable pupils tend to show a range of highly controlling patterns of relating. These pupils struggle to find ways of relating that help them to feel safe and therefore they move between different adaptations. You might also recognize several of the patterns described below within one pupil.

Pupils might show patterns of behaviour learned from the experience of dismissing caregivers – the *insecure avoidant patterns of relating*. These pupils strive to be more self-reliant within school. They can have a strong need to appear good and not to make mistakes. These pupils are reluctant to seek help or support when they are struggling practically or emotionally. They may turn away when someone approaches to help or look straight ahead with a blank, dazed expression as if they can't hear. Their expressed need is: 'I am fine. I don't need you.' This hides the need for emotional support that they are experiencing. School staff need to be emotional detectives with these pupils, recognizing the needs that are hidden. Context can provide important clues. Would you expect a pupil to struggle in this situation? Is this a time when a pupil might need comfort? Is anxiety or worry likely to be high because of the demands of the situation? Offering emotional support for hidden needs can help the pupil, over time, to feel more comfortable expressing this need. This includes providing regulatory support even when the child appears regulated. High levels of structure and routine can also help pupils with avoidant patterns feel safer with supportive adults (Geddes, 2006).

When pupils have had frightening experiences of their emotional needs not being met, these avoidant patterns can lead to *withdrawal from relationships and what is happening around them*, rather than self-reliance. This especially happens when something about the current experience reminds them of the earlier dangerous experience. This does not need to be a replication of the trauma. A teacher expressing some angry frustration with the class might signal to the pupil that things are about to get dangerous. He zones out from the current experience, sometimes to the point of dissociation. This is when the pupil's nervous system defends against the overwhelming stress of the situation by removing from conscious awareness what is being sensed or felt. This also means that the pupil is not able to signal the distress that he is feeling and therefore does not seek help. A key adult is in a good position to provide support at these times, recognizing what is happening and allowing the pupil to feel understood and supported.

Pupils might show patterns of relating that have developed out of experience of unpredictable, inconsistent caregivers. These are the *ambivalent patterns of relating*. These pupils can be very attention-needing, even clingy towards educators. They are inattentive to the task at hand because they are busy checking the availability of the adults. Anxiety increases if the adult is not focused on them, and they behave in a range of ways to ensure reconnection. They might talk excessively, follow the adult around, become confrontational or act as the 'class clown', all to draw attention back to themselves.

These pupils express the need for attention all the time, which means hiding times when they don't need support. They are reluctant to signal that they are emotionally okay and ready to focus attention on a task for fear that they lose the adult's availability totally. These pupils need a careful balance of attention and emotional reassurance with short times of being encouraged to manage without this support. They will need a lot of regulatory support for emotional distress that is close to the surface. Geddes (2006) recommends breaking down tasks into small steps so that pupils can manage brief independent attention to tasks without having to do this for too long. Frequent opportunities to be noticed by the educator, and extra support at times of transition, will also be important.

In addition to these insecure patterns of relating, vulnerable pupils can quickly escalate in their behaviour with increases in anger, aggression and control of adults and peers. These are the pupils that have very poor tolerance for increases in stress or arousal, even when these arise from exciting and positive experiences. The attachment pattern is described as *disorganized controlling*, a response to highly frightening early environments. These pupils are continually focused on signs of danger, often interpreting benign events as evidence that they are unsafe. They cannot tolerate uncertainty or unpredictability and will use a range of controlling behaviours to make sure the world is predictable. Those around these pupils can feel highly coerced. The pupils demand and force a response from the adults in order to reduce their own feelings of anxiety. This can be very effective when carried out in highly unpleasant ways which can be hard for the teacher to tolerate or to ignore; for example, rejecting offers of support by brushing it off in anger or mocking the teacher by telling him he is useless. This makes it hard for the teacher to respond in ways that the pupil needs. A priority for these pupils is for highly safe, predictable school environments with adults who can be calm and non-confrontational in their responses. High levels of empathy and understanding of these pupils can increase their feelings of being emotionally contained.

Noah's responses to the adults in his world would be classified as disorganized. He spent his first four years with parents who had significant substance abuse issues. They alternated between highly volatile behaviour and withdrawn, zoned-out behaviour. Noah and his three siblings were often terrified of being harmed when their parents were volatile, and of being abandoned when they would sleep all day or be zoned out from drugs. The children were taken into care when Noah was five years of age. His highly controlling and explosive behaviour as well as maladaptive self-soothing (picking and masturbation) resulted in multiple transitions in foster care. At school, teachers struggled to know how to respond to Noah's behaviour. He was very sensitive to any perceived criticism or changes in routine. His teacher reported feeling 'emotionally blackmailed' because she felt the only way to get through a day was to give Noah what he wanted and to remove any expectation of learning or compliance. She knew this wasn't good for either of them, but she wanted to avoid upset for the good of everyone in the class and to avoid the pain she could see when he entered a dissociative, shut-down state. She kept Noah close to her at all times. This made her resentful at times since he would not tolerate her leaving him to attend to other children's needs.

As Louise recommends with 'Team Pupil', this teacher needed a 'Team Noah' (Bombèr, 2016). She reached out to other staff members for help. She needed other adults who were available to regulate Noah when she couldn't. She started to warn him when she was going to set a limit or change something. She would predict that he might be scared and show his scared feelings with anger. She firmly insisted that she and others would help him manage but that she needed to help other pupils. She offered him a transitional object (one of her small stuffed toys) when she was working with others so he could remind himself that she didn't stop liking him when she was away from him; he still had a piece of her. She had to learn to tolerate his upset without fear that it was causing him more harm and to recognize that helping him with big feelings was going to be better in the long run than avoiding these. Together they created some spaces in the room where he could hide when he needed to. She made every effort to warn him when changes in routine would occur and to keep him close at these times. Her confidence and predictability helped Noah start to find different ways of being in relationship with her. With many, many repetitions, he began to have more good days than difficult ones.

This chapter has dipped into the relationship worlds of vulnerable pupils. Practical guidance and advice for helping these pupils can be found in a number of texts focused on providing attachment security in schools (Bombèr, 2007, 2011, 2016, 2020; Bombèr and Hughes, 2013; Forbes, 2012; Geddes, 2006; Golding *et al.*, 2013; Phillips, Melim and Hughes, 2020). This guidance is consistent with a DDP-informed approach, which will be explored in the next few chapters.

Conclusion

In this chapter, we have explored the impact of developmental trauma on pupils and the way that this can lead to some characteristic difficulties which impact on their schooling.

Children are born ready for emotional connections, innately ready for attachment and intersubjective relationship experience. When there is no response, or the wrong response, to their open and trusting invitations for connection, they experience fear. They quickly learn not to be open and trusting. They develop in ways that defend themselves from the pain of needing connection but not getting it. They avoid intersubjective experiences by adopting controlling behaviours and adapt attachment behaviours to miscue the adults about what they need. They learn to be selective about which needs they hide and which they express.

This early learning stays with the children as they grow and mature. Within school they remain vigilant to fear and hurt and this means that they are not open to change and difference. They do not recognize the open and available educator. Their nervous system remains set to defensive. They use all the controlling behaviours that they have developed in order to protect and feel safe. They do not have space left for curiosity and learning. In danger, safety trumps everything. Run, hide, fight become the imperatives, and learning moves to the background.

This becomes even more tricky when the school environment also provides normal and necessary limits and restrictions. The pupils, not safe with others, view these as more signs that the world is a mean place and that they are not good enough. They resist the discipline as they have resisted connection. Self-reliance and coercion increase as the pupils try to manage their own safety rather than being able to relax in the educator's good intentions.

Controlling relationships with others comes at a cost. It deprives the pupil of important relationship experiences needed for healthy development and recovery from trauma.

Liza notices Mr Watts smiling at her as she walks past the Head of Year room. 'What? What have I done?' she says in an aggressive tone and with a scowl on her face, avoiding the invitation to be in relationship with him. Mr Watts shakes his head in disbelief, raises his eyebrows and mutters under his breath, 'Why do I bother?' He continues with his marking.

When pupils are not experiencing the attunement and repair which regulate shame and make it manageable, they are left stuck in painful feelings come with a of lack of self-worth: 'I am bad, unlovable, unworthy.' When they are in situations which lead to disapproval from others, this sense of shame is triggered, and the pupils raise a shield to defend against the pain. Lying, blaming and minimizing defend against the sense of self as bad; when this fails, the pupil rages. Many situations in school can trigger these intense feelings, leading to some of the most challenging behaviours that educators must deal with. In addition, many of the traditional behavioural management strategies only serve to intensify the shame that the pupil is experiencing. Defensive behaviours increase as a consequence.

Overcoming pupils' fear of relationships is an essential role for educators supporting vulnerable pupils, as is overcoming their own fear of working with children who have such pain and frightening behaviour. The challenge for educators is to remain open to the pupils even when they are being met with defensiveness. When Mr Watts' smile is met with suspicion he might say, 'Ah Liza…you were walking past and so I thought I'd smile to say hello, and to see how you are doing. How's your morning been?'

In the next few chapters, we will explore ways in which educators can emotionally connect with pupils, leading to reductions in defensive behaviour and allowing pupils to feel safe enough to engage with learning.

CHAPTER 3

Building Connections

We have now reviewed some key difficulties that vulnerable children experience in school. Pupils are left with difficulties in trusting in relationships. They develop a shame-based sense of self and learn complex ways of relating to others that miscues their needs, leading to patterns of hidden and expressed needs. These difficulties can make these pupils hard to support and hard to educate. In this chapter, the focus will be on ways that educators can help pupils with this range of difficulties. This pays attention to building emotional connections with the pupils using the DDP principles as articulated within the DDP model. A summary of the principles and how they can be applied within education can be found in Appendix 1.

Difficulties with traditional support

Supporting vulnerable pupils is especially challenging because the educators are trying to provide behavioural support, guidance and teaching to pupils who do not trust them or their good intentions. As we have seen, the trauma that these pupils have experienced has led to a range of controlling behaviours. These behaviours can be very diverse: compliance, coercion, caregiving, self-reliance and entertaining. These all serve the same purpose of feeling in control of relationships so that these feel more predictable and safer. Even predictable anger and frustration from an educator, provoked by extreme coercive behaviours, feels safer to the pupil than waiting and wondering when the next angry outburst will come.

This is where traditional support runs into problems. Behavioural management as written into school behavioural policies aims to help pupils who display behaviours that are challenging for themselves and others. As explored in Chapter 1, vulnerable pupils find it hard to believe in the adults' good intentions. When education staff provide boundaries for relatively secure pupils, these pupils will be responsive to the limits being provided. They are responsive to the praise, rewards and consequences the educators are using to demonstrate approval and disapproval. They will also have internalized the values that parents have instilled in them and will be more likely to behave in ways consistent with these. We describe these pupils as well adjusted, because they are behaving within limits considered appropriate by the adults surrounding them. Even when they experiment with these limits through the rebellion and risk-taking of adolescence, they remain open to the support and guidance of the adults. These are the pupils who will be successful in school, achieving their academic potential. They will also be socially comfortable, able to form healthy relationships and open and engaged to connection with others.

Developmental trauma provides a very different experience. These pupils do not believe in the good intentions of others but view these intentions through the lens of their own feelings of worthlessness and shame. They are suspicious or fearful of the adults' intent to influence them. Adults are perceived as wanting to cause harm, wrecking their day by providing limits or confirming that they are liked less than the child who didn't push the limit. Opposition, confronting and ignoring the adult's attempt to influence them are the only ways to stay safe. Tragically, this protective stance means that these children are left alone in their fearfulness and mistrust and cannot access a new possibility for relationships.

Traditional behaviour management relies on adults' problem solving, based on understanding the environmental contingencies that make the pupil's behaviours more or less likely to happen. When a behaviour occurs in the context of certain conditions and is followed by certain consequences, it is more likely to happen again. A simple, but familiar, example is a pupil talking in class. The classmate responds and they are soon giggling together. The trigger for the behaviour is sitting next to the classmate. The response from this other pupil is rewarding; they are having a nice time together. The contingencies of talking to the classmate and his response makes it more likely that talking in class will occur in the future. The teacher, however, does not want the two classmates to be talking together; it is a distraction from the lesson. He has some choices. He can change the trigger by separating the classmates. He can ignore the talking and instead remind the pupils of the task at hand, rewarding them for attention to this. He can provide a negative consequence for talking. In all of these examples, the teacher is managing the contingencies to reduce the unwanted behaviour and increase the wanted behaviour.

Vulnerable pupils become anxious when the educators try to apply these ideas. They do not understand that the consequences and rewards are strategies focused only on behaviour while the staff member still accepts them unconditionally. Instead, these contingencies are viewed as signs of acceptance being conditional. Consequences are experienced as the adult being mean, unkind and unavailable. The pupil may meet what he considers to be unfair with anger. He may also become anxious that staff members have discovered that he is not good enough and will want nothing more to do with him. Even rewards can increase anxiety for these vulnerable pupils as, although positive, they are still an evaluation. Remember that the child who has experienced trauma does not see himself as having worth. Positive evaluations may feel like manipulation or a lie to the child who does not feel deserving. The pupil may just not be interested in any evaluation, positive or negative, from an adult. Being accepted by the classmate may be far more important. Anxiety then increases because the adult is thwarting this goal.

Teaching and classroom management will induce some anxiety in all pupils. Indeed, mild anxiety has been shown to improve performance (Bombèr and Hughes, 2013). It is important to remember, however, that vulnerable pupils are constantly in elevated states of anxiety. Their core state is one of high anxiety. We do not want to increase this further. Our goal should be the opposite; whether in supporting behaviour or increasing learning, we need to decrease anxiety in the pupils to improve their performance.

At times of high anxiety, the cognitive processing that allows the pupil to think and problem solve goes offline. Even if he could learn from limits, rewards and consequences when calm, this is no longer the case. The pupil is being driven by his emotional reactions instead. The teacher needs to find different ways to support the pupil's behaviour in ways that reduce anxiety and helps him to stay open to thinking things through and accepting adult support.

Regulatory-based behavioural support with emotional connection

Pupils do need behavioural support, but this needs to be provided in an environment which attends to their regulation and ability to connect. Educators need to offer the pupils the very experiences that they most fear – being understood and emotional connection. Only then will they be able to benefit from behavioural support so that they can internalize the values of the school. Educators need to find ways to build connections with their pupils, even though the pupils are behaviourally and biologically focused on staying disconnected.

A DDP-informed approach to regulation and connection

We are now going to explore how the DDP model can be brought into school environments (see Hughes, 2009, 2011; Hughes *et al.*, 2019 and the Introduction to this book for descriptions of the model). This can be described as a therapeutic approach. This does not mean that we are expecting educators to become therapists. It does mean that pupils can be supported in a way that can help them to benefit from all that school can offer.

Some pupils may also need help from a therapist and specific parenting practices to help them learn to trust. Therapy, parenting and school support can all be provided using the DDP model. If only the school is providing this approach, an opportunity is being missed, but the pupil will benefit from the experience of different relationships in school. If only the family is providing this DDP approach, then the school will miss out too! DDP is most effective when all those involved with a pupil are engaging in wraparound, consistent care. If pupils are surrounded by this approach at home, school and in the therapist's room, they will be getting comprehensive support with the trauma impact that they are experiencing. We will explore working with parents and networks further in Chapter 10.

DDP-informed schooling is part of the Dyadic Developmental Practice model. Educators need to understand the nature of developmental trauma and its impact on the pupil and especially the pupil's difficulties with relationships. With this understanding the pupil can become more relationship aware; valuing the attachment and intersubjective relationship experiences he needs which will help them to benefit from his schooling.

DDP-informed schooling is connection with behavioural support, alongside teaching. This means the school staff are taking on the multiple tasks of building trust, providing emotional connections, supporting behaviour and providing opportunities for learning.

Dan Hughes has described parenting for developmentally traumatized children as connection before correction. We have drawn on this idea within this book using the term 'Connection with Teaching' to acknowledge the importance of school staff attending to emotional connection before, during and after behaviour support and learning activities. It is important to note that the word 'teaching' as used here is referring to support which helps pupils develop prosocial behaviours by providing appropriate boundaries, limits and consequences within the context of highly warm and nurturing environments as well as referring to the teaching of the academic curriculum.

Behavioural support needs to be developmentally appropriate. Pupils vary in the rate that they mature. They can also be at a different stage in emotional development (the ability to understand and manage their emotional life), cognitive development (the ability to think based on their understanding of the world) and social development, which involves using both emotional and cognitive abilities to make and sustain relationships and to understand the self in relationship to others. Vulnerable pupils often have immature emotional and social development, with or without cognitive difficulties. Even if a pupil appears streetwise, or older than her years, this is based on a very thin emotional foundation. The pupils are slow in emotional development because their emotional needs have not been well supported in the past, and they are now less open to the emotional support of others. Energy has gone into defending themselves in what is perceived as an unsafe world, and this limits emotional growth. Emotional age also tends to reduce when we are under stress. Pupils become even younger emotionally when stressed; and if the adults become stressed by the impact of this, they may find themselves behaving in more immature ways as well!

Pupils will have more success when school staff provide a level of structure and supervision that is appropriate for their stage of emotional development. It is not helpful to expect more of a pupil than she can manage. When she fails to live up to these expectations, she will experience consequences that are likely to reinforce her identity as a naughty or stupid child. If the educator can provide a level of supervision and support matched to the pupil's developmental stage, then she will have more success. The pupil can then develop confidence that she is a good child who sometimes gets things wrong. Given the variability in vulnerable children's performance, educators must be constantly revising where their expectations must be that day or moment.

Jack was an 11-year-old boy whose ability to complete his work was quite variable. Some days he could pay attention, some days he fell asleep at his desk and some days he was quite hyperactive. At the start of the school year his teacher would provide work and expectations geared to his chronological age. She was confused because sometimes Jack was able to complete his work quite well and on other days not at all. Because he could do it sometimes, she believed that on days that he couldn't he was choosing to avoid work and she would provide consequences like staying in at break to complete his work or incentives such as extra computer time if he got his work completed during class time. As we have described earlier, neither punishment nor reward changed his behaviour because the variability in his performance was tied to how safe he felt. Jack lived in a household where there was a lot of yelling and fighting. His father drove a truck, and on the days he was away for work, life was calmer. Those were the days that he performed in class like an 11-year-old.

Once his teacher understood what Jack was bringing emotionally to school, she could support him more effectively. She was able to adjust her expectations both academically and socially. She was able to apologize to Jack for not understanding why he had difficulty some days and she reduced the pressure to perform when he needed that.

Central to helping pupils develop safety in connection is the attitude of PACE, which allows the educators to become attuned to the pupils through a stance of playfulness, acceptance of the pupil's inner world, curiosity about the meaning underneath the behaviour, and empathy for the pupil's emotional state. In this way, the adults stay emotionally engaged and available to the pupils, demonstrating their unconditional acceptance while also providing the safety that comes from appropriate boundaries and discipline.

Jack's teacher was able to use acceptance, curiosity and empathy (the ACE of PACE) in her conversation with him since playfulness would not have helped at that time. 'Jack, I first need to apologize for keeping you in to complete your work on days where you are tired or bouncy. I know that things can be tough at home some days and those are the days you have a harder time at school, and I was adding to this! I am so sorry. I was thinking, "This kid has a good brain but why isn't he using it? What can I do to make him use that good brain?" I wasn't realizing that when you are worried about your mum and dad there is no energy left over for learning. I have some ideas that might help you on those days, but I wonder if you have any ideas of what would help best?' Jack and his teacher compiled a list of ideas for those hard days, all of which involved connection and empathy.

Trauma and its relation to schooling

When supporting pupils who have been affected by trauma, it is important that school staff have a good understanding of this trauma and how it can impact on the pupil's development and day-to-day functioning. Being trauma-informed and responsive means that the educators can support the pupils in a way which helps them to feel safe and secure. This reduces the impact of trauma and increases the pupil's ability to engage with learning tasks. Sandra Bloom is a psychiatrist who is interested in the way that trauma can impact on hospital environments for adults experiencing mental health difficulties. She developed the 'sanctuary model' as a way of ensuring that the therapeutic environment was trauma-informed, including understanding the patients' traumas from childhood. The alternatives were environments organized by the trauma of the patients, which did not facilitate recovery from trauma and a return to mental well-being (Bloom, 2013).

We can think about Sandra Bloom's ideas in relation to schooling, where the difference between trauma-informed and trauma-organized can also be observed. Ordinary schooling, which does not take account of the traumas and attachment difficulties stemming from early experience, can easily become traumatized – in Sandra Bloom's model the school is seen as being organized by the trauma of the pupils. The school staff are affected by the difficulties that the pupil is having in trusting and entering relationships. They respond to the miscuing of the pupil's attachment needs and try to manage behavioural challenges without attending to the levels of shame that the pupil is experiencing. This can result in staff becoming defensive as they respond to the defences displayed by the pupils. As school staff become more trauma-informed, they will be more responsive and can support the pupils emotionally so that they maximize their ability to engage with learning. The staff member stays open and engaged to the pupil and is able to return to this when he notices himself becoming more defensive. Baylin and Hughes, writing about parenting, say, 'Parents who can resist the natural tendency to respond defensively to a child's defensiveness and can recover effectively from inevitable moments of losing empathy with a mistrusting child are the trust builders these children need to have' (Baylin and Hughes, 2016, p.73). The same is true of Team Pupil (Bombèr, 2016).

When trying to support and teach a pupil who is becoming defensive to your most gentle of interventions, it becomes difficult to stay open and engaged to the pupil. The pupil's defensive responses pull the adult into his own defensive responding in turn. Defensiveness breeds defensiveness. However, if the educators can find a way to stay open and engaged, or to notice their reaction and return to this open and engaged stance, the pupil will not be able to stay defensive. Open and engaged also breeds open and engaged. This is central to DDP-informed schooling.

A useful analogy for staying open and engaged is provided by the image of a river flowing between two banks to represent integration, as suggested by Dan Siegel (2010). If we stay in the river, we are integrating our own brain functions and relationships and are able to facilitate integration for others. We can think and respond optimally (see Figure 3.1). Dan Siegel suggests that:

> Integration is the linkage of different parts of something. When we integrate within a relationship, for example, we honor differences between ourselves and the other person. Then we promote linkage through compassionate understanding and communication. In the brain, integration happens when we honor the differences between our higher and lower regions and then link them, or between our left and right sides, and then link them. (Siegel, 2014, p.55)

This integration allows us to have a sense of harmony and be flexible and adaptive towards ourselves and others. Being open and engaged puts us into the free-flowing river where we can adapt to what the pupil needs as we respond flexibly and helpfully. We notice and make sense of what the pupil is doing, and this understanding guides us to provide her with what is needed. Notice that in this state the adult is taking the time to understand the pupil rather than moving to try to change the pupil's experience. Thus, the adult can behave in coherent ways, having energy to change and adapt while also providing stability. This flexibility allows adults not to rush into trying to reassure the pupil or to solve the problem the pupil is presenting. Once the adult understands the pupil's experience and communicates this understanding, then reassurance becomes a way of letting the pupil know that the adult gets it and that he has hope that they can get through this together. The adult is not trying to 'fix' the problem by changing the pupil's experience. From this position, adult and pupil can jointly find a way forward, if this is appropriate to the situation.

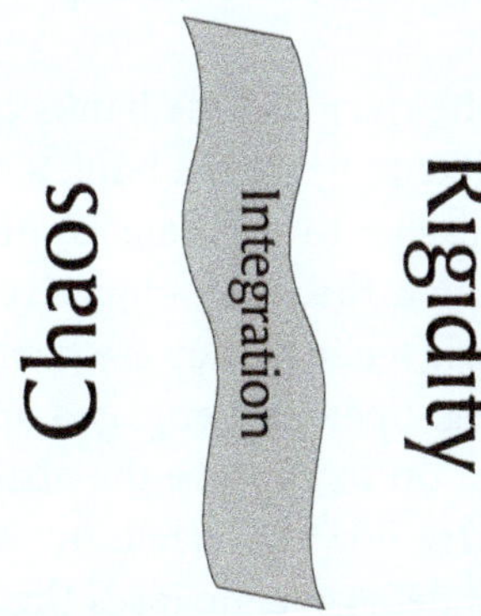

Figure 3.1: River of Integration (adapted from Siegel, 2010)

When educators move from this integrated state, they will be more defensive. When they move out of the river and onto the banks, their behaviour towards their pupils can be quite different. The banks of the river represent the times when adults have lost flexibility and are less able to adapt to what the pupils need. The two banks represent rigidity and chaos respectively.

On the bank of rigidity, the staff member might become very focused on achieving a task. He becomes stuck on this task and can see only one way of achieving this. Siegel equates rigidity with being boring and predictable. This is a rational response, but without the creativity that emotional engagement would bring. Jack's teacher was being rigid when she focused solely on getting him to complete his work. She had no tolerance for his variability in performance. She was making judgements about him (he is lazy, deliberately choosing not to listen) without paying attention to the factors that were making his engagement in learning difficult.

Chaos is on the other bank. Siegel suggests that chaos occurs when things are out of control, overwhelming and unpredictable. In this state, we might expect to see more emotionality in the staff members' responses towards the pupil. If Jack's teacher had operated from this river bank, she would not have been able to regulate her own frustration and may have expressed her strong feelings with little thought. She would likely have allowed her frustration to get in the way of liking or forming a relationship with Jack. Given Jack's sensitivity to adult anger, he would have picked up that his teacher was frustrated with him and both he and the teacher would have become stuck in their own emotional experiences, reducing the opportunity for learning for both of them.

Movement between the river and the banks can be led by pupils or the educators. We don't like to be on the bank alone, however, and it is easy for both pupil and teacher to gravitate towards the same defensive strategies. This closes down the intersubjective relationship as each becomes lost in the intense feelings they are trying to manage.

The difference between open and engaged and defensive becomes very important as we go on to explore the attitude of PACE, which ensures that the river is free flowing. When the staff member moves to either of the banks, he is defensive; he loses the attitude of PACE and instead becomes punitive, evaluative or judgemental.

A teacher described her response to a ten-year-old pupil. Natalie engages in extremely controlling behaviours which escalate even further when she becomes triggered. The teacher noticed that, if not careful, he would find himself barking commands at Natalie, and thus escalating her arousal even further.

In such situations, the relationship becomes less connected and the pupil's mistrust increases. When the adult stays open and engaged, the river flows. He can maintain the attitude of PACE or repair the relationship when this attitude is temporarily lost, the connection is strengthened, and the pupil's trust increases. This provides a relational foundation from which attention to teaching and learning can take place.

DDP-informed schooling is trauma-informed rather than trauma-organized. In understanding the trauma of the pupil, and the pupil's defensive responses, the staff member becomes able to stay in the free-flowing river rather than follow the pupil to the river banks, and stays open and engaged when the pupil's responses are pulling him into becoming defensive.

A teacher described how when 15-year-old Adam became agitated in her inclusion room he would dart about erratically. She commented, 'My heart would beat fast. I would choose to override my fear response by focusing on grounding myself, sitting down, changing my breathing, engaging in a mundane activity, while giving intermittent eye contact, smiling occasionally. Adam would then come join me. As I breathed a sigh of relief, I could sense my social engagement system coming back online.'

When educators can remain open and engaged to what they and their pupils need, this helps the pupils to trust in the staff member and to become comfortable with reciprocal intersubjective relationships, being open to influence as well as influencing. Educators will have to regulate powerful feelings of shame in the pupil and meet hidden as well as expressed attachment needs. Now true education can begin.

Skills needed to support pupils who fear connection

Staying in the river and connecting with pupils depends on educators' ability to make sense of their pupils' emotional experience and to respond to this. Their responses need to accept and have empathy for this inner experience.

Let's focus on this internal experience for a moment. What we think and feel is our internal experience, and it is important to hold on to the fact that our internal experience is separate from our external behaviour. What we think and feel is neither right nor wrong, it just is. How we demonstrate what we are thinking and feeling through behaviour might be acceptable or unacceptable, but is not the emotional experience leading to this. It is easier for education professionals if the pupils express their distress as this can inform interventions, but many hide their real needs and can remain unnoticed in the school context, often leaving them more vulnerable to mental health difficulties in the future. Louise knows a young person who has described how all through school she was 'the good girl' and now she just can't keep this persona up any more as it is too tiring. Trauma unravels over time.

Young children do not understand their internal experience as adults do. They need time with parents making sense of this to notice and understand it themselves. They will have big thoughts and feelings, but only with sensitive responsive parenting will they learn to recognize these and accept them for what they are. Their behaviour will be a reflection of how good they are at noticing and regulating their internal experience and turning to others for support with this.

When their self-regulation is poor, pupils will be at a disadvantage at school. There are many stresses during the school day and within the school environment. The pupil with poor regulation ability will be in a perpetual stressed and dysregulated state. For some pupils, this will be obvious through their dysregulated behaviours. What may be less obvious is that this is not intentional – they simply do not know how to regulate themselves, nor how to let others help with this.

Lee spends much of the school day running around and laughing manically. He has to touch everything. Without constant supervision he gets into trouble, putting fingers into the power sockets and roughly handling the school gerbils. Lee is not being naughty; his nervous system is in a perpetual state of high arousal and he does not know how to regulate this. His behaviours demonstrate this in a very obvious way.

There are pupils who work hard to keep a lid on this dysregulated emotional state. This may look like regulation, but it takes a lot of effort to keep it inside. When regulated, negative emotional experience becomes smaller and less influential. Without this regulation, the pupil is trying to hold on to emotional experience which is getting larger. No wonder there is little energy for learning. The pupil end the school day exhausted and often ready to explode, which he will often do at home. The team supporting the pupil are perplexed at hearing reports of this meltdown when they have seen no evidence that the pupil was struggling all day. Some staff may even misunderstand this dynamic. They may suspect that the parents simply need to provide more boundaries. The teacher is missing the pupil's hidden needs and judging the parents unfairly as a consequence.

Alternatively, some pupils might keep the lid on for much of the day, but then something happens, and they can't hold on to it any longer. The resultant outburst can be as intense as it is unexpected. With the pressure valve released a little, and with the fear of what this display of emotion might lead to, the pupil quickly reasserts control. The team supporting her are again perplexed at where the outburst came from and how the pupil can appear okay so soon afterwards. The expression of emotion was real. The quick regaining of control gives witness to how hard the pupil works not to give life to emotional expression that is perceived as dangerous.

Grace was quiet and unassuming. She would often appear fragile, crying in the inclusion department, but then from time to time would rage, throwing tables and chairs over in certain lessons. After a few minutes, she would return to her more fragile self, prone to crying. Staff, assuming that these were behavioural choices, would feel angry and frustrated with Grace. They didn't understand the regulation difficulties that were impacting on these behaviours.

Connection allows us to help pupils with this. When we notice, understand and connect with the internal experience of the pupil, we can co-regulate this emotion. This can reduce the behavioural challenges that the pupil presents, but even more importantly it will build her trust with her educator. The pupil will then be able to be in the classroom in a more regulated and less stressed state. This will be conducive to engaging with activities and learning. As trust builds, the pupil will, over time, learn how to regulate her emotion for herself and will feel more confident to seek support with this when needed. As pupils move through school, we expect them to become more confident learners needing less support from their support team. Attention to connection also allows them to become more confident regulators, managing their emotional experience in order to stay engaged with the teaching.

Alongside early co-regulation, a parent is helping the child to learn that her experience makes sense, and that it can be named and talked about. By reflecting with the child on what she is experiencing, the parent is co-constructing her experience. A recently overheard conversation with a mother and young child illustrates how we co-construct our children's experiences when we are attuned to their inner world.

A young mother was out shopping with her child who looked to be about three years old. The child was getting increasingly cranky and demanded some juice. His mother handed him a juice box and he threw it on the floor wailing, 'I want orange juice!' His mother tried calmly to explain that he had already drunk the orange juice and all that was available was apple. He was having none of it and continued to scream for orange juice. His mother could have scooped him up and left the store embarrassed by his behaviour or returned the anger and told him that there was no juice for kids who screamed. Instead she said, 'Oh sweetie I am sorry you are disappointed, and I can't offer you orange. We have stayed out too late with all this shopping, and when you are tired you get your grumpy pants on! You are one tired and grumpy boy right now, aren't you?' His wailing subsided and she pulled him to her for comfort.

In this short interchange, the boy's mother helped him understand his behaviour. His upset wasn't really about juice, but it did reflect fatigue and likely over-stimulation while out shopping. His mother helped connect his behaviour with his inner experiences so that next time he might be able to tell himself or his parents the same story. If she had left embarrassed or met him with anger, he would have missed learning about his feelings and how they were contributing to his behaviour and be less able to regulate himself.

We expect pupils attending school to have some awareness of their internal experience. Emotional literacy involves building on these capacities, developed out of good early experience, as in the shopping example. When pupils arrive at school without this early experience, some important developmental building blocks will be missing from their foundations. Educators need to be sensitive to this missing development otherwise their expectations of the pupils will be too high.

Teaching a pupil emotional vocabulary when the pupil has not had intersubjective experience of their emotional states will be like learning to read individual words but not being able to make sense of what is being read. This is why it is so important to give these pupils relational experience first, to be explicit about emotions before teaching emotions.

There are two key skills that teaching staff need in order to facilitate emotional connection:

- The ability to be mind-minded towards self and pupils.
- The ability to stay regulated so that they can maintain an attitude of PACE.

In this and the next chapter, we will explore these two abilities in more depth.

The ability to be mind-minded

As previously discussed, in order to connect with the pupil, staff members need to be able to understand the pupil's internal experience: what the pupil feels, thinks, believes, desires, fears and wishes for. It is this that the staff member will accept in order to support emotional connection. Doing this rests on a skill which we begin to learn when we are at the preschool age. This is the ability to mentalize. In particular, educators need to be able to know the mind of another or, as psychologist Elizabeth Meins coined it, to be mind-minded (Meins, 1997).

Another psychologist, Peter Fonagy, has written about the ability of mentalization (Fonagy *et al.*, 2002). This relies on having good 'theory of mind' – the ability to understand that you and others have minds, with their internal world of thoughts, feelings, beliefs and desires. Theory of mind is something which typically develops between the ages of three and four years. It is a maturing ability which also relies on the relationships that a child is experiencing. Theory of mind and the ability to mentalize combine into what Fonagy described as our reflective functioning. Children who have parents who are not interested in what they are internally experiencing are likely to be slower developing a theory of mind; they have weak mentalization abilities and therefore reduced reflective functioning.

Theory of mind helps us to understand ourselves and other people because we can understand what we or they are thinking and feeling.

This makes behaviour more predictable. A child notices her mother is crying. She therefore predicts that her mother is having an emotional experience; she is upset. She looks around and sees that their pet cat has knocked a vase onto the floor. She guesses that the broken vase has upset her mother. With this understanding the child can show some empathy to her mother. Without understanding, it is difficult to empathize. Without some experience first of her parents connecting with her emotional experience, it is likely that a child would find this much harder to make sense of. It is because others connect and have acceptance for children's internal experiences that they are able to reciprocate and do this for others in turn.

With this continual experience from the parent early in life, the child is discovering her own mind. The child is learning to organize her experience, and this will eventually help her put into words what she is experiencing. This further increases the child's capacity for regulation that has begun to develop within the relationship with an attuned, sensitive parent. Notice how relationship, regulation and reflection are all closely linked.

Regulation and reflection will be much weaker if the children do not have experience and trust in a relationship that is unconditional in its capacity to connect with the children's early experience. Without regulation and reflection, a child will find it hard to manage emotional experience without getting overwhelmed. This applies to positive emotion – think of an overexcited toddler, for example – as well as to negative emotion. If a child can't soothe herself, nor tell others what she is experiencing, she might dysregulate, demonstrating challenging behaviour at the verbal or physical level. Some children who have experienced very angry parents, when they have displayed these types of behaviours in the past, might dissociate – switching off and shutting down.

When pupils lack capacity for regulation and reflection, they arrive at school ill-equipped to manage the school day, to interact with adults and peers and to engage in learning. They will need experiences similar to children who have had the benefit of healthy adult relationships before they can meet the expectations school holds for them. Educators will need their own well-developed capacities for regulation and reflection so that they can introduce these to the pupils.

In order to connect with pupils, the staff member first has to be able to make sense of his own internal experience. Noticing what he is thinking and feeling with empathy for himself can help him to become more regulated. In the following example, a teacher is reflecting on his own experience during an incident when he became angry with a pupil.

It had been a long, wet week and I was tired, but Friday was here at last. I was aware of Ellen, pale and thin, sitting at the back of the classroom. I did know that she had been having a tough time, moved into foster care with little notice, and not knowing when she would be going back home. I am ashamed to say that this was not, however, at the front of my mind as I struggled to keep the class settled and focused for one more day. I have always prided myself on my ability to keep a class interested, but I was feeling distracted today. The weekend ahead was going to be difficult and my mind drifted to the worry of what might be in wait for me.

For most of the lesson Ellen had been disengaged but quiet. I paid little attention to her, but when the visitor entered the room, she became noisier. I heard her banging her chair about and was irritated. I didn't want the visitor to witness me in poor control of the class. I was also aware that her key person was not around just then. She had left the classroom a short while before. I felt cross – just when needed she was not around.

When Ellen finally exploded, I guess my irritation, anxiety and, yes, my own anger got in the way of any understanding about what was going on for her. I strode to the back of the room aware that she was now hiding under the table. I was not going to accept this behaviour. Needless to say, it did not go well!

With empathy for self, the staff member can remain open and engaged to the pupil. It is now time to focus on her internal experience. He has to make sense of what is happening, through clues in the pupil's behaviour. This curiosity lets him figure out what the pupil might be thinking or feeling. He then accepts this experience, knowing that it is neither right nor wrong, it just is. With acceptance, he can show empathy for the pupil's experience. The pupil feels understood and not judged for this experience. This connection also helps her to regulate her emotional experience. Through connection, the staff member is co-regulating with the pupil, and emotion can reach a tolerable level. Only now will the pupil be ready for learning.

Returning to the example of the teacher and Ellen. Here are the teacher's reflections once he was regulated and able to think about what she might have been experiencing.

Ellen was living with a mother who was increasingly poorly because of mental health difficulties. As Ellen was only six years old, I can only imagine how anxious and afraid this must have made her feel. Earlier in the week her mother had to go into hospital and Ellen moved to an unfamiliar foster carer. I am guessing she was afraid; who was this person, and would she be kind? She must have also been worried about her mother. I guess that Ellen took care of her mother a great deal; I am wondering how it must have felt not knowing what was happening to her. Maybe she felt guilty that she had not looked after her well enough.

Now I am thinking this through, it makes sense that she would not be very focused in class. The visitor entering the classroom may have seemed like a further threat, or maybe she worried that this person was going to take her away as well. I think all these feelings erupted at once into that explosion of behaviour. Now I think about it, if I had been her, I would have hidden under the table as well.

Conclusion

In this chapter, the focus has been on how to support pupils in school to increase their sense of security and to help them to manage despite poor developmental abilities to regulate and reflect. This requires more than traditional behaviour management.

Dean arrives in his maths class jumping about, squealing and talking loudly to his friends. Ms Critcher shouts at him to sit down and be quiet. She warns him that if he continues messing about, he will build up even more behaviour points and will probably get excluded as he must have a lot by now. Dean gestures at her and laughs hysterically. Ms Critcher sends someone to call senior management. Dean is left in a dysregulated state and knowing that once again he is in trouble.

Dean needs his educators to be mindful of connection with teaching. This helps the pupils to experience and feel safe with emotional connection and makes behavioural support more palatable while providing regulation.

With this in mind, Ms Critcher approaches Dean differently. She smiles, walks over and greets Dean personally. She can see he is not ready to settle yet, so she thinks it might be helpful for him to move some boxes of books for her. 'Wow, you have a lot of energy this morning! I need some energy as these need moving. Let's move these...' Learning becomes more achievable.

The model that is informing this approach is Dyadic Developmental Practice (DDP) as developed by Dan Hughes. The educators strive to provide an emotional connection with the pupils. This then allows the pupils to manage behavioural support with reduced feelings of shame, and less fear that they are not good enough. As the pupil uses this connection for regulatory support and to make sense of experience, he in turn becomes more able to engage with school and to learn and achieve. To achieve this emotional connection, school staff will need good reflective functioning. They will need to be mind-minded so that they can make sense of the pupil's internal world.

CHAPTER 4

Supporting with PACE

In the last chapter, we explored the importance of emotional connection to help vulnerable pupils cope and get the best out of school. Emotionally connecting with pupils relies on the capacity to remain emotionally regulated alongside the ability to be mind-minded, to make sense of the internal world of the pupil. When in an emotionally regulated state, educators can use this understanding to help them connect to the pupils. This is where PACE comes in.

The ability to maintain an attitude of PACE

PACE is at the core of supporting vulnerable pupils to thrive in school. This attitude facilitates a connection between pupil and staff member which is not possible with a narrower focus on managing the behaviour or teaching the pupil. Behavioural support is important in order to help a pupil to settle to learn. If it is not done within an atmosphere of PACE, it will reinforce the pupil's sense of shame and his belief that adults will not be interested in him or continue to support him. These pupils attend school in a perpetual state of feeling not good enough and expecting others to want to get rid of them. Many of these pupils have already had more experiences of moving school than pupils typically experience. It is not hard for them to imagine that they will have to leave this school too. This, together with other fears, keeps them in a perpetual state of anxiety. The connection that PACE brings builds the trust and security in the relationship that has previously been missing from the pupil's experience of school. With this connection, the pupil will cope better with the normal boundaries and discipline that school provides and will be more able to engage in learning.

PACE was suggested by Dan Hughes as a way of helping the adult remain emotionally engaged and available to the child (Golding and

Hughes, 2012). PACE helps parents to demonstrate to the children that they are available and sensitive to their needs. The parent becomes attuned to the child through a stance of acceptance, curiosity and empathy. Playfulness at appropriate times provides an opportunity to increase the fun and joy in the relationship. PACE combined with unconditional love for the child means that the parent is meeting the emotional needs of the child to be loved, nurtured, protected and understood.

Teaching staff can hold the same attitude in school. All pupils will benefit from the increased understanding and emotional support that this attitude can bring. Vulnerable pupils need educators to hold this attitude to increase their sense of safety in school. The emotional connection that the attitude brings allows the pupils to experience more secure relationships within which they feel understood and supported. This allows the co-regulation of emotion that they need to reduce the stress that being at school brings. It also provides co-creation of experience that allows the pupils to make sense of what they are experiencing, reducing the sense of shame and threat that this experience otherwise brings.

When holding the attitude of PACE, educators will naturally talk with the pupil in a more lilting, rhythmic voice. This is more like storytelling than lecturing. In a gentle, sing-song voice, with an open, warm, expressive face: 'It was all getting a bit much for you just then in maths. It was so, so hard. I am here now, so we can figure this out together. I wonder why it felt so hard today? What might have got in the way? I know you usually like your teacher and the subject. Hmm… we need to get our heads together and see what we think…' The pupil gets the experience of the other being interested in the story of what is happening or has happened to him. In sharing this story with the teacher, the pupil is able to understand his experience more fully.

Nine-year-old Jaz was shouting angrily at her friend that she was no longer invited to her birthday party and they would never be friends again. Her teacher moved over to see what the matter was, puzzled because Jaz was usually a quiet and co-operative pupil.

Teacher (in an animated voice that matched the energy of Jaz's upset): 'Jaz, you are so upset right now! I wonder what has happened to make you so upset with your friend? What could it be?'

Jaz (crying and angry) shouted: 'What do you care anyway!'

Teacher (dropping her voice slightly and using acceptance and empathy): 'Oh boy, Jaz, you must be feeling as if nobody is caring about you right now. Not your friend and not me. That feels horrible, doesn't it, when you think people don't care?'

Her teacher didn't reassure or contradict Jaz's experience, just tried to name and organize it for her. She also introduced for Jaz the concept of not being cared for as being behind her anger, a co-construction of her narrative.

Jaz (still crying but moving more into sad tears): 'Well it's true, nobody does care.' (And then back to anger as she tried to defend against her brief experience of vulnerability) 'I hate you and everyone!'

Teacher: 'Oh Jaz, you don't hate everyone! Hate is such a strong word.'

Jaz: 'You don't care! Nobody cares. I hate you!' (Responding now with more anger as her teacher moved to reassurance and correction rather than staying with her previous focus on Jaz's inner experience).

Teacher (recognizing her mistake): 'Jaz, I am so sorry. You really do hate everyone right now when you experience us as not caring. Hate is a strong feeling and, clearly, I am not doing something right to show you that I do care. You are also not sure whether your friend cares about you. It's so scary to feel not cared for. So scary. No wonder you are mad! No kid should be uncared for, should they?'

Jaz, her anger dissipating, looked down and shook her head, likely experiencing shame now that her anger had been expressed.

Teacher (in a soft voice): 'Jaz, I am so glad that you were able to show us that you were angry with us. You don't often show how you are feeling inside, and I am so glad you could today. You might be worried now that I am upset with you for yelling. You might be wondering, "Have I blown it? Now people won't care for sure because I told them I hated them."'

The teacher's guess was based on what she knew about Jaz's likely avoidant attachment pattern.

Jaz (still looking down) mumbled: 'Nobody likes me.'

Teacher (although she wanted to argue with Jaz, she was able to remind herself not to correct her and to stay with the sadness expressed in the statement): 'Jaz, how hard that is to feel as if nobody likes you. I think you worry a lot about what people think about you and try so hard to be a good kid. I wonder if that's your way to make sure you don't make people angry? How exhausting that must be. Would you like some help to figure out whether your friend is angry at you? Maybe I can help you get back to playing together?'

Jaz, still looking down, shook her head. Her teacher had asked too early while shame was still not integrated.

Teacher: 'I tell you what, you come with me right now. We are going to do some reading next. I'll give out the books. Why don't you snuggle into the cushions in the library to read? I'm going to think some more about how to help you with your worries about people not caring about you. I'll let you know when I have figured it out!'

Jaz was not yet ready to engage with people or learning and her teacher recognized her need to disengage for a while. She gave her a place in the classroom where she could feel more separated (remember, shame makes us want to hide) but kept the connection open by telling her that she was going to continue to think about this problem. You will also notice that there were no consequences given for yelling. Understanding was all that was needed here. The teacher, after handing out reading books, did approach the friend who had been involved in the upset to make sure she was okay about what had happened.

'Abbi, Jaz had such a big upset earlier, didn't she? You might be puzzled and wondering what you did wrong – or angry at her for yelling at you. Are you okay? I think Jaz sometimes finds it so hard to believe we all like her, even if we are frustrated and mad with her. She needs a bit more time this morning, but at lunchtime I would like to help you guys figure out what happened and get back to playing together. Would that be okay?'

Educators will strive to adopt an attitude of PACE, to maintain this attitude even when they are beginning to feel challenged by the pupils and thus defensive towards them, and to return to the attitude at those inevitable times when the attitude is lost under stress. The ability to do this is strengthened when the educators have good ability to stay emotionally regulated themselves. Emotional regulation strengthens PACE, whereas dysregulation weakens it. In the final chapters of this book, we explore self-care, social support and self-understanding. These all help to strengthen educators' capacity to stay emotionally regulated when under stress.

PACE rests on the mind-minded ability of educators to become attuned to the pupil's inner experience. Jaz's teacher could see that underneath the anger was a feeling of being uncared for. She didn't know all of Jaz's history but knew enough to understand that Jaz was a child who had not had consistent or nurturing parenting. She also recognized that Jaz tried hard to please adults. It was very likely that not feeling cared for was a big part of her inner experience. The teacher's attuned response helped Jaz to feel connected. She began to shift from an angry response to a sad one in response to her teacher's regulated behaviour. Her anger spiked again briefly in response to a misattuned response of reassurance and correction. Again, because her teacher didn't get angry, Jaz's anger could be regulated, and her behaviour could change. Her shame would take longer to regulate, but with repeated support from her teacher to put feelings into words, Jaz could learn over time to regulate, reflect and express herself without fear of repercussion on her relationships.

Notice that PACE is an attitude, a way of being. It is not a behavioural strategy designed to change the pupil. The staff member tries to maintain this attitude, however the pupil responds. If the pupil is not able to enter a conversation about this, the staff member can simply use PACE on behalf of the pupil. The attitude as backdrop to the relationship will provide the pupil with a greater sense of being unconditionally accepted, however he responds. Thus, if the educators are generally curious and understanding about the pupil's inner world, acceptance and empathy will come through in the way they are with the pupil. The pupil, in turn, will experience being understood without pressure to change what he is thinking and feeling.

In this way, the staff member does not use PACE to get pupils to talk, to open up, or to behave differently. Jaz was not expected to stop shouting or get back to playing. Her teacher was set just on understanding. The staff member changes her responses towards the pupil, without expectation that the pupil will change. PACE is a way of being to help pupils feel more secure. At its best, PACE is a habitual way of engaging with the pupil, not a technique to turn on and off as needed.

Sometimes, when pupils are verbal and at a developmental stage where they can join in the curiosity about their inner world, they might listen to the staff member and join in with some exploration of their experience. It is important that the staff member matches the pupil's mood so that the pupil can feel understood. Thus, if the pupil is sad, the staff member will talk quietly and slowly. If the pupil is angry, the staff member will talk without anger but with more vitality and intensity, as in the example with Jaz. With this understanding, the pupil might feel ready and able to think with the staff member about what has been going on for him.

If the pupil is not able to listen and join in, perhaps because of immaturity or because of the level of shame he is experiencing, the staff member continues to hold the attitude. Pupils are being introduced to the intersubjective relationship through this attitude of PACE. This is a relationship that they will have sought as infants, but the response of their parents was frightening or neglectful. They have since turned their back on relationships. These pupils will not always welcome PACE with open arms. The staff member needs to be PACE-ful on the pupil's behalf until he is ready to engage in the relationship.

The DDP principles for a PACE attitude

The DDP principles are helpful for educators to be mindful of when working to hold a PACE attitude (for more information about these principles see Appendix 1):

Affective-reflective dialogue

There is an affective and a reflective part of providing PACE.

The *affective* is the way we both experience and express our emotional states. To connect with pupils, educators must match their affect, without getting caught up in the emotion themselves. Imagine being with a friend who is feeling sad. You will be no help to him if you are overwhelmed by his sadness too; neither will it help if you are happy and jolly. The friend will be helped if you can communicate that you understand his sadness and have empathy for it. Words alone will not do this; the affective experience of your friend needs also to be matched. This is communicated through matching tone of voice, intensity and rhythm, the non-verbal elements of relationships, and empathy which is communicated both verbally and non-verbally.

The *reflective* is communicated through words. Putting words to experience will increase understanding of that experience as well as helping the pupil to regulate in the face of the experience. It also helps the pupil to feel accepted. He is not being judged for his experience but is being understood. A story emerges from this reflection which is shared between the two of them. It is the way that secondary intersubjectivity can occur – the forming of a story from a perspective different from that of the child. The child might think the reason for their behaviour is because they are a bad kid. When the adult can mentalize and put words to how behaviour reflects underlying experience, the child can form a different understanding.

Follow-lead-follow

Intersubjective relationships are based on interactions which are reciprocal and co-operative, and very different from the controlling interactions that the vulnerable pupils are more used to engaging in. PACE helps to support the pupils to become more used to intersubjective ways of relating to others. This attitude helps educators to adopt a follow-lead-follow approach to interactions. Most typically within education, educators expect to lead their pupils, guiding behaviour and learning. Secure pupils are confident following the staff member's lead. Vulnerable pupils will find this deeply uncomfortable. For these pupils, relinquishing control to follow the teacher's lead feels deeply dangerous. If the educators allow this degree of control from the pupils, nothing changes; the pupil is left in a state of insecurity and the defence remains in place. If the educators try to take control back, they end up entrenched in control battles which are invariably won by the pupils who are expert in this way of interacting. Educators can't lead the pupils, neither can they follow. To move out of this status quo, educators need to find a way to combine following and leading. They choose when to follow the pupils' initiatives and when to lead with initiatives of their own. The next step is determined by the responses of the pupils to this following and leading. This is described as 'follow-lead-follow'.

Mr Parker noticed that Colin was playing with Lego rather than finishing his maths questions. He knew that if he were to direct Colin back to maths there would be a power struggle. He joined Colin on the carpet.

Mr Parker: 'Colin, I see that you are playing Lego. What are you building? I see that you might want to be an architect when you grow up since you love to build things.'

Colin: 'What's an architect?'

Mr Parker: 'A person who designs what buildings look like – on the outside and the inside.'

Colin: 'Okay. Cool.'

Mr Parker: 'How do you decide how to build?'

Colin: 'I don't know.'

Mr Parker: 'Maybe it's just a natural skill you have.'

Colin: 'Maybe.'

Mr Parker: 'I know another natural skill you have.'

Colin: 'What's that?'

Mr Parker (playfully): 'Avoiding doing your maths!'

Colin, smiling, continued to build his Lego.

Mr Parker: 'I think you might want to say to me, "Mr Parker, I am ignoring you; I'd rather go with the conversation about the architect. That's something I do like!" I was wondering if there was anything you were finding hard about maths, something I could help you with? Maybe it's just too hard for your brain to resist things you do well like Lego. It's probably saying "Colin, stay away from the maths – for your own good! It makes you feel dumb." Trouble is that I have to find a way to teach you this stuff. Especially if you are going to be an architect. Imagine if you didn't know geometry and how to calculate stuff! Your buildings might be wonky!'

Mr Parker played Lego for a couple of minutes with Colin, following his lead again.

Mr Parker: 'Okay let's get this maths done! Let's find a way to tell that voice in your head that is telling you that you can't do maths that it doesn't know what it's talking about!'

PACE helps the staff member to better understand and accept the pupil's internal experience, what she is thinking and feeling, her beliefs and wishes, her fears and doubts. With this understanding, the staff member can be sensitive and responsive to the pupil's behaviour and interactions. He does not have to impose his own demands on the pupil but can be more responsive to the pupil's wishes, all the while holding his adult authority. Adult guidance becomes founded on a unique understanding of the pupil and her wishes, strengths and challenges. The pupil in turn will experience the staff member as having her best interests in mind as she feels understood by this staff member.

Follow-lead-follow means that the staff member ensures that he knows the pupil first before guiding her in a direction that he believes will be helpful for her, when guiding both behaviour and learning. As the pupil experiences feeling understood, she will in turn be able to follow the staff member's lead, helping her to develop her own understanding, influencing her sense of security and opening up new ways of interacting with adults and peers. As Dan Hughes writes, 'Following and leading means that we step back from proving that our position is the correct one. It means being committed to understanding both positions and then seeking a common path that meets the needs and wishes of both' (Bombèr and Hughes, 2013, p.224).

Talking to, for and about

PACE helps us to talk with pupils in a way that increases our understanding of them. However, many vulnerable pupils fear this understanding. They will not join us in these conversations, or they simply do not know what they are thinking or feeling. The educators need to find ways to know the pupil, and to help him to feel comfortable in this knowing. Sometimes we need to stop talking to the pupil, taking the pressure off him and allowing him to listen to us talk about our sense of what he is experiencing. This involves the educators holding the attitude of PACE without putting the pupil 'on the spot'. This does involve some guesswork and is therefore based on the staff member's understanding of and her relationship with the pupil. She can wonder aloud about what the pupil might be experiencing with no expectation that the pupil will respond. The pupil can quietly witness the staff member understanding him, giving small verbal, or often *non-verbal*, responses which can guide the staff member in adjusting her guesses in tune with the pupil. The staff member might wonder aloud by talking to herself or with a colleague. The pupil witnesses being 'talked about' without having to engage. The staff member reflects and the pupil listens. The storytelling attitude is important here to reduce any sense that the staff member is lecturing the pupil; instead, it conveys an attitude of deep interest.

George, an angry nine-year-old, had been sent to the principal to cool down. The principal greeted George with a smile and invited him into his office.

Principal: 'Hi there! You seem to be angry and your teacher seems to be angry. What is going on?'

George scowled, shrugged his shoulders and turned away from the principal.

Principal: 'Oh boy, I think you are saying to me, "Stop talking to me! What do you care anyway!"'

The principal gave the child the space he was asking for and sat at his desk, talking to himself. 'I wonder what it could be that has made George so very angry? He came to school today in a great mood. I saw him help one kid off the bus and hold his backpack and he wasn't mad then. Then he went to class and managed all morning. I do know that it takes George a lot of energy to manage in class, working and listening to his teacher. I wonder if he just got to the end of his energy? I wonder if his teacher asked him to do something he didn't want to do and that just used all of that energy up?

Just like that. I am going to think about this some more but first I need a glass of water. George, would you like one?'

George, looking down, shrugged slightly.

Principal: 'I'll take that as a yes! Stay right there. I'll bring us a cookie too and we will figure this out together when I get back.'

To deepen the affective elements of the dialogue even further the staff member might 'talk for' the pupil. This means talking as if she is the pupil – 'If I were you, I would be thinking/might say...' The staff member has a go at being the pupil, expressing for him what he might find hard to put into words. It is important that this is done based on good understanding of the pupil. We are not wanting to tell the pupil what we would like him to think but trying to put into words his own experience. Notice the difference between 'If I were you I would say I am happy to be picked to read my work to the class because it means the teacher is proud of me' with 'If I were you I would say I am scared that the teacher has picked me to read my work. She thinks my work is good, but what if she is wrong or I can't do good work again?' In the first, the teacher is articulating what she would like the pupil to feel, while in the second, she is using her understanding of what the pupil feels to help him express his insecurities. Talking about and for pupils means helping the pupils to experience us as understanding them, including their deepest fears and worries. As Dan Hughes says:

> When you try to express what the child or young person is experiencing like this, you're giving your pupil the gift of your mind (and words) to help them to notice aspects of their own minds more clearly, which they are then able to communicate about more clearly. (Bombèr and Hughes, 2013, p.211)

Rupture and repair

The use of PACE to connect intersubjectively is only possible if the staff member can stay open and engaged. When pupils become closed, defensive and/or hopeless, it can be easy for the staff member to join them in this closed, non-engaged state. The educators also become defensive through their experience of feeling irritated, frustrated, hopeless and so on. All these responses will close down the intersubjective relationship.

When the staff member loses the attitude of PACE and instead becomes punitive, evaluative or judgemental, the relationship is less connected and the pupil's mistrust increases. When the staff member stays open and engaged by maintaining the attitude of PACE, the connection is strengthened and the pupil's trust increases.

Educators like all of us are human, with our fragilities and vulnerabilities. No adult will be able to stay open and engaged all the time. Breaks or ruptures in the relationship are a normal part of experience. Both staff member and pupil must find a way of managing these. Discovering that a relationship can rupture but can then be repaired is a powerful learning experience for a pupil. This helps the building of resilience; after all, the pupils will need to manage many relationships in the future, including all the conflict that goes along with this. For a pupil with only fragile trust and little sense of safety, ruptures are hard to cope with. Shame can quickly increase, leading to behaviours that can further disrupt the relationship.

There will be ruptures – they are inevitable – and the educator's job is to take responsibility for repair. Sometimes, this involves the staff member apologizing to the pupil; if the staff member genuinely feels that she got something wrong, it is helpful to acknowledge this. Over and above this, however, repair is about letting the pupil know that the relationship is still strong.

This also means that the repair is not about the pupil's behaviour; that can be supported later. It is about the relationship. By repairing the relationship, the staff member is communicating that the pupil is accepted unconditionally, and the staff member will continue to support the pupil in all the ways he needs. This will include supporting the pupil to manage any consequences because of the behaviour. This demonstrates that whatever has gone wrong the pupil is worth bothering with.

Pupils' responses to PACE

PACE, together with these other DDP principles, therefore helps pupils to increase their security as they experience themselves being understood and accepted. With this increased security they can come to understand themselves more deeply, sometimes revising their sense of who they are and what they expect of others. With this deepening security, their attachment needs, often communicated through controlling behaviours, can relax. This allows exploratory systems to activate and the pupils become open to learning.

Sometimes pupils will struggle with the experience of being this deeply understood. This feels alien and frightening to them. They may fear being exposed and being found wanting, that the staff member might discover that they do not accept the pupil after all. The pupil might try to avoid this intersubjective experience. They will feel exposed and try to distract the staff member. The relationship is not intersubjective because attention is not shared, and each has a different intention – the adult to understand; the pupil not to be understood. In the same way that a horse led to water will not drink if it does not feel safe, the pupil offered a relationship will resist this until he experiences some safety and trust in this relationship. PACE takes time and patience.

Pupils may resist the relationship when the staff member is trying to make sense of what is a very difficult experience for them. An easier starting place might be with the more relaxed playful moments that come and go during a school day. When staff member and pupil can share a fun or enjoyable experience, the pupil may be more open to the intersubjective connection between them. Co-regulation of affect and co-construction of experience can still happen, but because it is focused on less shame-based parts of the pupil it may be easier for the pupil to tolerate. Playful moments can provide an oasis in a day that feels like a walk through a desert – hard, tiring and with little end in sight. Holding on and treasuring the playful, fun times can carry the staff member and pupil a long way through the desert.

Unpacking PACE

We have been describing PACE as a whole. This is how it is best understood. Here we will describe each of the components of PACE to help you understand it fully. This is a bit like telling you how to drive by describing all the different actions you will need to take. The ability to drive might disappear as you think about each separately; but you will then combine these together again. The whole will emerge as the parts recede into the background.

P = Playfulness

The first part of the PACE attitude is Playfulness. Educators can help pupils to develop security in part by helping pupils to be playful. This is not about providing appropriate toys and activities, important though these are. For playfulness to build security, it needs to develop the relationship. The staff members help the pupil to experience joy in the relationship. Experience is amplified when it is shared in a playful way. It dramatizes that the pupil is special and lovable. Fun and play are protective; a pupil can't experience shame while being happy and joyful. Playfulness provides optimism that things can be different. The pupil discovers his strengths and uniqueness; he experiences having a positive impact on another within a reciprocal relationship. This builds trust as the pupil enjoys feeling connected. Relationship-building playfulness is an important part of the support that the pupils need.

A = Acceptance

Perhaps the hardest part of using PACE is being able to accept without evaluating the pupil's inner experience of thoughts, feelings, beliefs, wishes and desires. Educators need to be aware of the inner life of the pupil, understanding it without trying to change it. When this inner experience is distressing or difficult for adults, it is understandable that they move into trying to reassure or talk the pupil into feeling something different so they themselves can feel better. The pupil may experience the adult's diversion with anxiety: 'It must be bad if my teacher can't handle it.' Or they may worry that they are not good enough or pleasing enough for the educator. Shame can then settle in further. When the educator can tolerate and embrace the feelings that come with mistrust, the child can start to recognize that adults can be safe and interested in them and will start to trust them. Shame then can reduce: 'My teacher can handle all of my parts.' We may wish this experience was different so that it is more comfortable for the pupil and the staff member. Security comes, however, from having adults who accept the child's internal experience without evaluation. Sitting with the uncomfortable is part of providing a secure base.

C = Curiosity

Support that builds relationships is support that is also curious and reflective. Through an attitude of not knowing and a desire for discovering who the pupil truly is, the educators can understand the pupil more fully. If the team supporting the pupil are not curious, they are more likely to make rapid judgements about the pupil, and this is more likely to lead to non-reflective action. This in turn can shut down relationships. Curiosity is an act of discovery that can lead to responsive, non-judgemental care.

E = Empathy

Curiosity leads to a different understanding and thus a deeper acceptance of the pupil and his experience. The pupil experiences this increased understanding and acceptance through empathy. Empathy builds secure attachment. The pupil feels more secure when inner experience is understood, accepted and empathized with. It is only with this experience of security that attachment systems can settle and the pupil's exploratory system can become active. Exploration is essential for learning. Empathy is central to helping pupils get into a state for learning.

PACE as a way of being

PACE can be an emotional compass for educators, helping them to remain open and engaged to themselves as well as to their pupils. When educators are feeling frustrated, despairing or a sense of failure, it is important that they are PACE-ful towards themselves. In this way, they can find a sense of equilibrium again, with support from others if helpful, and then calmly return to PACE for the pupil.

PACE becomes a way of being rather than a technique. The staff member wants to be with and to understand the pupil without an immediate motive to change him. PACE allows the staff member to get alongside the pupil and to support and share the experience the pupil is having, trusting that change will come out of the process as the connection between staff member and pupil becomes stronger.

Using PACE to try and change the pupil will weaken this connection. When a pupil experiences the staff member as trying to change him, he is more likely to be oppositional and non-compliant. The pupil is helped when the staff member has no immediate agenda beyond empathically connecting with the pupil through understanding and acceptance. When the pupil perceives the staff member as wanting to know him, he is more likely to be engaged in the relationship, and behavioural change might indeed follow when correction is not the focus. If it doesn't, the staff member continues to accept the pupil and the emotional difficulty he is struggling with, holding on to hope that this will become easier over time.

There are verbal and non-verbal elements to PACE. The verbal element is the content, what the staff member wants to understand. The non-verbal elements carry what the staff member is feeling. It is important that our verbal and non-verbal expressions match. Sometimes an educator may be 'talking' PACE but her non-verbal communication is conveying something else – perhaps frustration or disappointment in the pupil. When an educator notices this discrepancy between the verbal and non-verbal, she might reflect on her own experiences. Perhaps she is experiencing some frustration or disappointment or is anxious about loss of authority or worried about her sick child at home and can't be open to the child's experience. Maybe she is using PACE in the hope that the pupil will change rather than being PACE-ful without expectation of the pupil. This lack of acceptance is likely to be picked up by the pupil who will become more defensive in response. He might become angry or withdrawn as a consequence. When this happens, the staff member needs time and compassion for herself and support from colleagues as she works at understanding the pupil more deeply, as in our example of Mrs Jenning in Chapter 2. As she accepts and is supported with her own struggles with this, she is likely to find a deeper acceptance for the pupil. Now PACE will be conveyed in a way that the verbal and non-verbal match. The non-verbal components reflect a way of self-expression that is unique, deepens and makes the communication more trusted, and, most importantly, is received authentically by the pupil.

It might be helpful to think about how the elements of PACE link together, so that it is appreciated as a whole rather than a series of elements. Notice that there is no starting point, but that it is a circular process of combining the elements into a whole.

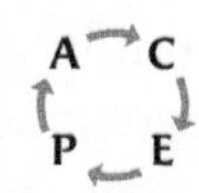

Notice how ACE will always be present, starting with any of these elements, and P will come in and out as appropriate.

It can also be helpful to think about how curiosity can deepen acceptance and empathy (A and E). The staff member responds to the pupil's mental state with light acceptance and empathy: 'You are having a hard day today' or 'You are enjoying yourself today.' The staff member's curiosity about

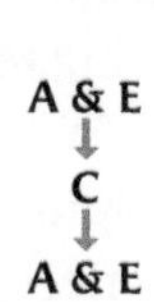

the pupil's experience can then increase her understanding, leading to a deeper acceptance and empathy response. 'It is so hard when you get your sums wrong. I wonder if it feels as if you will never learn this?' or 'You are loving the way that sand feels as it trickles through your fingers.'

Introducing PACE to pupils

Pupils will respond to PACE in different ways. Some pupils respond positively straight away, and the educators experience a stronger connection with them. Other pupils might resist the feeling of closeness that PACE brings. It may feel too strange to them, not fitting their sense of who they are. Empathy can expose the pupil to being known in a way that is unsettling. Older pupils might comment on how the staff member is reading their mind. The staff member will need to approach these pupils more slowly; lighter PACE can gradually deepen over time, allowing the pupils to get used to being known and to feel safe in this experience.

At the annual DDP conference in 2016, Jon Baylin described PACE as surprising the brain. The child has adapted to a world where negative reactions and rejection are anticipated. When the adult does not respond in this way, the child experiences something which is surprising and unexpected. Novelty allows new learning and adaptation to occur.

It is helpful to think about how parents naturally have a PACE-like attitude to their infants and young children. They accept the child and what the child experiences and try to make sense of this experience so that they can nurture and soothe or stimulate and play with their child. They have no expectation of the child, they just strive to be with him in a way that supports and connects. As the child matures, the parent begins to make this more explicit, telling the toddler what he is experiencing so that the toddler can come to understand himself more deeply. Only with the older child does the parent ask the child how he is feeling. Now the child can join the parent in wondering about his mental states; it becomes natural to be curious and to express what is being felt.

When introducing PACE to vulnerable pupils in school, it can be helpful to keep this developmental sequence in mind. The staff member notices the pupil's ability to make sense of internal experience. Does the pupil need the staff member to be with him, as with an infant, to help them to know what they are experiencing as with a toddler, or can they wonder with the pupil as with an older child? As the educators developmentally match the pupils, they will be able to connect with them in a way that the pupils are ready for. Over time, the pupils will learn to reflect on their experience and will be comfortable to experience it. At times of stress this fledgling ability to connect will reduce again and the staff member can return to sitting with acceptance for the pupil without any pressure for the pupil to talk about what he is experiencing.

PACE before discipline

When PACE is used as a technique in the hope that the pupil will change his behaviour, the educator is not experiencing acceptance. The staff member might, for example, decide to use empathy rather than have a genuine curiosity from which empathy naturally arises. 'I know this is hard for you but...' The staff member is trying to use PACE in order to bring about change. PACE as technique is likely to lead to resistance. Pupils will react to this with shame, as they experience not feeling good enough. This only strengthens the behaviour that the staff member hoped would change.

When the educators sit alongside the pupils, understanding and accepting their experience, empathy will naturally emerge. The pupils experience a sense of being good enough. This in turn can lead to feelings of guilt and genuine remorse for behaviour that has been challenging. The pupil wants to make amends and does not need to be coerced. Rather than 'This is so hard, but...', PACE with true acceptance of the pupil's experience can lead to behaviour change, but this is not something that is forced by the staff member. The essence of PACE is being able to be with the other without expectation of change.

PACE does not mean that educators will tolerate behaviour which is unacceptable to them. Discipline is still needed. PACE is an attitude that also sits alongside discipline. PACE helps to continue an emotional connection while the discipline will support the pupil's behaviour, helping the pupil to behave in a way that is more comfortable for him as well as everyone else. This helps the pupil to experience unconditional acceptance even though discipline is present.

Through the connection that PACE brings, the pupil will experience shame being regulated. Now the pupil can experience guilt and want to make amends. The connection with the staff member provides the continuing support needed to help the pupil to do this. Consequences become collaborative rather than imposed by the adults, and the ongoing PACE before, during and after discipline allows the pupil to continue to feel understood and accepted. It also allows any relationship ruptures caused by the discipline to be repaired.

When the pupils were being called back into school after the lunchtime break, the lunchtime supervisor, Mrs White, noticed that six-year-old Siobhan was still absorbed with something by the flower bed. As she got closer, Mrs White noticed that Siobhan was trying to make something with a pile of sticks she had gathered. Aware that all the pupils were nearly inside and back with their teacher, Mrs White told Siobhan to put the sticks down and hurry up. Siobhan reacted immediately. Still holding one of the sticks, she ran at Mrs White, who thought she was about to be hit. Her instant response was to be cross with Siobhan. Luckily, Mrs White was part of 'Team Siobhan'. She knew something of the difficulties that Siobhan had and how they as a team had decided to support her.

She quickly but calmly spoke to her: 'This is so, so hard. I get that. You are letting me know loud and clear that it is a big ask to have to follow us grown-ups. I can see how hard it is. I think I surprised you as well. You were so busy, maybe you hadn't known that we were all going back into school and then suddenly I was there trying to move you along. What a shock! Right now, I want to do all I can to help you know that I am on your side. I must ensure that everyone is safe when I'm the adult in charge. Carrying sticks like that is not okay but we will work this out together. I know we will.' Siobhan dropped the stick and came up to Mrs White, giving her a big hug. 'I'm sorry, Miss. I don't want to hurt you.' Gently Mrs White disentangled herself from Siobhan. 'I know you don't. Maybe tomorrow you can stay close to me at lunchtime. I can let you know when it is nearly time to go back into school, so that you will be ready.'

PACE alongside teaching

PACE does not mean that the teacher will abandon education. It is being sensitive to the additional support that the pupils need in order to engage in learning. The teacher continues to promote learning while, alongside the support staff, maintaining an emotional connection with the pupil. The attitude of PACE can help the pupil to engage with learning, relaxing hypervigilance and reducing the fear of getting things wrong that make engagement difficult.

Of course, PACE takes time. It can be hard to imagine how this can be built into the day alongside all the educational tasks that need to be achieved. It is true that an attitude of PACE means slowing down and taking the time to understand the pupil before deciding how to respond. In doing this, however, the response given to the pupil is likely to be regulating rather than dysregulating, reducing stress rather than increasing it. In the long run, this can save considerable time. Moving hastily to enforce a rule or insist that a pupil completes a task can lead to a level of stress and dysregulation that will take time to soothe. Helping a pupil to maintain a regulated state in a lower stress environment can ultimately mean that the pupil spends longer on learning tasks and the teacher has more time with the class as a whole.

The teacher is responsible for the whole class and many pupils will need his attention. Seeking understanding can only be brief. Acceptance and empathy can be high, but sometimes deeper curiosity is harder to achieve. Therefore, it is important to have support staff who can assist the teacher. When a key adult is involved, their time can be used to seek a greater understanding. They will also get to know the pupil at a deeper level, thus being better able to make sense of what the pupil is struggling with. The team supporting the pupil can work together to ensure that the pupil gets the individual attention needed while a PACE-ful attitude is maintained for the whole class.

Conclusion

In order to support vulnerable pupils in school, the teachers and support staff need to have an attitude of PACE towards the pupils. Playfulness within the relationship helps the pupil to experience safety in relationship and to experience the joy that this can bring. Acceptance conveys that the pupil's internal world is understood and not evaluated. Curiosity helps to find this understanding, discovering the story that is the pupil. This understanding is conveyed to the pupil with empathy. PACE is experienced by the pupil as emotional connection. It might feel strange and worrying to begin with, but over time the pupil's experience of PACE will help him to feel safer and more secure.

The following example illustrates this.

All the class were seated, and Liam was nowhere to be seen. Miss Baker asked the others where he was. They shrugged their shoulders. The door burst open and Liam stood there with a big grin on his face. Miss Baker was annoyed as he was holding her up. She had so much to get through before 3.30pm and it was already 2.30pm. One of the other teachers had made a comment about her time keeping and so she was especially sensitive about this right now. 'Where on earth have you been? You are wasting everyone's time. Get into your seat quickly and stop grinning about it. It's not funny!' At this Liam slumped into his chair, deflated.

About 15 minutes into the lesson another teacher popped in to pass on a message. Liam seemed preoccupied. The other teacher explained that Liam had just bumped into his little sister as they had been doing a tour of the school. Liam and his sister were living in different foster placements at this time. Miss Baker felt terrible. She started the class on an activity and went over to Liam, who turned away. 'I've just heard that you bumped into your little sister just now...' Liam shrugged and looked into the distance. 'I'm sorry that I jumped to conclusions too quickly. I should have asked you whether you were okay.' 'It was nice to see her.' Liam looked at Miss Baker with big, sad eyes. 'Ah, it was nice to see her. I wonder whether you feel a few feelings seeing your little sister – pleased to know she is okay, sad not to be living with her, mixed-up feelings might be in there too.' 'Yes, it feels kinda muddly if you know what I mean.' 'Yes, muddly. Thanks so much for letting me know... It's a big ask to get on with work when there are muddly feelings about. I get that. How about I sit next to you and we do this work together? Maybe we could then make a card for your little sister, to pass on later?'

CHAPTER 5

PACE: Frequently Asked Questions

In this chapter, a range of common questions which educators ask when discovering and exploring PACE will be considered.

Why do I need to use PACE in my teaching? I have taught many pupils who have achieved in school without this attitude.

Secure pupils will do well in school with well-intentioned teaching, however this is done. PACE, however, is an attitude which can strengthen any relationship. We all want to be understood and accepted for who we are. When a pupil experiences safety in relationships, she will develop resilience. A PACE attitude from an educator will increase well-being even when the pupil is not needing to heal from trauma and a fear of relationships.

A traumatized pupil can only start to learn when she begins to feel a level of safety within the school and in the different relationships she encounters – safety which is taken for granted by the more secure pupil. PACE is an essential part of the teaching experience which can give this sense of safety. The relationship needs to be experienced by the pupil as important to the staff member; only in this way can the pupil start to develop trust and thus can become open to relationships as well as to learning. A vulnerable pupil needs something extra from the support she is receiving in school, meaning that traditional teaching is not enough.

I am using PACE, but the pupil is not changing.

It is understandable that educators have a strong motivation to see the pupil engage in school and learning. They want the pupil to be successful, happy, healthy, to achieve his potential. They know that disengagement in school will reduce this. They also know that a high level of behavioural challenge will impact on all the pupils. Educators can experience feelings of frustration, failure, hopelessness and even anger when their attempts with the pupil are not leading to positive changes. However, to achieve a happy, healthy and successful life, pupils need to be able to trust, connect, enter intersubjective relationships and experience only low levels of shame. Narrow goals for behaviour change, even if they can be realized quickly, are not likely to achieve this for the pupil. Pressure to teach the pupil without taking the time for the emotional support can end up increasing stress for all the pupils. Teaching by the long route is needed to help the pupil with 'connection' as well as teaching. PACE will help the educator to stay regulated, connected and open and engaged to the pupil. This ultimately will help the pupil to change in positive directions. This is not a quick fix but a journey that the adult is going on with the pupil.

I am trying to use PACE, but it is so difficult. What can I do?

PACE is hard, but worth the effort as you notice the pupil growing in security and engaging with learning. Some people use PACE very intuitively; it comes naturally to them. However, many of us must really work at this. With commitment and practice, we can improve in our ability to maintain the attitude of PACE. The dual capacities for emotional regulation and mentalization will support the use of PACE. If the educator has weak capacity for emotional regulation and struggles to be mind-minded towards the pupil, he will be weak in PACE. The effort to use PACE will, however, help him to strengthen these capacities. We all start somewhere. If the educator makes the effort to adopt an attitude of PACE, he will find that he grows in his ability to regulate and mentalize.

Good self-care, social support and self-understanding will also help a staff member to strengthen his emotional regulation and capacity for mentalization. Attending to a staff member's own needs will strengthen his attitude of PACE. The final chapter of this book provides guidance for looking after yourself. Bombèr (2016) discusses 'Team Pupil' looking out for one another too (see also Jennings, 2018; Tranter *et al.*, 2018).

When I use PACE, the pupil gets angry and tells me to stop it.

It is very difficult when you are working hard to help a pupil and your attempts are being thrown back in your face. It can lead to concerns that you are failing or being unhelpful.

PACE is an attitude that connects emotionally with the pupil. Vulnerable pupils have learned to defend against such connections because of the pain and fear that they have experienced when they have been emotionally open to parents in the past. PACE can therefore evoke the pupil's vulnerability, and the pupil resists this, anticipating more pain and fear. She does not experience safety in feeling sad and being open to comfort. The anger is a way of defending against this emotional vulnerability. As the pupil develops safety over time, she will begin to feel greater trust in the team supporting her and allow herself to be vulnerable, and confident in their support at these times. If the staff member can maintain the attitude of PACE and accept the pupil's feelings of anger, she will, over time, feel less angry and be more open to emotional connection.

At these times, it is also worth being curious about the pupil's regulation at the point at which you are expressing empathy and curiosity towards her. It might be you need to find ways to help the pupil feel calmer and more soothed. This can be different for each pupil. You will need to reflect on what works for this pupil. The key adult will know the pupil well and may be able to spend some time with her, going for a walk, engaging in a soothing activity. (For more ideas to help with regulation see Bombèr, 2020; Forbes, 2012; Howard, 2013.) When the pupil is more regulated, she may then be open to some gentle PACE or some wondering aloud near to her.

I am trying to have a PACE attitude, but the pupil seems to be getting more distressed.

This can feel like a step backwards. However, as was explored in Chapter 1, pupils who have experienced a lack of comfort early in life adapt by blocking the experience of social pain; this is pain that arises from within a relationship. When a pupil begins to find safety in a relationship with an educator, she does not need this adaptation any more. It is safe for the pupil to experience pain and sadness because she now trusts in the comfort. The pupil will begin to allow herself to be more vulnerable; to experience pain and distress that she had previously blocked and to turn to the staff member for comfort with these experiences. The pupil will be more emotionally distressed because she trusts the staff member to help her with this. She no longer needs to suppress this distress behind anger and oppositionality. Commonly, the first tentative explorations into distress are brief and you might notice an oscillation between vulnerability and anger as the pupil moves towards and then retreats from these experiences. You might want and hope that the pupil can be happy, but it is also important that you can stay open to emotional distress. Providing a safe space within the school where the pupil can go to at these times is also important. This needs to be a quiet area away from the hustle and bustle of everyday school life. It is helpful if it includes sensory comfort such as blankets and cushions. Educators are often creative about how to create a safe space. For example, tents, yurts and sheds have been used, as well as finding a corner, area or room within the school that can be designated for this purpose. Ideally, it will be big enough for the pupil and an adult. At the least, an adult needs to be nearby. The space is for gentle connection, time with a safe adult allowing the pupil to recover from the distress and regain a sense of safety. This also avoids the pupil experiencing the discomfort of being seen by her peers when in a distressed state.

When distress in a pupil is seen as a sign of failure or as PACE not working, you can become defensive. This is a sign to the pupils that their trust was misplaced. When this happens, you need to attend to the relationship again, providing a repair to the rupture any defensiveness might have caused. Without such a repair the pupil is likely to suppress the emotional distress again and revert to previous adaptations in anticipation that staff members will not be available or comforting.

I think that the pupil is responding to our PACE attitude but then she will do something which just spoils it and it feels as if we are back at the beginning again.

This is so hard. To feel you are making progress and then to see it moving backwards can make any educator doubt what he is doing. However, progress is rarely straightforward, and ups and downs are likely to be common. Just think about developing a new habit or skill yourself, and how inconsistent progress can feel. It is with practice that the new becomes habitual. Any new learning requires new neural pathways to be formed within the brain. As the skill or habit is practised, these pathways strengthen or, in neurological terms, become myelinated. Consistency only comes with practice. An analogy might help to understand this. Imagine taking a daily walk through a field; if you walk across the field in the same way several times a path will begin to form. At first this path will be unstable; if you walk a different way for a few days the grass will grow back, and the emerging path will disappear. The more that you take the same path, however, the more stable it becomes.

It can be harder to cope with the ups and downs than when no progress is being made. When the pupil is doing well, the staff member can relax. He can start to enjoy the relationship he is offering to the pupil, and which is now being received. He feels the satisfaction of the pupil engaging in learning. But the pupil then feels a need to retreat from the warm feelings that comfort and joy in a relationship can bring. She is still uncertain that she deserves this and fears that she might lose what she is starting to like. She does something to create distance again. This might be a way of testing the staff member; is this a part of me that will drive you away? Alternatively, she might be ensuring that she can still manage without the thing that she believes she doesn't deserve. At these times, it is easy for the staff member to lose confidence. He might doubt that any progress observed was real. He might despair, unsure that he can go through it all again. This can be experienced as a 'dopamine crash'. The warmth and connection that was present in the relationship with the pupil leads to increased dopamine, allowing the staff member to feel good about this. The disruption to the relationship as the pupil retreats again can lead to a crash, as dopamine rapidly reduces. This can feel worse than not experiencing the dopamine reward at all. It is hard to continue offering PACE with the discouragement and pain that this can bring. Knowing about this possibility can help the staff member to remain steady, enjoying the ups and supporting the pupil through the downs.

The pupil seems to manage me being curious but hates it when I am empathic.

Sometimes educators can use empathy as a technique without feeling it. Feelings of frustration and anger, or a sense of failure, can make genuine empathy difficult. At these times, rather than trying to force empathy, the educator might try to be more curious and accepting of his pupil's experience. This will increase understanding, leading to deep feelings of empathy for the pupil which can be communicated with genuine feeling. Educators may try to 'fake it until they make it' but this will not be helpful for expressing PACE, which needs to come from the core of the self. This might be a time when educators need helpful people in their life who can have PACE for them and their experience of the pupil; as they feel connected and emotionally supported by others they will be able to 'make it' without any need for fakery.

Another possibility is that the pupil is struggling with the intensity of the relationship that is provided with PACE. A lack of empathic support when younger can lead some pupils to feel anxious and confused when they experience empathy from staff in school. They mistrust the adult's intention; they anticipate a trick to get them to behave, or some children may fear that this is a precursor to being hurt. Empathy evokes feelings of vulnerability, a state that traumatized pupils try hard to avoid. Most of the defences they have built up over the years are to avoid feelings of vulnerability and they have learned not to want or need empathy from others.

Sian worked with one pupil who would scream at her, 'Stop using that voice! Just shut up!' The young boy, who had so much mistrust, was terrified of the vulnerability it evoked in him. The team first needed to provide empathy indirectly, such as talking about him, writing notes (e.g. I'm sorry that you are having a hard day today) that allowed verbal expression without the non-verbal expression and sometimes, if he would allow it, playfulness: 'Here comes my annoying voice; quick, cover your ears!' These indirect ways of providing empathy allowed the team to not be controlled by his fears. They could give him what he needed but in ways that were respectful of the time he needed to trust in it. It is only with a gentle persistence, over time, that the pupils will start to feel comfortable with these experiences.

When direct empathy is provided, think about how you convey it. When we communicate empathy, we tend to be quite animated and musical in our communication. We use intonation and rhythm in speech to convey what we are feeling. This is called prosody. Pupils who struggle with empathy will need less prosody in the voice. This means being more matter-of-fact in our speech. Prosody can increase as the pupil becomes more tolerant of empathy, but for a while she might need this lighter empathy.

For my pupil, empathy is helpful but curiosity just isn't accepted. She calls me a freak and a witch.

When a pupil appears unsettled about curiosity it is worth reflecting on the pupil's early experience of others making sense of her feelings and thinking. If the pupil is not likely to have experienced much of this, it can be disturbing when someone appears to know what is in her mind. Experiencing curiosity can also be a worrying experience for a pupil who has grown up with a sense of not being good enough. Some pupils feel frightened when they experience another as 'reading their mind'. They can feel out of control. It is important that the educator is attuned to how much to 'wonder aloud'. This will be dependent on the responses of the pupil.

It can also be helpful if the adult clarifies her motives with the pupil: 'Oh my, you thought I was a mindreader, like I was a witch or something. No, certainly not. I just do all I can to try and understand the pupils in my care as I want to ensure that I get to know them well. I hope I can make school easier for you, as school can be a big ask.'

The staff member needs to think about how to express acceptance for the strangeness and perhaps fear of this that the pupil is experiencing. Bigger empathy and lighter curiosity might be helpful until the pupil becomes used to others talking about her inner experience. Curiosity can be expressed less often and more tentatively; for example, 'Oh Sarah, it is so hard to figure out what is going on in your brain, isn't it? You may want to say to me, "Stop trying! You may not like what you find out!" I'm sorry it's so hard. I am going to make guesses about what you are feeling because I think it is important that we figure this out. My guesses won't always be right, so I will check them out with you. I am guessing right now you are feeling a bit worried, that it feels uncomfortable that I might "know" what you are feeling and thinking. Is that right?'

The pupil might also be helped by hearing classmates wonder about each other's inner experience. Let her witness this without the intensity of having to hear it about herself. In a similar way, indirect curiosity can be provided using stories, pictures and puppets. Pupils can be helped by this sort of one-step removed approach.

Louise worked with a pupil who was having to move schools, a situation that understandably made him feel very anxious. It was hard for Louise to be curious with him. He would become very quiet and unresponsive. He would also be distracted by other things around him. Louise therefore talked to Tolstoy, a tortoise puppet. She noticed how sad Tolstoy was feeling and how he showed this by disappearing into his shell, speaking in a whisper with occasional tears. Now the child could listen to Louise. He focused intently on the puppet, stroking his head. He then took his friendship bracelet off from his own wrist and put it carefully over Tolstoy's head. It was clear he was identifying with the feelings that were being expressed by Louise for Tolstoy.

When I ask my pupil what she is feeling she just shouts at me that she doesn't know.

The team supporting the pupil might be helped by thinking about how they are talking with the pupil. Are they expecting the pupil to know, without accepting that the pupil might not know? Are they losing the storytelling tone in their well-meaning efforts to question the pupil? In these cases, pupils can experience the pressure of expectation. The staff member might wonder with the pupil without the expectation that she should have the answer. The pupil might then become curious herself. If not, the staff member can accept this and wonder on her behalf.

It is also important to be mindful about the pupil's emotional maturity and early experience. With immaturity and poor early experience, the pupil is unlikely to be able to respond to curiosity about her internal experience. In this case, the pupil may need to be told what she might be experiencing without expectation that she will be able to do this for herself. This can be done indirectly by the adult wondering aloud about what the pupil's internal experience is, making guesses about this and talking to himself about what he is guessing.

Talking for and about her can be helpful in organizing her inner, emotional world.

When Evie's teacher was guessing for her she made a number of guesses in a way that tried to organize her inner experience. 'Evie, I think you try so hard to keep people from knowing you. You might want to say to me something like: "Miss, stop trying to figure me out! You won't like what you see, you know. If you know how I really think and feel, you won't like me any more." Oh boy, no wonder you don't want to answer my questions if you think that will be the result. Am I right about that?'

Evie looked down and nodded her head briefly. Her teacher responded with empathy and as if Evie had been able to tell her in her own voice: 'Evie, thanks for telling me. That was so hard to do. It is so hard to believe others won't like you for your thoughts and feelings.'

When I try to be playful with the pupil, she just gets over-excited or spoils it in some way.

The team supporting the pupil might reflect on how they are being playful and whether they are mindful enough about regulation as well. Are they expecting too much from the pupil? Is the pupil becoming over-aroused? Are the activities too much for the pupil?

PACE is much more about joy in relationships than activities. Small playful moments are equally if not more important than sustained experiences. In fact, pupils can experience a strong need to put distance back into the relationship after a long period of connection. Small moments, however, can be accepted without anxiety.

I just can't be PACE-ful all the time. When I get cross or start lecturing, I feel so disappointed with myself.

Educators have strong motivations to do the best they can for their pupils. It can be hard not living up to their own expectations of being open and available to their pupils. It is alright to lose PACE sometimes. This is just being human. Some educators find this hard to accept, and consequently put a lot of pressure on themselves. It is natural to move from open and engaged to defensive. When educators can recognize how normal this is, they can have compassion for themselves. This will help them to become open to the pupil again.

It is also helpful to remember that however difficult things have been, the educator is always able to repair. This means letting the pupil know that she is still unconditionally accepted. The staff member needs to help the pupil know that the relationship is more important than anything else that has occurred between them. When the adult has made an error or mishandled the situation, an apology can be vital in letting the child know how important he is to the adult. Relationship repair provides the staff member with something he can do to restore the relationship even after the most difficult of times. 'Paul, yesterday I wasn't very helpful to you. I was a bit cross and spoke to you in a way that perhaps made you think I didn't like you. I let my worry that we were not going to get our work done bubble over. I am sorry that I made that mistake.' Such a statement can repair the relationship and also communicate that mistakes are about being human and don't result in the loss of a relationship.

PACE just isn't working.

When educators stress that PACE is 'not working' they can be experiencing a mixture of feelings: a sense of failure; disappointment that this isn't the answer they were looking for; hopelessness that nothing seems to make a difference. While PACE is a very helpful way of introducing connection to a pupil, it is not an answer to the many challenges that the pupil will often continue to present. It can be hard to tolerate the relentless and sometimes very frightening behavioural ramifications of trauma. We all want the behaviour to stop so that we, the child and the other pupils can feel better.

If the focus has become too narrowly focused on the behaviour, then it is likely that the staff member is experiencing less acceptance for the pupil. The motivation to change the pupil is getting in the way of understanding and having empathy for where the pupil is right now. When acceptance reduces, it can make curiosity more intrusive and empathy more misattuned, as it is not matched to how the pupil is feeling.

If we can keep our focus on the relationship, the pupil's feelings of shame, fear of connection and the need for regulation, we will help the pupil to increase feelings of security over time. Having a team around you that understands trauma or colleagues to talk with is so important when it doesn't feel as if progress is being made.

How can I have PACE when I am responsible for so many pupils?

PACE is a way of being; it can be used lightly or intensively. Modelling this way of being will be helpful for all the pupils. When they observe you seeking understanding before responding; having empathy for feelings behind difficult behaviours or struggles to learn; and accepting feelings while still holding limits and expectations, they will be learning this way of relating too. This does not mean having to have in-depth discussions with a pupil over every small thing. It does mean that holding an attitude of acceptance, curiosity and empathy, a brief wondering aloud, a small guess or just inviting the pupil to know that you understand that they are struggling with big feelings may be all that can be done in the moment. Similarly, playful interactions which allow the whole class to enjoy being together will be a positive experience, facilitating a healthy atmosphere to work within.

Sometimes a pattern of behaviour is observed that deserves more thinking about. This might be a time to take the pupil to one side, ensure that he is regulated and then do some deeper thinking with him. These moments of more intensive PACE will increase your understanding of the pupil. The lighter-touch PACE will become easier as pupils are better understood.

The pupil has learning difficulties. Will PACE still be helpful for her?
All pupils, whatever their ability or disability, will benefit from educators who want to connect emotionally with them.

The team supporting the pupil need to have realistic expectations of what they might achieve; if they are looking for PACE to somehow fix the pupil then they are likely to be disappointed. PACE can build connection and security, but it will be a slower process. The pupil is likely to find life more stressful, and therefore progress can feel as if it is going backwards at times. The pupil is dealing with a double blow of trauma and disability and so the journey will be longer.

Good support for the team is an essential part of caring for a pupil with a disability. A team around the pupil and family can ensure that everyone is providing the pupil with what he needs. With good support around them educators will be able to stay with the attitude of PACE and to notice improvements, however small.

I am supporting the pupil in school but life at home is still problematic. Am I doing more harm than good?
It is a concern when pupils are going from school to homes where it is feared that parenting is not good enough. Finding ways to work with the parents, offering them the support they need and working together with networks will be an important part of supporting the pupil. Educators can have an important role to play in helping the pupil get what he needs at home and school. Holding an attitude of PACE can help educators to understand the struggles of the family and can reduce any feelings the parents might be experiencing of blame or judgement. In their communications with the family the educators can provide a relational experience of PACE, and in experiencing this, the family members are more likely to hold this attitude with their children. This will help to provide a healthy environment for the pupil to live in.

Ms Todd was meeting with Lisa's mum, Ella, who came in looking cross and was quite abrupt in her manner. Ms Todd wanted to discuss Lisa's attendance which had fallen off recently. She decided, however, to start the meeting by checking in with Ella. 'I can see you are upset. Help me to understand what is going on.' Ella was taken aback. She was expecting to be in trouble for not getting Lisa to school. Ready to defend herself, she was disarmed by Ms Todd's interest in her. She was able to tell her about the difficult time she had been having recently, with a sick mother and Lisa's brother needing medical attention. Ms Todd's empathy for her felt supportive and together they could now think about how to help Lisa get to school each morning, with support from some of the other mothers. This relational experience for Ella meant that she knew how powerful it is when others are interested in you and your experience. She was now more likely to use this attitude with Lisa because she had first had the experience herself.

Educators sometimes worry that offering pupils a different relationship experience at school will put them at a disadvantage when they must adapt to different relationships at home. Pupils can adapt to different relationship experiences and will not be disadvantaged by experiencing healthy relationships in life. This can contribute to their resilience and offer some mitigation when other relationships are less healthy.

CHAPTER 6

Supporting Behaviour, Supporting Peer Relationships and Providing Education

Earlier we discussed the importance of emotional connection and building trust when connecting with vulnerable pupils. Unfortunately, educators can't assume that security in relationship is already there as a backdrop for the education and for the behavioural support that all pupils need. In this chapter, we deepen the exploration of how to provide education and behavioural support when pupils don't trust their educator's motives or intentions.

Exploring behaviour support

Behaviour management is an important part of the role of the team supporting the pupil. This is reflected in the whole-school behaviour policies. These are written to provide a map for the school staff to use to ensure that all pupils are helped with their behaviour and are in the best state possible for learning. These behaviour policies rarely include attention to the relationship, beyond an encouragement to give pupils positive experiences of the educator via rewards and praise. All pupils will benefit from a relational approach to behaviour policies – after all we are all part of a social species born into relationships, with an innate need to be social. For pupils who have been hurt by relationships, not including the relational context in behaviour management is a serious omission. They need behaviour support rather than behaviour management. This means additional relationship support to help them do what many pupils of their age can already do – settle to learn (Bombèr and Hughes, 2013). Behaviour support needs to start with offering pupils the experience of safe and trustworthy relationships. This includes acceptance for the pupils' difficulties in believing in this support, and patience while the pupils develop this trust over time.

Traditional behaviour management tends to have a focus on the behaviours that pupils are displaying and provides ways of reinforcing the desired behaviours and reducing the less desirable ones. The importance of having a positive relationship with the pupil is emphasized, but there is an assumption that the pupil wants or can form such a relationship. Essentially it is assumed that the pupils feel safe in school and that they want and are seeking approval from their educators.

These assumptions do not hold true for pupils who have experienced developmental traumas. These children are in a dilemma about how to manage needing connection from adults who they expect will harm them. The behaviours that they develop to manage this conflict make it difficult for them and their educators to form the connections they will need to learn. These pupils anticipate danger, not safety. As they move through school, their motivation is to maintain the hard-won controlling behaviours that they developed at home and have been refining ever since.

Behaviour management strategies can be helpful when children experience being unconditionally loved and have trust that their parents only have good intentions towards them. Secure children remain open to their parents' comfort and support. They have complete trust that their parents love them unconditionally and that they will make everything alright when it feels as if the relationship has gone wrong. As they mature, children feel safer because these boundaries are there. They are internalizing the values and standards of their parents.

The same process of internalizing the standards and values occurs when children enter school. Children need to depend on support from educators while discovering their independence. Pupils move from needing the external controls from the educators to internalizing the standards being displayed to them and managing their own behaviours within these standards. They will make mistakes, mess up, go too far, but the secure pupil will have trust that adults will help them pick up the pieces when this happens.

Pupils who have experienced trauma anticipate that adults won't support them with difficulties but will rather be mean towards them ('You don't care about me') or look for ways to get rid of them ('You just want me gone'). They will view behavioural boundaries and discipline as being indicators that they are not good enough.

Because of these fears, the pupils experience high levels of stress, which quickly overwhelm their already fragile regulation abilities. They dysregulate quickly, often through displays of anger and temper. These triggers are sometimes hard to see, but they usually centre around interpretations that others disapprove of them and do not want to be with them. The triggers can be as subtle as a slight change of facial expression or not having a request met quickly enough, or they can be as obvious as a staff member giving attention to another pupil, or needing to attend to a task that requires the pupils to work alone for a while. The pupils do not want to behave this way, although it can seem that they do as they hide under tables or run out of the classroom. They have become highly anxious and are emotionally overwhelmed. Pupils make sense of their challenging behaviour by blaming themselves – 'I am a bad or crazy kid' – which further increases their anxiety and shame. Now, when it seems furthest away, the pupils need adult support most. This is a relationship which can help the pupil to regulate, and eventually to move from communicating through behaviour to reflection, and being able to put feelings into words.

Relationship

It is at the challenging times that the pupils need connection most. This is hard for educators, who need to find ways to connect with the pupils at the times that they most want to put some distance between them. These are often times when the whole class has been disrupted and the teacher is focused on getting everyone settled again. Sometimes the teacher also feels resentful that the pupil has caused this, leaving them with the aftermath. With the support of a key adult for the pupil, the staff team can work together to manage these situations. The pupil needs safe relationships with each member of the staff team, but it is the key adult who will develop the deeper relationship. They will be ideally positioned to step in when the pupil needs them, allowing the teacher to manage the class.

Teams supporting the pupils can hold an openness to the relationship even at these difficult times. Over time, this will build trust and the security of knowing that they are acceptable to their educators, that they are unconditionally accepted. As we will explore in the next section, educators need to have PACE for themselves, and relationships that they can turn to, in order to maintain their resilience in the face of these challenges. Looking after yourself is an essential part of supporting the pupils.

Regulation

While pupils can display behaviours that feel very targeted, manipulative and intentional, many of these behaviours stem out of dysregulated emotion and shame. Not being able to use support at these times, the pupil does the only other thing he can do – he uses the Shield against Shame (see Figure 2.1). His behaviour dysregulates as his emotion becomes overwhelming, but he turns this outward, attacking others.

Some pupils may dissociate rather than lash out. These pupils are often missed by educators because their behaviours are less challenging. It will still be important to notice and support these pupils with their emotional experience. Dissociation is a form of dysregulation and signals that the pupil is completely overwhelmed.

Emotional connection is the first step to help the pupil to regulate. There is no point trying to help the pupil reflect, with the aim of changing the behaviour, when dysregulation is driving it. This just sets the pupil up to fail and increases the sense of shame and inadequacy. The emphasis on the regulation of the pupil's internal experience means that this approach to behaviour support is regulatory based rather than behaviour based. Behaviour is still supported, but this behaviour support is successful because it is based on the pupil being helped to regulate.

Providing regulation support takes time and relies on a good understanding of what works for the individual pupil. It is a challenge to provide this support while also teaching a class. The key adult might be called for to give the necessary time to the pupil when it is needed. Spending time with the pupil and providing regulatory support also builds understanding of the pupil. The key adult learns what works and what doesn't and is ready to assist the pupil as needed as well as help the teacher understand the pupil more fully.

Reflection

Once the pupil's arousal level has come down, she can be helped to reflect on what happened to cause her upset. A more mature pupil is developmentally able to reflect on her behaviour but might need help with regulation first. A younger or more immature pupil will need the staff member to help her reflect, as happens with toddlers. The teacher may tell a story about what happened and might guess as to the underlying experiences, as in the following example.

Ahmed was in preschool. He had experienced a very difficult morning culminating in throwing things, spitting at his teacher and tearing paintings off the walls. His teacher had called his key worker to help her. By the time she got to the classroom, Ahmed was quieter but still angry. He was hiding behind the coats muttering and tearing pieces of paper. The key worker sat on the floor facing away from him to decrease the intensity of the relationship. She recognized that Ahmed was probably now expecting trouble, and direct communication would probably cause a re-escalation of his behaviour. She began to talk in a storytelling voice, weaving empathy for and curiosity about his experience.

'Ahmed, you have had a tough morning! I am so sorry it's been so tough! Mrs Thomas told me that you are having one tough time. Throwing things and spitting and yelling is a clear way of telling us, "I am mad, mad, mad!" I wonder what made you so mad? Do you have any guesses? You probably don't yet. When we get mad like that it's hard for us to think about anything else. Our body just takes over and lets everyone know how mad we are. Even if there is part of your brain that says "Oh oh! I shouldn't be doing this!", your body doesn't listen, does it? It just has a mind of its own! I wonder what it could be that made you so mad?'

Ahmed is quieter and not tearing the paper or muttering any more, so his key person started to make guesses to help him wonder about himself.

'Mmm, I wonder what could have happened to make you so upset... Maybe something happened with your friends? Maybe they didn't want to play the way you wanted to play? Or maybe it started even before you came to school? Were you able to have breakfast this morning?

Ahmed mumbled, 'No' (while looking down).

The key worker immediately responded with acceptance and empathy. 'Oh, being hungry can really make it difficult for anybody to control their upset. There is even a new word for that – hangry – a made-up word that includes hungry and anger. I love this new word because everyone can get hangry from time to time. Are you ready to come with me and we can find you something to eat before we figure this out a bit more?'

Ahmed nodded and his key worker took his hand and led him out of the classroom. Once he had eaten, she could begin to discuss how to repair what had happened in the classroom.

'Okay Ahmed, are you ready to talk to me about how we are going to fix things in the classroom? You might be worried about going back there in case Mrs Thomas is angry with you or your friends are cross too. I'll do some checking before we go back, but I think Mrs Thomas might be more worried than angry. I'll make sure. We will need to figure out how to put the things back on the wall and if you are able to say sorry to Mrs Thomas for spitting at her. I'll help you if you don't know how. I was also wondering if there is something going on at home that makes it hard for you to have breakfast in the morning. I will talk with Mrs Latimer later today to see if there are ways that we can help your parents. Let me know when you are ready to go back to class.'

For an older or more mature pupil the story can be created together. The pupil is regulated and has experienced the staff member as supportive towards her. She is now able to sit with her and think about her experience.

Again, the team supporting the pupil need to work together. The teacher can provide some reflection, but this will be limited by the demands of the whole class. A light acceptance that the pupil is having some strong feelings and the teacher wants to support her with this can be conveyed. The key adult can work with the pupil to make a deeper sense of this experience.

Using PACE and having a storytelling attitude at this point can further strengthen the connection between staff member and pupil. This does mean starting with the pupil's experience and making sense of this before helping the pupil to consider the viewpoint of anyone else involved. We tend to ask children to consider how their actions have impacted others well before they are ready to do so: 'How do you think Sarah felt when you did that?' The question is often more of a statement, communicating the adult's irritation or anger. The child when still upset or fearful of the adult's answer will not be able to reflect on her own or other's experiences. When we can first communicate curiosity and empathy for the child's experience, the child will begin to regulate and be ready for reflection.

This is a slowing down in support. It often takes time to understand.

The temptation, once a pupil is calm again, is to focus quickly on the consequences of what has happened: 'See how you hurt me'; 'Notice how upset Polly is.' This is well intentioned. The staff member wants to help the pupil understand the consequences of her behaviour in order to make amends, and to reduce this happening in the future. These well-meant intentions go awry, however, when the pupil's shame increases, levels of stress build up and dysregulation threatens once more. Staying with the pupil's own experience for longer both strengthens the connection between staff member and pupil while providing further regulatory support. Now the pupil is ready to reflect on the consequences of her behaviour. Instead of shame, she can experience guilt and remorse. The staff member is on hand to help her with this, supporting her efforts to make amends.

One of the strengths of this approach is that the consequences for the behaviour can also be part of the building of the relationship. Instead of educator-imposed sanctions, the consequences can be collaboratively worked out between them. As in the example with Ahmed, teachers might figure out what the pupil can do to make amends and discuss consequences that logically follow the behaviour that caused the upset. The teacher had softly but clearly communicated her expectation that Ahmed help tidy up the class and apologize to the teacher. It is important as in the above example to figure out what the staff member can do to support the pupil with this. The staff member might also reflect on whether there is anything he could do differently to support the pupil in the future. Perhaps the pupil needed more supervision, less freedom, more support to manage friendships and so on. The key adult's knowledge of the pupil and the teacher's awareness of what is happening within the classroom can help them to work in partnership to figure this out.

Supporting peer relationships

School is a challenge for vulnerable pupils for many reasons. Fear, hypervigilance and a constant need to feel in control mean that the pupils are rarely regulated enough to engage in learning. Struggles to feel safe with staff members mean that the pupils find it hard to use relationships to calm their high arousal.

Alongside these challenges, the pupils are also needing to fit into a peer group of same-age pupils when they are emotionally more immature. The pupils are like square pegs trying to fit into round holes.

Thirteen-year-old Tina still loved playing with her teddies and dolls at home. She had names for them and they all had special roles. She expected friends to join in with these games. As this was very different from what her peers wanted to do, she was seen as odd. Tina's foster carers were saddened to see how Tina was increasingly avoided by her classmates. Invitations to visit were politely declined and she was rarely invited to parties.

Finding enough safety to engage with learning is difficult. Fitting into peer groups is difficult. Having to do the two together presents a near insurmountable challenge. The teacher is left trying to provide a learning experience for the whole class while also finding ways to meet the needs of the traumatized pupil. As the pupil moves through school, the differences from her peers become more pronounced. As well as meeting the pupil's need for emotional support, the team supporting the pupil also needs to provide social support; helping the pupil learn to co-operate, manage conflict, and relax her need to control her peers. Without this support, the pupil can end up socially isolated, struggling to fit in and recognizing that she is not accepted by classmates.

One of the major reasons why these vulnerable pupils fail in peer relationships is because they have not learned how to engage in reciprocal relationships. They manage relationships through a range of controlling behaviours which can leave them isolated and unpopular. A lack of good early relationship experience has left them ill-equipped to understand the viewpoint of peers, to experience empathy for how the other is feeling and from this understanding to engage in supportive and co-operative relationships. These pupils need help to experience empathy and understanding for others. Without good early relationship experience they cannot be taught how to do this. First, they need to experience empathy from another. As they become comfortable with this experience, they can then start to discover empathy for themselves. Only now will they be ready to journey out into the new territory of experiencing empathy for others; only now will they be able to enter successful peer relationships.

Catherine was a ten-year-old pupil who had had multiple transitions in her young life. She wanted so badly to have friends, but it was so difficult for her to find a comfortable way to be with others. She wanted to dominate conversations, would be intrusive in joining others' play and would get upset quickly when her ideas for games were not followed. One day, her teacher observed Catherine insisting that two of her classmates do what she said. Predictably, her classmates got angry, told her they didn't like her and ran off to the other side of the playground. Catherine angrily shouted at them, 'You guys are stupid and ugly!' Her teacher felt so badly for Catherine as she knew how much she wanted a friend and how predictably she made it hard for others to be her friend. She approached Catherine wondering how to get her to see her friends' experience of this interaction. She responded first with empathy: 'Catherine, I see how upset you are. You really wanted to play with your friends, and it didn't turn out the way you wanted. I'm sorry.' She sat quietly with Catherine for a minute or two not expecting her to talk. She then said, 'Do you have any ideas why Paula and Jess got upset with you?' Catherine shook her head angrily, saying, 'They hate me and they are stupid. I don't want to be their friend anyway!'

The teacher returned to empathy, saying, 'I'm so sorry this friend stuff is so hard. Let's figure out what happened. Are you ready to do that with me?'

The teacher led Catherine into wondering what it might be like for her friends not to have any say in what games they chose or how they were playing. 'Do you think it's possible that Paula and Jess didn't think it was fair that you got to decide *everything* about how you were going to play? I wonder if they thought: "Catherine doesn't seem to care about what we think and feel, so we are going to play somewhere else!" I don't think you intended to make them upset, but I could see why they might be if they thought you didn't care about them. Can you?'

Catherine was calm enough at this point to see her teacher's point and mumbled, 'Yeah, I guess.'

The teacher was delighted. 'Great! That means we can work together to figure out how to take turns when you play!'

A DDP-informed approach to socially supporting the pupils has advantages, not just for the vulnerable pupil but for the whole class. An atmosphere of curiosity, empathy and acceptance can help pupils to become more tolerant of each other, and of differences between them. Playfulness can help to create an environment of fun and laughter, with which all can join in. Discovering each other's stories and learning to emotionally connect with each other's struggles and successes will help pupils become more socially open to each other, leading to greater relationship success.

Providing education

When supporting vulnerable pupils, education can seem like a distant goal. Helping the pupil to feel settled in school must come first, and this means attending to safety. Until pupils feel safe, they will not be in a state for learning, prepared as they are for defensive responding. Curiosity and exploration will reduce if the pupil is ready for fight and flight at a moment's notice. Hypervigilance to the wider environment also comes at the cost of attention to the task in front of him. It becomes more important to know who has just entered school, what the expression on the educator's face means and whether the other pupils are going to fight him than to understand the learning task. Establishing safety, stabilizing arousal states and managing the environment around the pupil all precede education. Relationship, regulation and reflection not only provide behavioural support but also help the educators to work with the over-aroused nervous systems of the pupil so that defensive states reduce, and the pupil is ready for curious exploration. Now he is ready to learn.

It is also important to be aware that stress can reduce and then can increase again. Happenings at home or changes in school can all send the pupil spiralling back into high arousal again. Progress can feel as if it is going backwards as a pupil apparently settled to learn suddenly becomes inattentive, absent or challenging. Educators need to step back at these times to think about the context for this change. They can then go back to an earlier level of support until the pupil is ready to manage without this again.

Pupils who don't feel good about themselves are also challenged by school because they often do not expect to succeed. Secure pupils will often thrive from the challenge of not knowing, enjoying the journey of discovery before them. They want to do their best, but they are also able to learn from their mistakes. These pupils can maintain an optimal level of arousal for learning, are confident to explore independently but also secure enough to seek support when needed. Insecure and frightened pupils do not have these advantages. Anticipating failure, they may be reluctant to try; mistakes can send them spiralling into shame and they remain ready to assume that others will give up on them rather than support them. These pupils may do better in environments which offer errorless learning, allowing them to build confidence in their abilities. Homework, tests and exams will present a big challenge, with the evaluation that inevitably accompanies these. Pupils fearing failure will often opt out or sabotage these opportunities. Better to be seen as lazy, awkward or oppositional than to be revealed as stupid and useless. Until the pupils feel confident in the teacher and able to use the support on offer from members of their support team, it will be difficult to help them with these educational challenges.

Many pupils with developmental trauma experience have additional learning needs because of neurodevelopmental difficulties, stemming from factors such as foetal alcohol effects and genetic problems. This can lead to problems with executive function. Many of these pupils will be of normal intelligence, but this executive dysfunction can lead to difficulties with cognitive processes such as impulse control, understanding cause and effect, problem solving, attention and organization. This can all add to the challenges that pupils have in school.

Regulation-based education with PACE

We have explored the critical importance of relationships within school for vulnerable pupils. Safe relationships can help pupils to feel safe in school and to learn to trust in the support available. That safe relationship also needs to help pupils to regulate. Without regulation, no education is possible. For optimal learning, pupils need to be relaxed and settled – a state dependent on regulation (Bombèr and Hughes, 2013).

When you are using a regulation-based approach to support, you will need to be mindful of the arousal level of the pupil. As stress increases, arousal also increases, and this will change what the pupil is open to. Bruce Perry suggests that there are five arousal states to be considered, each of which changes the way the pupil behaves. Each state is governed by a different part of the brain, with the lower arousal states being able to use higher brain regions that are open to thinking. As arousal increases, lower brain regions take over, leading to increasingly more instinctive behaviour – behaviour that is out of the pupil's control (Perry, 2006). We will explore these arousal states in the following example.

Ten-year-old Faith has arrived at school looking tired and without her school uniform. The teacher decides to check that she is okay and to talk to her about her lack of uniform. It is only later that morning that the social worker phones the school to let them know that Faith was removed into care suddenly the previous evening.

How might Faith respond to the teacher governed by the arousal state she is experiencing, and how might the teacher respond?

- *Calm.* Arousal is low. Faith does not want to talk about the previous evening, but she tells the teacher that she wasn't at home that morning and therefore she did not have her uniform to put on. She is worried about what the other children will say and wishes she could go home. Notice that while Faith is upset about the change, her arousal is low. She can be rational and therefore is open to reflection. She is likely to be able to explore her wishes and worries with the teacher. She is open to PACE and is likely to feel supported by the teacher.
- *Aroused.* Faith does not want to talk about the previous evening. She protests that she is tired and just wants to be left alone. When asked about her uniform, Faith tells the teacher it is not her fault. She sits at her place and refuses to say anything more. Faith's emotional arousal is increasing, and this has made her more rigid towards her teacher's questions. She may be able to engage if the teacher uses PACE, but without too much expectation that she will be able to reflect, at least initially. She may respond to a bit of playfulness with acceptance and empathy. Regulation activities might also help, especially if these can also be nurturing, such as a regulating snack or drink. As her arousal comes down, she might then be able to reflect.
- *Alarmed.* Faith is angry with the teacher when she asks her if she is okay. She tells her she just wants to be left alone. When the teacher asks her about her uniform, Faith becomes angrier. She demands to be left alone as it is not her fault. Faith is getting more emotional and this is reflected in some defiance. Dysregulation is increased, leading Faith to anticipate that the teacher is not interested in her, only in her uniform. She therefore becomes defensive. Faith is unlikely to engage in reflection until she receives acceptance and empathy from the teacher, who is open and engaged to what she is feeling. This means

not being pulled into responding defensively towards her. This is likely to take some time. Opportunities for regulation will also be important, and she might respond to something nurturing.

- *Fearful.* Faith doesn't even let the teacher finish asking her if she is alright. She shouts at her that she hates her and that it isn't fair, they are always picking on her. She throws her school bag across the room and sits angrily at her place. Faith is now very reactive. She is angry, and this is reflected in her behaviour. If the teacher can provide simple but genuine acceptance and empathy for long enough, Faith may be able to calm a little. The teacher will need to be curious on Faith's behalf, wondering aloud and making some guesses about why she is feeling so strongly. Again, some help with regulation might also be supportive, but this is likely to need to be more physical, for example while they talk they could also walk, or the teacher might see if Faith will help with something that involves heavy lifting while they talk.
- *Terror.* Faith flares up at the teacher as soon as she comes over to her. She shouts at her that she is a cow and she hates her. Faith goes to leave the classroom. When the teacher tries to stop her, Faith flies at her, kicking and punching her. Faith becomes angry very quickly and is verbally aggressive and oppositional. This quickly turns into a fight response as the teacher tries to take control. The teacher can only ride the storm now, ensuring that they are both safe. PACE via A and E might provide some regulation for Faith, but with no expectation that Faith will respond quickly. The teacher needs to provide a sense of safety through voice and actions. As the storm passes and Faith's arousal comes down, she will need comfort and regulation. The teacher needs to find acceptance and empathy for Faith without becoming defensive.

It might be helpful to think of this as a volcano, as in Figure 6.1. PACE can be effective in reducing arousal during the build-up. During the eruption, the pupil needs to be kept safe but will be open to PACE as it subsides. Keep to A and E (acceptance and empathy) to avoid further eruptions, only involving the pupil in playfulness and curiosity as you move away from the eruption.

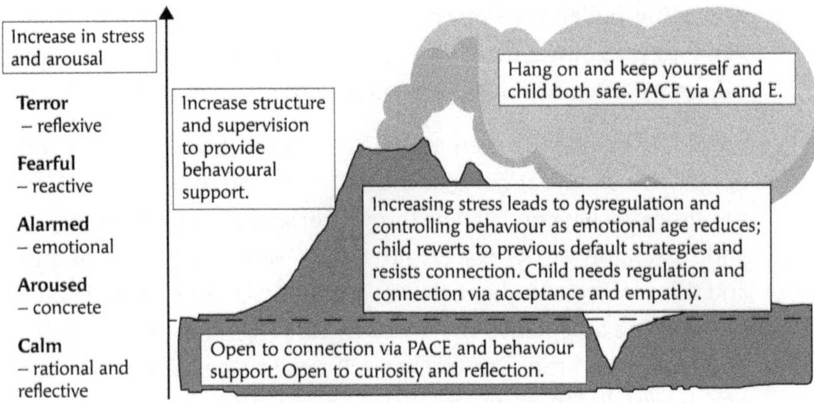

Figure 6.1: The Volcano of Arousal

This is challenging. You will need lots of PACE and compassion for yourself, supported by others who can hold PACE for you. This can help you to notice the impact the pupil is having on you (curiosity) and support you with acceptance and empathy for yourself. This will then help you to hold on to curiosity for the pupil. As you understand what she is experiencing and the thoughts and feelings she is likely to be going through, this will be displayed through your acceptance and empathy for her. The pupil will feel held by you as she experiences your genuine compassion for her.

In order to do this, you will be working hard to keep a lot of thoughts and feelings at bay, including frustration and anger with the pupil and a sense of failure within yourself. Give yourself time and space to process this after the episode. Talk to people you trust about this, and choose people who can be curious and playful with you and who will give you the acceptance and empathy you need. If you try and keep these feelings out of sight, they are likely to come back and disturb you when you least expect it. A word or look from the pupil or your colleagues can lead you to erupt in anger and frustration. You are left wondering how you could have dealt with the bigger behaviour so well only to blow it for much lesser behaviour!

Where do traditional behaviour management strategies fit in?

Behaviour support strategies can still be helpful, although may need some adaptation for this group of pupils.

Relationship

Some of the traditional strategies can help with the building of the relationship. Playfulness is part of PACE, and positive time together is part of most behavioural advice. Playfulness looks for moments of fun and joy; these can build towards finding positive activities and making learning creative.

Often for pupils, relationships with their educators are deepened in non-classroom times, field-trips, assemblies, school plays or sports. For vulnerable pupils, these types of activities are desperately needed but often avoided or sabotaged, further isolating the child and preventing learning from relationships. Such activities need to be taken more slowly and with careful preparation. This is because traumatized pupils are more comfortable with the familiar than the novel. If they are going to engage successfully in an activity, they will need to be prepared for what to expect. A simple story about the activity told ahead of the time, and repeated if needed, can help. Some educators will be familiar with the idea of social stories. They are often used with pupils on the autism spectrum and can be very helpful for these vulnerable pupils as well. Trauma leads to a fear of novelty, but stories can help the novel feel familiar. This allows the pupil to participate and enjoy activities that would otherwise be too challenging.

A second difficulty is that the pupil might not feel she deserves the activity. This can increase her stress and anxiety as she anticipates it all going wrong. If it is successful, the pupil remains anxious, often spoiling it when back in the classroom, as she reminds the staff members that she did not really deserve this.

The pupil might also struggle with the return to normal, and the reduced attention that often accompanies a return to usual routines. This can trigger fears of not really being liked or approved of.

If the pupil still has fragile regulation abilities, the additional arousal which comes with the excitement of something new might be hard to manage. Even positive arousal is difficult to regulate when regulation has not been fully developed. The pupil may be eagerly looking forward to the event, but once there just spoils it because the emotion dysregulates and behaviour deteriorates as a consequence.

Positive activities need to be built slowly and begin with the familiar to increase chances of success, and educators need to remain open to what might be contributing to their pupils' failure to engage in activities.

Regulation

Other behaviour management strategies can help with regulation, albeit with some adaptation. 'Time in', for example, is an adaptation of 'Time out', which is a well-known strategy that is not helpful for vulnerable pupils. 'Time out' is used to remove pupils from situations in which they are getting rewards for inappropriate behaviour. For vulnerable pupils, this can increase the fear of abandonment. The removal from the situation, and the staff team, can trigger fears that this time there is no way back – they have been discovered as hopelessly bad. They will not be wanted after this. Even worse is isolating the pupils at these times through seclusions or exclusions. At a time when the pupil most needs support, he is left to deal with the strong feelings evoked by the event on his own. He is psychologically and physically abandoned at the time of greatest need. Margot Sunderland described a simple adaptation of 'time out' to what she called 'time in' (Sunderland, 2008). The pupil is removed from a situation that she is struggling with but is brought closer to the adult. This is a task for the key adult who is now on hand to co-regulate the pupil's emotional arousal, increasing regulation and allowing her to return to the situation successfully, perhaps with additional adult support. Remaining close to a pupil at times of greatest disruption recognizes the strong feelings of shame the pupil is experiencing even if hidden from view. It demonstrates care and concern for the pupil which starts the process of regulating the shame and helping the pupil to reflect on his behaviour. Louise (Bombèr, 2007) talks about key adults as being bridge builders, helping their pupils find a way back to relationships that they have harmed. They assist the pupil to repair ruptures in relationships caused by their behaviour, an important lesson that they can make mistakes, get things wrong and make things right again.

It is important to reflect on the context for any strategy that is used. Given the pupil's earlier experience, is this likely to increase or decrease the pupil's feelings of security? Ignoring negative behaviour, for example, is a simple way of conveying to a secure pupil that the behaviour will not get her the desired attention. For the insecure pupil, it can convey another message entirely. The staff member unwittingly conveys that she is not worth bothering with as the pupil fails to distinguish between her behaviour as unacceptable and herself as acceptable. Ignoring can therefore increase shame and dysregulation.

Reflection

One very popular way of increasing a pupil's sense of accomplishment and therefore their self-esteem is through the use of praise and rewards. Instead of helping the pupils reflect and learn from their unacceptable behaviours, the focus is on positive behaviours. As these are praised and rewarded, social learning theory predicts that they will increase in frequency. The flaw in this plan for vulnerable pupils is that praise and rewards ultimately work because the pupils want and desire approval within a relationship where they do have some security, some sense of being accepted. When we take this desire away, we see pupils responding very manipulatively to rewards. They behave as requested until the point that they get the reward and then they revert back to previous behaviour. The reward is gained while the relationship was never anticipated anyway. Similarly, praise is viewed as a trick; after all, the staff member does not approve of them and so they cannot believe in this praise at face value. Global praise which tries to convince a pupil that she is a 'good kid' simply does not fit the pupil's sense of self and so must be rejected. Telling an insecure pupil that she is good at singing, for example, is likely to lead to the pupil refusing to sing.

Of course, we do want to help pupils to feel good about themselves, and to enjoy their accomplishments. We would like their self-esteem to increase. Praise and rewards are an important way of conveying this if we go cautiously. Praise needs to come from the heart and be a way of enjoying an accomplishment together. If it is used as a technique the pupil is likely to reject it, but if it is experienced as genuine joy in the pupil and what she has achieved then the pupil might be able to share in this. Rewards might be accepted if they are low key and descriptive. Reduce the global statements which the pupil can't accept and notice the small things. 'I like the way you sang that song, you really kept in tune during that tricky bit towards the end' is easier to accept than 'How great you are at singing!' The first is a moment in time which the pupil can enjoy without feeling she has to repeat it. The second creates too many expectations of what she might be able to do in the future. Consider that praise and rewards are evaluative. They represent judgements about the pupils' worth. This is likely to put them on the defensive. Pupils can experience approval (praise, rewards) for behaviour that they believe they can't sustain. They become anxious in the face of the educator's pleasure, anticipating times when the adult discovers how bad they really are. Thus, shame is triggered. Just think about the pressure on you if you are told you are good at something, especially when you find it hard to believe this. Will you be able to repeat it? Can you maintain this approval?

When adults evaluate vulnerable pupils, they are likely to trigger the already sensitive social monitoring system. The pupil will perceive danger and move into defensive responding. If educators are to help pupils stay open and engaged to the relationship, then they need to proceed cautiously with praise and rewards. A genuine thrill about what a pupil has achieved is less likely to feel evaluative. Additionally, a cautious, low-key use of praise and rewards that does not conflict with the pupil's global sense of self, alongside the strengthening of connection and relationship, is more likely to lead to change in self-esteem over the longer term. Pupils need stories more than they need praise and rewards; they need opportunities to make sense of their experience, rather than having this experience evaluated.

What is most important within behavioural support is that the pupils experience this as occurring within the context of an unconditional relationship. This is conveyed through the emotional connection the educators make with the pupils rather than any specific response to behaviour. If the educator focuses too narrowly on behaviour or teaching without attention to the relationship, several problems can occur.

First, a focus on behaviour or teaching instead of relationship will convey that these are most important. This does not build the pupil's trust in the adults, nor does it help the pupil to feel secure within the relationship. The pupil's expectations that she will not be able to manage her behaviour or achieve in learning additionally increase the chances that the pupil will experience shame with all the consequent problems that this can lead to.

Also, many behavioural strategies rely on consequences to convey approval or disapproval in behaviour or success in learning tasks. The pupils experience this as a reminder that relationships are conditional. Such conditional relationships can be lost. The pupil anticipates that the staff member will discover that she is no good at some point in the future. The consequences can trigger this fear. Consequences that are collaborative because they emerge from the relationship can be helpful to the child. The staff member is supporting the pupil to make amends for behavioural transgressions or to choose an appropriate reward for effort in a task. The pupil is worth bothering with, and the pupil's trust in unconditional love and support is increased. Consequences that are imposed by educators are more problematic.

Finally, the behavioural strategies tend to focus on providing predictability and consistency, so that the pupils learn from the consequences for their behaviour. This relies on the pupils learning from cause and effect. Predictability and consistency are important for vulnerable pupils, but these are not always things they have learned to trust in. When pupils have lived in highly inconsistent and unpredictable environments, they have not had the experience needed to learn about cause and effect. They have underdeveloped causal thinking. They therefore need predictability and consistency in order to start to develop this capacity. They are not yet ready to make the shift to learning from cause and effect. When effect (consequence) is disconnected from cause, the pupils will experience the consequences as the educators being mean to them. This will lead to further dysregulation rather than learning from behaviour.

Conclusion

Education is the main purpose of schools. When pupils arrive at school ready for this, educators can feel confident that they can help the pupils to achieve. Pupils with experience of developmental trauma will need many things in place before education is even possible. Feeling safe is a first priority. Providing a safe environment is part of this, but providing trustworthy relationships and offering regulatory support are close seconds. The pupils' challenges in feeling safe and secure in school are often expressed in their behaviour. Behavioural support is therefore an important part of teaching these pupils. It is this support that can help them to grow up into secure and well-adjusted adults, able to manage their own behaviour in relation to others. Traditional behavioural advice stresses this part of the education task, offering ideas for the teams supporting the pupils to manage behaviours that are challenging and to reinforce behaviours they would like to increase. When pupils have experienced developmental traumas, this becomes more complex. The teams supporting the pupil need to work together to find ways to build security and safety for their pupils as well as providing support for their behaviour. Emotional connection can be taken for granted with secure pupils but must be worked at when pupils have the insecurities and fears that developmental trauma brings.

It is also hard to engage in learning when fitting in with peers is so hard. Teachers and support staff need to help their pupils manage these relationships in addition to all the other support that is needed.

Like Catherine, who we met earlier, Sanjay was bossing his peers about at breaktime and they were complaining. Mr Richards walked over and knelt down with a warm, empathic face. 'Oh Sanjay, you really wanted to play Tag today and the others are not wanting to. That must have been so hard. I know how much you love that game. I wonder if you were feeling really disappointed about that? You have been trying so hard to get the others to understand how important this is for you. I get that.' Sanjay nodded and looked down. 'They won't play it. I want them to play Tag with me.' Mr Richards responded, 'I know. It's so hard. I wonder what the others might be feeling? I wonder what the others might be thinking? Shall we try and work it out together?'

Providing this level of support for pupils who are struggling so much is a challenge alongside all the other teaching and support tasks that are needed. It is necessary, however, if children like Catherine and Sanjay are going to get the most out of their education.

CHAPTER 7

Some Principles: 'Connection with Teaching'

At the centre of the DDP-informed education approach is the forming of emotional connections with the pupil. This provides a foundation on which behavioural support can build, providing a structure that can support education. PACE plus discipline can increase security for the insecure pupil. A platform for education is then built. Here we will present a set of principles for educating vulnerable pupils which are derived from an understanding of child development and the DDP model.

Principle 1: PACE is a consistent feature; discipline is brought in as needed. Both are required to support education

It is important that the educator strives to hold on to PACE even when they need to provide some discipline or limits for the behaviour of the pupil. PACE before and during the discipline will help the pupil to feel emotionally connected and unconditionally accepted.

The pupil needs to know that the relationship isn't being lost to him, and that he is still acceptable to the staff member even though she is not happy with some aspect of his behaviour. This is a message that is hard for vulnerable pupils to know. Disapproval with their behaviour is experienced as shame for self. PACE with discipline helps to maintain this connection when the pupil is at his most vulnerable – experiencing shame and fear. The continuing use of PACE can regulate the experience of shame and help the pupil to learn more effectively from the discipline.

PACE following the discipline can add to this learning, providing the pupil with a continuing sense of being unconditionally accepted. It also provides the staff member with an opportunity to repair any ruptures in the relationship which might have occurred because of the need for discipline. This means letting the pupil know that he is still accepted unconditionally and the relationship is still strong despite the limits set. The pupil gets the message that the teacher values her relationship with him even when discipline is necessary. An apology when the teacher has got something wrong with the pupil is also important in affirming this.

The following example illustrates the setting of limits with PACE.

The teacher sent Derek back to class early from break because he had thrown rocks at another pupil. He entered his classroom yelling, 'This isn't fair! She started it and I'm the one who is getting punished!' Rather than arguing or telling him to stop yelling, his teacher responded with acceptance and empathy before asking him what happened.

Teacher: 'Oh Derek, you are so upset! It sounds as if you think something happened that was unfair, and you are very upset about that! Things should be fair! I'm sorry your breaktime didn't go as planned. Tell me what happened.'

Derek: 'I was playing, and Jessica took the ball when it was my turn and she wouldn't give it back. I told her to give it back and she didn't listen.'

Teacher: 'I can see how that would be upsetting and feel unfair when you believed it was your turn. How did it get to throwing rocks?'

Derek looked down, experiencing some shame.

Teacher: 'Maybe you now wish that you hadn't thrown rocks, hadn't lost your temper like that?'

Derek nodded.

Teacher: 'It feels crummy doesn't it when we wish we hadn't done something?' (Notice that the teacher doesn't have to tell Derek that it isn't okay to throw rocks. Lecturing him about something he already knows will reduce the sense of safety.)

Derek: 'If she hadn't made me so mad, I wouldn't have lost my temper!'

Teacher: 'I wonder how we can help you hold on to your temper when someone upsets you? I don't think you feel very good when you are angry, and then when your anger goes away you certainly don't feel very good! Do you have any ideas what would help?'

Derek shook his head.

Teacher: 'Don't you worry, I have some ideas. At lunchtime we will spend some time together and I'll tell you my ideas. Then tomorrow we will try a breaktime with some adult help beside you to test them out. But today, you will stick close to me, so you don't get into more trouble. Deal?'

Derek mumbled, begrudgingly, 'Fine.'

Teacher: 'You may be upset with me for saying you can't go back out to break today. I don't want you to have any more trouble and I think this is the best way today. Tomorrow we will try again.'

With this approach, the pupil's sense of safety will increase and stress and arousal will reduce.

The teacher's acceptance and regulated approach helped Derek become less defensive quite quickly. She was accepting and curious about his experience before giving him a consequence of not going out again that day. The consequence was given in a way that communicated the desire to help him rather than punish him, and involved her support rather than isolation. When discipline can be delivered in this way, pupils will learn that their behaviour will be supported without a loss of relationship. With this safety, they will become more socially engaged within the classroom, becoming open to curiosity and exploration. Education will be more successful when attention is paid to connection with behavioural support.

Principle 2: Two hands of teaching, authoritative teaching

Research has demonstrated the value of so-called authoritative parenting for helping children to grow up into secure and well-adjusted adults (Baumrind, 1978). The term 'authoritative' is a bit confusing. It can be confused with authoritarian. Authoritarian parenting is low in warmth and nurture and high in punishment. This leads to children growing up insecure and poorly adjusted. Authoritative is not the same. It describes a parenting that is high in warmth and nurture, alongside the provision of clear structure and boundaries. This gives the children an experience where development of autonomy is encouraged, matched to their developmental age. This is unlike authoritarian parenting which discourages autonomy – a 'do as I say' approach – or passive parenting which provides few boundaries – a 'do what you want' approach. This same approach to supporting pupils can be provided by the teams supporting the pupils. An atmosphere of authoritative parenting alongside authoritative teaching is ideal, with good partnership between home and school.

Pupils need structure and boundaries so that they can exercise their developing autonomy under the supervision and guidance of the adults. Warmth and nurture, alongside acceptance and curiosity, provide the emotional connection. The provision of structure and boundaries matched to the pupil's development of autonomy provides the behavioural and educational support.

This can be considered as having two hands:

- *Hand 1:* provides warmth and nurture, allowing pupils appropriate autonomy matched to their developmental age. In other words, pupils are supported to make choices and to develop independence but only at a pace that they can cope with. This hand also contains the curiosity, allowing the staff member to wonder about and accept the pupil's internal experience. Hand 1 supports PACE.
- *Hand 2:* complements PACE, providing structure and boundaries – the support from the educators that pupils need to be successful. This can include consequences but stemming from understanding and used collaboratively with the pupils. The example with Cole in Chapter 1 illustrates the effective use of the two hands.

Two hands of parenting allow for:

- Connection with teaching. The educator might need to give a consequence for behaviour (discipline) and they will need to structure the teaching tasks. This is likely to be more successful when the pupil feels understood (connection). This is not finding an excuse for behaviour which still needs to be dealt with. It is not to replace the setting of learning tasks; these are part of education. It does, however, provide an atmosphere of warmth and empathy within which discipline and education can be successful.
- No discipline without understanding. If the educator responds without understanding, the pupil will feel less secure, and will not build trust. This is not about finding an excuse for the pupil's behaviour but is about explanation. The explanation helps the educator to get the consequences right.

Principle 3: The sandwich

Misattunements are a normal part of any relationship, including between an educator and a pupil. However, for vulnerable pupils these disruptions to the relationship can provide them with the evidence they are seeking that they are not good enough. This is especially true when the adult is providing discipline. The educators need to work to try and minimize these experiences of shame. This will mean providing a quick repair to the relationship at these times. In this way, these ruptures can present an opportunity for building trust with the pupil (Tronick, 2007). If a staff member can repair the connection with the pupil soon after the disruption, the pupil will feel more secure, learning that the relationship doesn't get lost for long. Interactions represent cycles of attunement–misattunement–repair which strengthen the relationship.

Sometimes behavioural support is more about regulatory support, as we have explored. This is not a time for discipline, but a time to help the pupil bring their level of emotional arousal back to a manageable level. Children being children, however, there will be times when the behaviour is pushing a boundary, getting into mischief, trying it on and hoping not to be caught. Discipline ensures that reasonable boundaries are in place and that pupils do experience clear consequences for their behaviours. Without this the pupils feel unsafe. Authoritative educators find a balance between nurture and discipline. Discipline, in the form of boundaries and consequences, is important, but it can be sandwiched between attunement and relationship repair (see Figure 7.1).

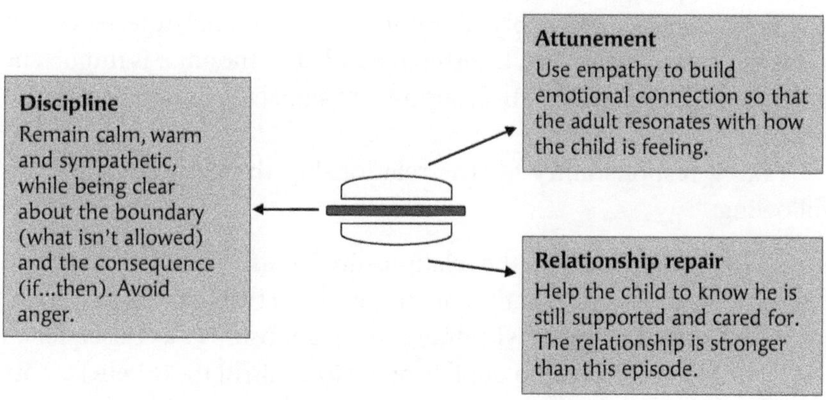

Figure 7.1: The Discipline Sandwich

Principle 4: Adult takes responsibility for the relationship offered to the pupil

It can be tempting to withdraw from the relationship with the pupil, especially when he is being especially challenging. 'I will come back when you are ready to apologize' can feel like a useful lesson. However, it is a message that the relationship is conditional. You can have a relationship with me only if you behave in a certain way. This will reduce the security a pupil is feeling. For a pupil who is already insecure within the relationship this is a body blow, confirming his worst fears that this relationship can be lost too. The pupil needs to know that the relationship is always open to him, even though at times he must also manage consequences for his behaviour.

There will be times when the educator needs to withdraw for other reasons. They may be feeling particularly angry and frustrated such that they cannot stay open and engaged to the pupil. They need to take care of themselves so that they can continue to support the pupil as he needs. When in this situation, the staff member needs to do this in a way which signals that the relationship is still strong and will continue to be open to the pupil. The staff member might, for example, tell the pupil that she is feeling angry just now and needs some time to look after herself. She won't forget the pupil and will support him just as soon as she can. In this way, the pupil gets the message that the relationship is still important, but sometimes adults must take a break for themselves.

All of this is useful advice, but so hard to put into practice. In the heat of supporting vulnerable pupils with their challenges it is hard to stay open and engaged. Inevitably educators' own emotional experience will get in the way at times. Relationship repair led by the adult is important following these episodes. This continues to signal the importance of the relationship to the pupil.

Taking responsibility for the relationship therefore involves the following:

- Not punishing with the relationship. Pupils who are insecure are quick to assume that they are no good and that they are not loved. If the staff member withdraws the relationship as a consequence or in anger, then the pupil is quick to confirm these beliefs. This increases insecurity further and moves the pupil further away from developing a trusting relationship. Judgemental disciplinary methods are therefore ineffective. (For example, discipline that conveys: 'I am disappointed with you, my relationship with you is conditional on your behaviour.')

- Looking after self when needed. This gives adults the strength and resilience to keep going. The adult is looking after the relationship with the pupil by taking care of herself before she reaches breaking point.

- Taking responsibility for relationship repair. Educators are only human, and it is inevitable that they will get cross or frustrated at times. It is important that these times are followed by relationship repair led by the adult that protects the relationship between them. Educators needn't be afraid to acknowledge that they got it wrong and that they are sorry, if this is how they are feeling. A genuine apology models that mistakes can be acknowledged. Repair following discipline also allows the educators to let the pupils know that they will continue to be there for them. The staff member lets the pupil know that while she doesn't want the pupil to feel bad about himself, she does want to support him to manage things differently.

Principle 5: Understanding without lectures, premature problem solving and rushed reassurance

Lectures are the opposite of stories. When we lecture someone, we are trying to teach them and provide them with new wisdom. Lectures about behaviour just do not work. Often this is because the pupils perceive this as a judgement about themselves. They feel they are a disappointment to the staff member, that they have let him down. Love feels conditional once again. Stories are an act of discovery together. The staff member is working with the pupil to understand what is going on.

Solving problems without understanding also doesn't work well. Think about the difference between a teacher nagging a pupil to get on with his work or wondering with him about why he is struggling. Rarely is work progressed when the teacher is on the pupil's back. When they figure out together why the pupil is reluctant to do his work, then progress can be made. The pupil might need some structure and supervision from the teacher; there may be a problem with understanding which the teacher can help with. This is problem solving at its best, based on a good understanding of what the pupil is experiencing.

Reassurance is also problematic if it is rushed or used to help the educator to feel better. Quick reassurance signals to the pupil that his inner experience is not accepted; he should not think or feel that way. This is invalidating of the pupil and therefore harmful to the relationship.

Often this type of reassurance stems from the difficult feelings of the educator. They are uncomfortable with the emotion the pupil is displaying and therefore want it to go away. The pupil proclaims that he is rubbish and will never achieve success. The staff member tells the pupil, 'Of course you are not rubbish; keep practising and you will succeed.' The pupil's feelings are being shut down because the staff member is finding them overwhelming.

In order to be able to be present with the child's emotional experiences, we may first need to take some time to care for ourselves. What do we need to do for ourselves to return to an open and engaged stance? We might then be able to communicate, 'I know you feel rubbish right now and it feels as if practice is not going to help. Those are hard feelings. I am here and am going to support you even though you feel rubbish. I am hopeful that in the future you won't feel like this, but right now I get that you can't believe this.' Such a statement communicates to the pupil that the teacher understands his experience and isn't going to argue or dismiss it, but the teacher holds out hope that things can be different.

Understanding the pupil therefore involves the following:

- Not lecturing. Lecturing is an evaluation rather than a desire to understand and can increase shame and defensive behaviour.
- Delaying problem solving. Pupils can rarely be talked into or out of behaviour. Remember that behaviour change comes from being understood within relationships so that boundaries are experienced with warmth and empathy. Pupils might be able to join in with some problem solving – how they might have managed something differently – but they will not engage with this until they really experience staff members as understanding them.
- Not rushing to reassure. Reassurance that tries to talk pupils out of what they are experiencing is not helpful. This is not acceptance. It is effectively saying to the pupil that you understand what they

are thinking and feeling, but they don't need to or shouldn't think or feel this way. Reassurance denies that thinking and feeling is neither right nor wrong, it just is. Reassure to give hope rather than to make yourself feel better.

Principle 6: Provide appropriate level of structure and supervision

Very often expectations of pupils are based on their chronological age. Phrases such as 'Act your age' or 'a nine-year-old should be able to...' show that an educator is judging the pupil based on what peers of his age can typically do. This does not consider the pupil's individual level of maturity and can lead to increased pressure for the pupil to manage a level of structure and supervision that is too low for him. Educators need to be mindful of the pupil's emotional maturity, adjusting their expectations in line with this. This is made more complicated because levels of immaturity can fluctuate depending on the level of stress being experienced. We all act younger when under stress, and this can be exaggerated in pupils who are emotionally insecure. Structure and supervision will therefore have to be adjusted in relationship to the pupil's current level of stress.

A balance must be found between too much structure and supervision, which does not challenge the pupil and hampers development, and too little structure and supervision, which overwhelms the pupil with too much expectation of what he can do. Pupils need sufficient challenge to progress, supported by staff members.

Notice that if the consequences are piling up it is a sign that the pupil needs increased structure and supervision, alongside empathy. If the pupil is remaining static, not developing in maturity or ability, then maybe too much structure and supervision is not sufficiently challenging him.

A Russian child psychologist called Vygotsky explored this in relation to what he termed the Zone of Proximal Development (Vygotsky, 1978). This is a complicated term but essentially means that children will make developmental progress when provided with some scaffolding. The children can do so much on their own, and a little bit more with support. If expectations are within the zone, the educator is holding the right level of expectations and the pupils are likely to progress. If, however, their expectations are outside this zone, the pupils are less likely to progress because expectations are too low or too high (see Figure 7.2).

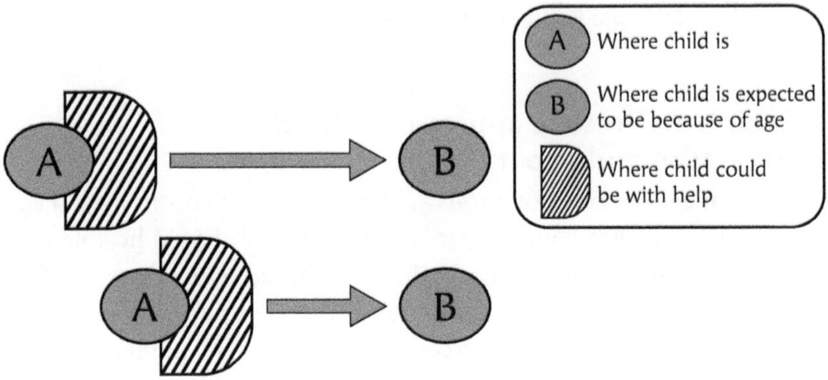

Figure 7.2: Zone of Proximal Development

Principle 7: Help the pupil to manage shifts between playfulness and authority

One of the hardest things a mistrusting child can do is to accede to the authority of the parent. These children have learned to control others as a way of maintaining their own safety. Giving up this control is not going to be easy. This means that at times when a parent needs to use her authority the child will revert to his own pattern of controlling behaviours. Baylin and Hughes (2016) point out that the shift from what they call 'companionship mode' to 'authority mode' can be especially difficult for vulnerable children.

The same is likely to be true with education staff. There are times during the school day when the teacher is relaxed, guiding activities in a fun, playful mode. The pupil can connect with the teacher at these times. The difference in power and authority between teacher and pupil is at its smallest. Time moves on and the teacher must bring the activity to an end ready for the next session. As the teacher moves back into authority mode, the pupil needs to adjust to the teacher being back in charge. These relational transitions can lead to very rapid shifts in the pupil towards anger and meltdown. The teacher needs to find a way to stay open and empathic to the pupil's struggles in letting him have a benevolent authority over her.

CHAPTER 8

Practising in the Moment

In the last few chapters we have shared a lot of ideas, and perhaps given you some insight into supporting pupils in a way that you are less used to. There is a lot of information to hang on to, and applying this in the moment can be challenging. In this chapter, we are therefore aiming to put this together for you – a guide to supporting the vulnerable pupil when the luxury of time to think things through is not available. We are basing this on a model that Kim developed to guide those parenting vulnerable children. This model informed by the DDP principles is called 'Parenting in the Moment'. Here we adapt this as a 'Practising in the Moment' model.

We hope that your reading of the previous chapters helps you to understand why we have put this together in this way. It is a guide and does not have to be followed rigidly. There are seven stages, but you may find yourself going backwards and forwards among these.

What you will see is that this is supporting pupils by the long route. In more traditional support we tend to move straight from stage 1 to stage 6, with stages 2–5 getting lost on the way. We miss out a lot that is helpful when we take this short cut. It is the longer route that will allow the pupil to develop security, to experience safety and build trust with the team supporting him. It is the long route to helping the pupil achieve educationally.

'Practising in the Moment' encourages you to maintain an attitude of PACE, to cultivate an attitude of curiosity that will increase your understanding, which will increase your acceptance and empathy. Look for moments of playfulness and pick your moments for using PACE with the pupils, bearing in mind their age, verbal ability and level of emotional arousal.

Practising in the Moment is a set of seven stages which summarize the DDP-informed approach to supporting pupils that is explored within this book. By keeping these stages in mind, it is easier to stay open and engaged with the pupil rather than becoming defensive. This in turn helps you to make emotional connections with the pupil while also providing some behavioural support. All of this provides the foundation the pupil needs to engage in education and to achieve her potential in school. Later in this chapter, we have included a diagrammatic version of these stages. Here we will summarize each one.

Stage 1

Notice what is happening. This is the moment when you realize that something is going on that a pupil might need your support with. It might be an increase in challenging behaviour; it might be the pupil signalling that he is troubled or worrying about something; it might be struggles with a learning task. You will need to make some immediate decisions. The first is: do I need to step in? You will decide whether the pupil needs your support right now or whether he is benefiting from managing this by himself. Sometimes watching and waiting can help you to choose the right moment to offer support. At other times, it is obvious that you need to get involved. If the pupil is demonstrating challenges that are impacting on him, you or the other pupils, you will need to consider what immediate steps you need to take to ensure everyone's safety. For example, if a pupil has grabbed a chair and is threatening to throw it, you will need to act to remove the chair and to ensure that the other pupils are moved to a safe place. Taking these initial actions can give you a breathing space to reflect on where to go next.

Stage 2

This may seem surprising, but we are going to suggest that you now pause for a moment and notice what you are feeling right now. A quick internal scan can help you to notice the impact the pupil is having on you. Notice if you are regulated. Can you stay open and engaged or are you in danger of becoming defensive? If you are becoming defensive, do you need a break, or can you get back to being open and engaged? If you could do with a break but this is not possible, at least you can be compassionate to yourself. Obviously during the behaviour, you may not have much time to do this, but just taking a moment to notice can help you to stay regulated. It may also be helpful to notice your reactions to reflect on later with more time and with a trusted other. This will all be part of building your resilience.

Stage 3

Now it is time to focus on the pupil. Notice how aroused he is. Where on the arousal continuum do you think he is? What does this mean for his emotional age right now? What capacity for thinking and reasoning is he likely to be open to? Is he open to some playfulness with you? If not, use simple A and E (acceptance and empathy) responses. This is light A and E as you have not yet used your curiosity to figure out what the pupil is experiencing. Simple statements like 'I can see you are having a hard time right now' will convey to the pupil that you are present and available to support him. This thinking will guide you on how to use your relationship with your pupil at this moment. Should you focus on regulation, or is the pupil open to reflection? If you think regulation might be helpful, you will also need to judge at what sensory, or emotional, level this needs to be. Sometimes pupils will regulate with your gentle and empathic presence. At other times, they may also need some sensory activities to help with this. Food, drink, exercise or calming activities can all help the pupil into a more regulated state. If you have previously explored what is helpful for the pupil at a sensory level, you will have some ideas about what might work right now.

Stage 4

At this stage, you can fully engage your curiosity and understanding. Figure out what might be going on for the pupil right now based on your previous experience and with knowledge of his past experience. Wonder about what he is feeling and thinking. What is your best guess about what the pupil's internal emotional experience is at this moment? Remember that internal experience is neither right nor wrong, it just is. You are not going to judge it, but you will accept it. If the pupil is open to and able to reflect with you, it might be possible to gently wonder with him. Wonder what is going on for him right now and see if he can give you some clues. If this is not possible, use your curiosity on his behalf. Deepen your understanding so that you can help him to know that you get it.

Stage 5

Now you can deepen your A and E because it is based on your curiosity and understanding. Use acceptance and empathy to connect with the pupil around the best guess of what his emotional experience is. Think about how you can help him to know that you get it. This is a time for focusing on the pupil's experience. He will not yet be ready to think about his actions and how these have impacted on others. You also can't rush to focus him on a task he is struggling with. To do either of these prematurely is likely to trigger shame and further increase his emotional arousal.

Stage 6

At some point, as your pupil is calm and regulated, and when he is able to think about himself, you will judge that the time is right to focus his attention on others on whom he may have had an impact. If he is feeling supported and understood by you, any sense of shame will have regulated and he might now be experiencing some feelings of guilt. This is the time that you can support his feelings of remorse and can think with him about how to make amends. Alternatively, he may be ready to think with you about the task that he has been struggling with or a worry he is grappling with. He may be ready for you to support him with this. Here and in the next stage consequences can be considered collaboratively by the two of you. You might help him to think how he can put things right with any upset he has caused. You might consider together how he is going to catch up with the work. You might support him to do some problem solving around a worry he has. You will then think about whether you need to do anything further. Are further consequences or actions needed or is the pupil on track for making amends or being able to focus again?

Stage 7

Repair of relationships and achievement of tasks happen in this stage. If all has gone well it is likely that there is no rupture to the relationship between you. The pupil will experience your unconditional acceptance for him and his experience. However, sometimes you will have reacted to things less well as you have tried to support the pupil. Take responsibility for any mistakes you may have made. Let him know that it may have felt tough but the relationship between you is stronger. Together you have got through it. You can also, following on from the previous stage, help the pupil to repair any relationships with others who may have been impacted by his behaviour. Often this repair is part of the logical consequence for the pupil. Many pupils, who have felt supported through the connection with the staff member, will now be experiencing some guilt and remorse and will want to make this repair. Finally, you can help the pupil to finish a task and to experience a sense of achievement.

In the sister book to this one, written for parents, Kim wrote a story based on a real-life event told to her by a child and parent (Golding, 2017). This illustrated the 'Parenting in the Moment' sequence. Here Kim is going to reimagine this event from the perspective of the teaching assistant to illustrate 'Practising in the Moment'. In the original story, Benjamin goes home for the rest of the day. In this example, the team supporting the child decide that they will help him to stay in school. For those interested in reading the original story, it is reproduced at the end of this chapter.

A DIFFICULT DAY AT SCHOOL, REIMAGINED

It is a hot day in the summer term. The children are all a bit fractious as the end of term approaches. Seven-year-old Benjamin has always found school difficult, and this is increased as the children become more unsettled around him. As his stress increases, he is finding it harder and harder to stay regulated. He nearly blew before lunchtime, but the teaching assistant managed to step in and provide him with some calm time out of the classroom. Unfortunately, this hasn't lasted. An argument over who has the football leads to Benjamin hitting two of the other boys. Benjamin sits with the headteacher in her office to have his lunch. This gives his support team some time to decide how to support him for the rest of the day. After some discussion, including wondering whether Mum should be called to take Benjamin home, it is decided that the teaching assistant, Miss Rogers, will work with Benjamin in the support room. This means he will stay in school but won't have the challenge of going back into class. They are not yet sure what consequence to give him for hitting his classmates. They suggest that Miss Rogers sees how the afternoon goes and they will then decide before end of school so that Benjamin knows the plan before going home.

Miss Rogers has some strong feelings about what has happened. She is disappointed with herself that she didn't help Benjamin to calm down enough before lunchtime. She had then judged he would be alright out in the playground with the other children – a decision that was clearly wrong! She also notices she is feeling angry with Benjamin for disrupting the plans she had for the rest of the morning, and of course for hurting Jack and Billy. They have five more minutes before all the children are back in class for the afternoon. Miss Rogers uses this time to reflect with the team on how she is feeling, along with a cup of tea to help her feel calmer!

Benjamin is still very cross as they walk together. Miss Rogers is not sure how she will settle him in the small room they are heading for. She has an idea, and luckily the school hall is empty just now. She takes Benjamin to the hall and gives him some time on the gym equipment, which is already out for a class later that day. She makes sure that he does some climbing and hanging on the ropes to help him to regulate. They then make their way to the support room, picking up a drink and biscuit on the way. Miss Rogers now thinks that Benjamin is ready to talk about what happened.

'So, breaktime was hard today?' Miss Rogers gently comments. Benjamin's head immediately goes down, but he does not run away.

'It's tough being at school when you're feeling hot and tired, isn't it?'

Benjamin looks up 'Yes, and it was so noisy. I hated it.'

Miss Rogers nods sympathetically: 'Yes, it is much harder for you when they are noisy. I wonder why they were noisier today?'

'Mrs Jones said that we were all feeling hot and tired. She told us that it is harder not to argue when you are hot, but we should try hard.'

'Do you think that is why you were finding it hard? Were the children all arguing?'

Benjamin thinks about this: 'Not all of them, but Justine and Carol got very cross when they were gluing. I think their model broke.'

'Well, Benjamin, no wonder you were feeling wobbly today. That was a lot to cope with, wasn't it?'

Benjamin hangs his head again and then whispers, 'I hit Jack and Billy.'

'I know, Benjamin. That is why we decided it would be better for you to spend some time with me rather than going back into class.'

'I didn't mean to hit them, but they wouldn't let me have a turn with the ball. I had waited ages.'

'It sounds as if you were trying to be patient, but then you felt very cross with them, didn't you?'

'Yes, and I tried to get the ball from them...' Benjamin hesitates and then whispers, 'And then I hit them.'

Suddenly Benjamin brightens: 'Can I make them cards? You know, to say sorry. Can I make a card for Jack and Billy?'

Miss Rogers smiles: 'Well, that sounds like a great plan. I will get the card and pens out and you can make them before we tackle that number work that Mrs Jones wants us to do. Maybe tomorrow you can go back into class and give Jack and Billy their cards.'

Benjamin looks pensive, and then looks at Miss Rogers with a sense of urgency: 'No, not tomorrow. I want to give them the cards today. I don't want to wait until tomorrow.'

Miss Rogers looks puzzled: 'Well, we could, but I wonder if Jack and Billy are still feeling a bit upset with you. They might find it easier to like your cards tomorrow when everyone has calmed down.'

'No, that won't do,' proclaims Benjamin. 'We must give them today. You see, I don't want Jack and Billy to be upset all night!'

Miss Rogers smiles. 'Do you know Benjamin, that sounds like a great plan! Jack and Billy might not want to talk to you today, but we can give the cards to them and make sure that they know you are sorry.'

Practising in the Moment as open and engaged support

Notice how this sequence of stages helps you to stay open and engaged to the pupil. Any feelings of defensiveness, your own or the pupil's, are noticed and you use curiosity to move out of, or avoid moving into, a defensive attitude. When educators don't take a moment to take care of themselves and become overly focused on managing the behaviour or achieving a task without ensuring that they have a connection with the pupil, then defensiveness is likely to follow. The staff members will have the best of intentions. They want the pupil to behave well and to achieve academically, not just because this is their job, but also because they know this will ultimately be more helpful for the pupil. That desire to be helpful can lead them into more coercive teaching approaches for fear that waiting will put pupils behind and reflect badly on them as a teacher. Teachers become vulnerable to blocked care for their pupils, which further reinforces the pupils' mistrust of them. This will be discussed further in Chapter 12. If educators are aware of being more anxious or punitive in their interactions, talking with colleagues or administrators can help return them to an open and engaged way of being. The above practice model is applicable for colleagues, managers and supervisors to help the educator feel that they are being noticed, understood without judgement, felt with the others' empathy and offered solutions when and if appropriate.

Practising in the Moment: 'Connection with Teaching'[1]

This cycle demonstrates a sequence that is helpful to take when supporting a pupil. By keeping this in mind it is easier to stay open and engaged with the pupil rather than becoming defensive. This in turn helps to make an emotional connection with the pupil while also providing some behavioural or teaching support. When an educator connects alongside teaching and behavioural support, the pupil will experience unconditional acceptance as well as the safety which empathic boundaries, discipline and teaching can provide.

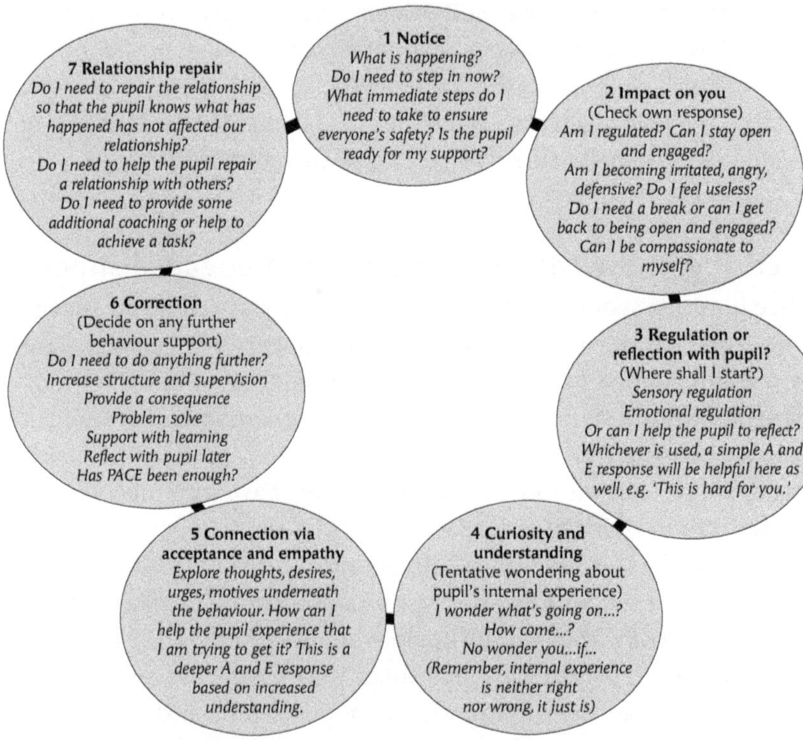

Figure 8.1: Practising in the Moment – 'Connection with Teaching'

Conclusion

It is our hope that Practising in the Moment can guide the teams supporting the pupils towards a more open and engaged teaching within which they can use PACE to connect with their pupils and with each other. This provides a foundation for behavioural support where

1 Adapted from Golding (2017).

a healthy balance between connection and teaching/disciplining is found – a balance where any teaching or discipline that is used serves to strengthen the relationship further because it is collaborative rather than coercive.

A DIFFICULT DAY AT SCHOOL[2]

It is a hot day in the summer term. The children are all a bit fractious as the end of term approaches. Seven-year-old Benjamin has always found school difficult, and this is increased as the children become more unsettled around him. As his stress increases, he is finding it harder and harder to stay regulated. He nearly blew before lunchtime, but the teaching assistant managed to step in and provide him with some calm time out of the classroom. Unfortunately, this hasn't lasted. An argument over who has the football leads to Benjamin hitting two of the other boys. It is decided that it would be better for Benjamin to go home than for him to continue to struggle and his mum is called.

Mum puts down the phone with a sigh. This afternoon was not going to be the afternoon she had planned. She quickly phones the friend she had planned a coffee with. She reflects on how she is feeling. She is a bit frustrated that she must fetch Benjamin. Fleetingly she wonders if they could have managed him at school without the need for him to come home. She is okay though – her empathy for how hard Benjamin is finding school remains high. She thinks how to help him. She knows that Benjamin is finding school difficult at the moment, and she anticipates that his emotional regulation will be very fragile after such a difficult morning. Instead of jumping in her car to collect him she decides to take the time to walk to school. She hopes the walk home will provide some regulatory support to help Benjamin to settle.

When she arrives at school Mum greets Benjamin with a quick hug, acknowledging that it has been a difficult morning. She does not talk about it any further but instead they walk home chatting about what they see. They notice the birds singing and Benjamin is very pleased when he recognizes the blackbird. As they get towards home Mum notices that Benjamin is becoming unsettled again. She guesses that he is anticipating a talk about school. Quietly she tells him that they will have a chat later, but for now she just wants him to have a snack and something to drink. She guesses rightly that he has not eaten much of his lunch. After a round of toast and jam and a milkshake drunk through a straw, Benjamin is calm again.

2 Reproduced from Golding (2017).

'So, school was hard today?' Mum gently comments. Benjamin's head immediately goes down, but he does not run away.

'It's tough being at school when you're feeling hot and tired, isn't it?'

Benjamin looks up: 'Yes, and it was so noisy. I hated it.'

Mum nods sympathetically: 'Yes, it is much harder for you when they are noisy. I wonder why they were noisier today?'

'Mrs Jones said that we were all feeling hot and tired. She told us that it is harder not to argue when you are hot, but we should try hard.'

'Do you think that is why you were finding it hard? Were the children all arguing?'

Benjamin thinks about this: 'Not all of them, but Justine and Carol got very cross when they were gluing. I think their model broke.'

'Well Benjamin, no wonder you were feeling wobbly today. That was a lot to cope with, wasn't it?'

Benjamin hangs his head again and then whispers, 'I hit Jack and Billy.'

'I know sweetheart. That was when Mrs Jones called me. She isn't cross with you, but she thought it would be better for you to be at home this afternoon.'

'I didn't mean to hit them, but they wouldn't let me have a turn with the ball. I had waited ages.'

'It sounds like you were trying to be patient, but then you felt very cross with them, didn't you?'

'Yes, and I tried to get the ball from them...' Benjamin hesitates and then whispers, 'And then I hit them.'

Suddenly Benjamin brightens: 'Mummy, can I make them cards? You know, to say sorry. Can I make a card for Jack and Billy?'

Mum smiles: 'Well, that sounds like a great plan. I will get the card and pens out and you can make them while I clear up a bit. We must be sure to remember to take them with us when we go to school tomorrow.'

Benjamin looks pensive, and then looks at Mum with a sense of urgency: 'No Mum, no, not tomorrow. We must take the cards to school today. I don't want to wait until tomorrow.'

Mum looks puzzled. 'Well we could, but what's the hurry? It would be easier to take them with us tomorrow.'

'No Mum, that won't do,' proclaims Benjamin. 'We must go back to school today. You see, I don't want Jack and Billy to be upset all night!'

Mum smiles and ruffles Benjamin's hair. 'Do you know Benjamin, that sounds like a great plan!'

CHAPTER 9

Helping the Adolescent in School

Supporting adolescents in school brings an additional range of complexities. The young people are managing education alongside the developmental changes happening at all levels. Physiological changes alongside increasing cognitive maturity and changing social relationships all contribute to a life stage which is all about developing independence, revisiting self-identity and preparing for adulthood. This can be especially challenging for teenagers who have experienced developmental trauma. Teams supporting these students have an important part to play as they move through secondary school, helping them to achieve academic qualifications while supporting them with the competing challenges which can assault them. A DDP-informed approach to educating teenage students can be more challenging because of the additional complexity of this life stage, combined with a changing school environment. This can, however, represent a last chance to reach these students before adulthood – to give them the experience of healthy relationships to take forward into life, work and adult relationships.

Moving into adolescence

Entering adolescence tends to coincide in western countries with a move to secondary school. These schools are generally larger, with higher expectations for self-organization and independent study. They require the students to navigate a larger number of relationships with adults and peers. Young people often make a jump in maturity as they move to the 'big school', rising to the challenges the setting poses.

Vulnerable children are already emotionally immature because of the impact of the trauma on emotional growth. The gap between them and their peers can grow even wider as the peers jump while the traumatized youngsters stand still. At a time when the peer group is becoming increasingly important, the vulnerable students are very aware of their difference from their peers, and this can impact negatively on their changing sense of identity.

Now, more than ever, these students need key adults in their life who can help them make the transition to secondary school and adolescence and to cope with the many demands that this life stage brings. It is not always easy to reach these students. If adults don't take the time to know and understand them, don't demonstrate their trustworthiness and don't offer them safe intersubjective experiences, the students will soon turn their backs and look elsewhere for a safe base. Adolescence brings many new experiences and an enlarged peer group within which students can seek this base. An opening-up world has safe challenges, but also risky adventures into drugs, sex and criminality without the guidance of safe adults.

Young people entering secondary school and adolescence will benefit from adults around them who are prepared to take it slowly. They need educators to emotionally connect with them, who will get to know the students in their care and take the time to understand before they respond. This can be a challenge in busy secondary schools with their multiple demands on the educators. A DDP-informed approach can guide these young people into secondary school while they are still open and receptive, helping them to find a path through this stage of their education which will not only provide learning opportunities and qualifications but will also help them socially and emotionally. Making the most of education relies on these relational aspects as much as it does on the teaching of the curriculum.

The complexity of adolescence

Adolescence represents a complex life stage. The young people are encountering new experiences, learning to rely less on parental support and more on each other, and starting to think about their future – who they want to be and what they want to achieve. Secure adolescents will thrive on the novelty and additional challenges that this can bring. Their increasing cognitive maturity allows them to adjust to different demands for self-study, organization and planning. Their increasing emotional and social sophistication allows them to fit into expanding peer groups, and to seek out close friends and companionship from within this.

Heather Forbes (2012) paints a picture of how trauma can impact on this life stage when writing about the fictional 'Billy', representing all traumatized pupils in school. She says:

> Trauma impacts a child's ability to concentrate, organize, and process information. So by age sixteen, Billy may still be unable to keep his backpack organized, his note-taking skills are probably non-existent, and he likely has no ability to plan out the timing of a four-week project. His level of frustration with school has been continually building since the second grade, and by now he hates learning and has no tolerance for doing work he believes is 'busy work'. At this point in his academic career, Billy is truly viewed as nothing short of a problem student in the classroom. (Forbes, 2012, pp.44–45)

Vulnerable adolescents are often changing physiologically and cognitively while remaining emotionally immature. This immaturity can become more pronounced as the stress of not managing well increases. Drives towards independence, to make sense of self in relation to peers and to fit in and be liked, accepted and wanted within the peer group all continue unabated, while emotionally the students are still needing a high level of support, structure and organization from adults. Opportunities provided by technology, social media and contact with a wider range of peers alongside a strong need to be seen as successful and able to cope can lead adolescents down roads that are risky.

Alongside this, adolescence is a time of revisiting your sense of identity, of exploring life stories and of envisaging who you will become. This brings the young people back into contact with difficult life experiences that they need to make sense of all over again. While they may have seemed comfortable with this during middle childhood, new understanding that comes with increasing cognitive maturity can make this a troubling exploration. If project work at school also touches on themes resonant of the student's own history, this can add an additional stress, which the team supporting the pupil are not always aware of.

With a complex range of needs alongside resistance to accepting adult help, these students are often viewed as problematic. It is easy to understand why educators might back away from relationship with these students as they try to get them to fit with the school's policies and procedures. New ways of relating to and supporting these students are needed, informed by our understanding of the impact of trauma. If staff don't find the time and energy for these students, they are missing the last big opportunity to help them onto new, more hopeful life paths (see Bombèr, 2007; Forbes, 2012; Gott, 1999; Howard, 2013). Forbes again puts this succinctly:

> Instead of asking children to make a better 'choice' in their behaviours, it is time that we ask ourselves to make a better choice in the creation of their environments. We must develop stronger relationships that will increase their window of stress tolerance and hence increase their capacity to learn, thrive and succeed. (Forbes, 2012, pp.21–22)

A DDP-informed approach to supporting vulnerable students in secondary school rests on understanding the clashing of developmental trauma and adolescence. This has been explored only briefly here but is looked at in more depth by others (Forbes, 2012; Golding *et al.*, 2016; Perry, 2009; Staff, 2016).

The complexity of the school environment

As adolescence represents an increasingly complex life stage, school is also providing an increasingly complex environment where the young people spend large parts of their day. The secure base of primary school, with single classrooms and a small number of adults to relate to, is replaced with large schools, complex timetables and many adults guiding education. The students must navigate around large educational sites alongside many other students in what can be noisy and crowded environments.

Ted was standing in his oversized uniform looking at his diary. Which week was it? And which period? Where did they say the drama studio was? He looked perplexed as 15- and 16-year-olds bounced down the corridors squealing and laughing confidently past him. His bag was knocked off his shoulder as he shuffled along hoping he would bump into someone else from his form group to ask.

Even getting to school can be a challenge, as often these schools are further from home and students are expected to use public transport to reach them.

Vulnerable students are likely to struggle with having to relate to a range of adults with the inconsistencies that this inevitably brings. Increased stress levels can push them back into controlling behaviours learned when young, combined with a reluctance to seek or use adults for support. Fear of peer judgement can mean that they do not want to reveal the struggles that they are having. They may want to hide that they are finding it hard to remember and find their way around the school or are feeling overwhelmed emotionally and at a sensory level with the noisy, busy environment. Needing additional support can make students highly self-conscious in front of their peers. Fears of losing credibility and status are high at this life stage.

All the additional stress that this brings will lead to vulnerable students being less likely to arrive at lessons organized, calm and ready to learn. This threatens further the weak executive functioning skills which hinder these students in their ability to plan, problem solve and foresee consequences. Expectations for independent study, homework and project work become unattainable as students spend more time in hyper-aroused and inflexible states. They are unable to adjust to what is needed and fearful of being seen to need adult support.

Finding a whole-school approach to helping vulnerable adolescents benefit from secondary education will be a challenge. Large staff teams, complex leadership and management structures and many competing demands on the staff make it hard to keep these students in mind and to ensure that all staff members are adopting a consistent approach. Helping secondary schools to adopt a relational approach to educating their students will benefit everyone and is essential for the vulnerable students. Louise writes:

> Let's get relationship back on the map in secondary schools. *Relationship security is at the heart of what is needed to engage our exploratory systems, that is, our capacity to learn.* We would be wise to start investing in relationships between staff and pupils if we want to see academic success; to invest our limited resources into allocating key adults to build relationships with vulnerable pupils; to allow permanency for these key relationships, not chopping and changing, but remaining over time, to create small, consistent teams around pupils to build safety,

security and stability. (Bombèr, 2016 from the foreword of Golding *et al.*, 2016, p.9, original emphasis)

A DDP-informed approach to educating adolescents

As with younger children, understanding the difficulties of vulnerable teenage students in school is an important starting point. Knowing how their dysregulated nervous systems work is essential in finding a school approach that will be helpful for them. This, combined with understanding that traumatized adolescents relate to educators based on assumptions that they are not good enough and that the educators will be uncaring towards them, can begin to shape the adults' approach to relationship building. Without attention to relationships, all the other means of support that the teams supporting the pupils adopt (rewards, praise, discipline) will be viewed as controlling and evidence that assumptions about educators are correct.

A DDP-informed approach views relationships as key to unlocking the potential of these disadvantaged students. Emotional support cannot be handed over to school counsellors or therapists but needs to be a part of the educational approach of all school staff. The teams supporting the pupils are guiding the students towards independence and educational success. They are also providing emotional and social support, allowing the students to use needed dependence and appropriate independence. The vulnerable student might be very accomplished at avoiding and resisting the educators' discipline and boundaries; they may have sophisticated controlling behaviours to provide a sense of artificial safety; they may have learned to hide their difficulties from view, using arrogance or withdrawal as defences to keep adults at bay and peers on side. Beneath all this is an emotionally overwhelmed student who needs adult support even if he can't acknowledge this. Even though there is less time to connect with the students alongside all the demands of school, even though the students' defences are highly honed and entrenched and their resistance to adult support can be strong, educators need to find ways to continue to offer relationships to the students.

This means remaining open and engaged, even when students are pushing staff members into defensiveness. The vulnerable adolescent, experiencing the additional stresses of secondary school, is likely to return to a nervous system alert for danger, even if the middle school years have been calmer. Only an open and engaged attitude from the staff members will soothe the nervous system and allow the student to be regulated and safe enough to respond.

> One of the important tasks therefore for all adults who are supporting traumatized adolescents is to help develop the self-regulatory capacity of the adolescents, by creating environments which are regulating, by using the relationship to co-regulate and by gradually helping the adolescents to move away from survival and towards relationship. With their thinking brain back in charge, these adolescents will have the flexibility to manage the stresses they encounter and to seek help for this when needed. (Golding *et al.*, 2016, p.205)

The educators need to provide a regulating presence, allowing the student to use the co-regulating support when able to. This means not rushing the student to think about her behaviour, especially when this has impacted on others. When levels of shame and dysregulation are high, premature guidance is likely to increase these further. Time for regulation and to experience having her own emotional reactions understood and accepted are essential before the student will be ready to think of others, experience remorse and want to make amends.

Educators need to find opportunities to wonder about the emotional lives of students. They are more likely to tolerate this curiosity when they are away from their peers. A PACE attitude provides genuine interest in the student's experience (the reflective part of the student's story discovered through curiosity) and the emotional impact of this experience (the affective part of the story supported through acceptance and empathy). The staff member can help the student to co-create an understanding of day-to-day experience, both in and out of school. If talking with the student is too intense, the staff member might find ways to talk about the student indirectly, expressing acceptance, empathy and curiosity for her so that she gets a sense of being understood and valued. Notes and other forms of indirect communication can be helpful. Adolescents will also respond well to playfulness in these interactions. The staff member needs to be careful not to convey any criticism or advice through the playfulness. This undermines the experience of joy in the relationship that playfulness is offering. Finding ways to enjoy the relationship with the student is the aim.

There are lots of reasons that PACE is difficult. Staff members need support for themselves and good self-understanding if they are to be successful in adopting this way of being with their students.

Some students are harder to connect with than others. Stress and multiple worries can also interfere with good intentions. Sometimes ideas sound simple but are hard to implement. This is especially true when memories of difficult relationships in their own adolescence are triggered, as the following example illustrates. Fortunately, Mrs Kay was able to reflect on her difficulty and find a way back to the PACE attitude.

Mrs Kay was having a hard morning. She was struggling with a headache. The class was restless, and she was aware that the school inspectors were visiting. When she saw Lucy passing a message to Keith in her Year 10 English class, she felt very irritated. She removed the note, placing it on her desk, and warned Lucy that any more trouble would land her in detention. She struggled through the rest of the class and was relieved that the next session was free from teaching. She decided to go to the staffroom to take some pain killers before attending a planned meeting. As she took a short cut through the school grounds, she spotted Lucy and Keith not in their lessons. Following the incident in her class, she felt cross with Lucy. She suspected that she was the instigator, distracting the generally studious Keith from his lessons. She called them over to her.

Mrs Kay: 'Where do you think you two are going? I think both of you have places to be right now – French, isn't it?'

Keith and Lucy: 'Yes Miss.'

Mrs Kay: 'Off you go Keith, if you get a move on you won't miss too much, but don't let me see you out of lessons again. Lucy, stay, I want a word with you.'

With a glance to Lucy, Keith nodded and walked back towards the school. Lucy stood sullenly in front of Mrs Kay. She didn't look at her.

Mrs Kay: 'Well, young lady, what do you have to say for yourself? First you are passing notes in my lesson, and now you are distracting Keith from getting to his class. Did you talk him into leaving school with you? Is that what the note was about?'

Lucy looked down at the ground and stayed silent.

Mrs Kay: 'Well, don't you have anything to say?'

Lucy: 'It's not fair, Miss. You always pick on me. I was worried about Keith.'

Mrs Kay: 'I only "pick on you" if you deserve it. I haven't seen you trying to do any work yet today. If you're worried about Keith, then you shouldn't be stopping him from getting to his lessons. You may not see it as important, but Keith is trying to do well in this school.'

Lucy, clearly angry, said nothing. Her head went down again.

Mrs Kay: 'I will see you after school for detention. Now get to your class or I will make it a double detention!'

They each went off in different directions. Mrs Kay was feeling frustrated. She was now going to be late for her meeting and there was no time to go to the staffroom. As she retraced her steps, she took some deep breaths. She tried to focus on the meeting ahead, but her mind wandered back to Lucy. She struggled to like this pupil. She wondered why. Lucy wasn't majorly disruptive, but somehow, she never felt respected by her. Just like Frances, she thought, recalling her own sister during her teenage years. She was surprised, as she had never thought of this similarity before. She then remembered the note. It was still lying on her desk, unread. She wondered what it said. She was passing her classroom and so she slipped in and picked up the note. She read it as she walked to the meeting room. Lucy was clearly worried about Keith and something that had happened the previous evening. She wanted to know he was okay and that he wasn't going to 'do anything stupid'. Mrs Kay was beginning to think she had misjudged the situation. As soon as she could she sought out the head of pastoral care, Miss Clover, and asked her about Keith. She discovered that Keith's father was violent, and that Keith was very protective of his mother. He had been to see Miss Clover that morning to tell her about an incident the previous evening. She was going to check in with him again at lunchtime. 'And I am going to check in with Lucy,' thought Mrs Kay. She realized that she had acted without fully understanding the situation. At lunchtime, she asked Lucy to come to her classroom for a chat.

Mrs Kay: 'Thank you for coming, Lucy. I bet I am the last person you wanted to see this lunchtime?'

Lucy looked down at the ground and said nothing.

Mrs Kay: 'I can understand that you don't want to talk to me. I imagine you are just expecting me to be cross with you again. I think I was a bit hasty this morning. I would like to understand what was happening.'

Lucy: (angrily) 'It's like you said. I was distracting Keith, okay! I'll come to your stupid detention, just leave me alone, right.'

Mrs Kay: 'Lucy, of course you are cross with me. I can see why you felt picked on. I didn't try to find out what was going on this morning. That was my mistake. I've read the note you were passing to Keith and I can see that you were worried about him. I would like to understand now. It seems Keith is a good friend?'

Lucy: 'He's not my boyfriend. I've known him for years. We're just friends, right!'

Mrs Kay: 'I'm sorry, I wasn't suggesting he was your boyfriend, but I can see you care about him. It seems as if you have been worried about him today?'

Lucy: 'That's none of your business.'

Mrs Kay took a breath. This was just how Frances used to be towards her. She could feel herself getting angry.

Mrs Kay: 'I know you are cross with me Lucy, and I can understand why. I wasn't listening this morning, but I am now. I am guessing that your worry about Keith made it hard for you to focus on our class this morning. I can see you wrote the note to check if he was okay. I don't know why you were out of class when I saw you earlier, but I am realizing that it was important to you.'

Lucy: 'I just wanted to see if he was alright.'

Mrs Kay: 'You are really worried about him, aren't you? Did you take him outside to talk to him?'

Lucy: (beginning to shout) 'No, I followed him. He went outside.'

Mrs Kay: 'Oh, Lucy, I didn't get it. I hadn't realized Keith had gone out first. Why wasn't he going to his lesson?'

Lucy: 'He was angry, with his dad. I thought he was going to find him. I wanted to stop him.'

Mrs Kay: 'I think I'm understanding. Miss Clover told me a little. So, you knew Keith was angry, with his dad, and you thought he was going to leave the school. So, you went after him. To check he was okay? To stop him?

Lucy: 'I didn't want him to get into trouble. I wanted to get him to come to French. Look, it's his business. I shouldn't be telling you. Can I go now? I'll come to the detention.'

Mrs Kay: 'I want to help. You are a good friend to Keith. He needs friends. We can help him too. I know he is talking to Miss Clover. You don't need to do this alone, Lucy. You can talk to me. We can help.'

Lucy: 'What, and get another detention?'

Mrs Kay took another breath. Frances, again, she thought!

Mrs Kay: (smiling) 'Ouch, I deserved that, I guess. I really wasn't listening this morning, was I? It's going to take time for you to trust me. I just want you to know I am here if you want to talk. It's hard to see your friends going through a hard time. No more notes in class, eh, but I'm glad you are there for him.'

Lucy: 'You're alright, Miss. I'm sorry I did that.' She smiled: 'I'll make sure you don't see me next time!'

Mrs Kay: (laughing) 'Well, I'd prefer if you talked to him at break. I think you would like *The Mill on the Floss* if you gave it a chance.'

Lucy: 'Actually I've read it and I did like it. I like reading.'

Lucy started to talk animatedly about the book.

Mrs Kay: 'I had no idea you liked reading so much. You have lots of great thoughts. Why don't I see these in your essays?'

Lucy: 'I'm not good at writing things down. I'm not clever like Keith.'

Mrs Kay: 'I think we are both underestimating you today. If you can bear more time with me, I can help you. Let's get your good ideas on paper. I run a help group on a Thursday. Want to come? We can swap it for the detention. I think we will both enjoy it more.'

Lucy: 'I'll give it a try...maybe. Thanks, Miss.'

A consistent relational approach will, over time, soothe the aroused nervous systems of the students, communicating safety and reducing stress. The students will feel of interest and value to the educators and they will become more open to educational experiences. In order to reach this stage, the educators will need resilience and patience. At first, the vulnerable students may feel more vulnerable. They can react to this by creating more distance between themselves and the staff member. This can be through angry and aggressive behaviours, through avoiding the staff member or simply by not turning up to school. Part of the relational approach is to support the anxiety that students feel when beginning to experience being understood and valued. This can be hard and hurtful as the defensive responses of the students can feel rejecting. Good teamwork and support for the staff is essential.

In order to benefit the vulnerable adolescents within school it will not be enough for lone staff members to have gained understanding and ability to use a DDP-informed approach. A whole-school ethos is needed, with a consistency of approach supported by senior leaders within the school. With support throughout the staff team, individuals can become the champions who invest in training and developing the skills needed. They can then pass these on to colleagues. Often it is the less well-paid support staff who provide the individualized, key adult support for students. The expertise of these individuals needs developing and recognizing so that they become essential support for vulnerable students and a knowledgeable resource from which the whole school can benefit.

Conclusion

Supporting adolescents with developmental trauma to get full benefit from their secondary school education can be both a challenging and highly rewarding experience for school teams. Recognizing the complexity of adolescence and how this is impacted on by earlier traumatic experience is an important part of the knowledge base the teams supporting the pupils will need. This means being alert to the needs of the students, whether these are expressed or hidden from view. Behaviours can provide important clues to understanding a student as long as educators don't get too caught up in them, challenging though these might be. In the following example, the tutor focused on the behaviour, missing Clara's strong need for support at this time.

Clara was slumped over her desk in form, head in her hands. She was the last one out as the first buzzer went, moving very slowly to the next class. Her form tutor shouted at her, telling her to get a move on as she couldn't build up any more behaviour points! Clara turned around and screwed her face up at Miss, swearing under her breath. 'You come back here right now!' said the form tutor in an attacking tone. Clara continued walking, faster now, head down, ignoring her form tutor. 'You get back here right now, I'm warning you!' 'Right, that's it, I'm calling senior management!' Clara then kicked the plaster and swore more profusely as she ran off site.

If this tutor had spent some time understanding what was going on for Clara, this episode may have gone very differently.

Clara was slumped over her desk in form, head in her hands. She was the last one out as the first buzzer went, moving very slowly to the next class. Her form tutor got down to her level and quietly said, 'I can see you are not okay – something is going on – help me to understand...', in a warm, empathic tone. Clara looked up tentatively as if to check her form tutor's face. From beneath her long hair she saw her empathic eyes. 'It's all going wrong...' 'It's all going wrong?' 'Yes, they have spread it all over the school...now everyone knows...' 'Something has been spread all over the school about you?' The dialogue that continued revealed that someone she thought she could trust had spread rumours about her over social media. She felt completely alone and so overwhelmed. She had no idea what to do. Together with her form tutor they figured out that she needed to have some pastoral support this morning while this was looked into.

In addition, teams need to look at the school environment through the eyes of their most vulnerable students. Understanding the complexity of the secondary school environment can begin a journey towards creating safe school environments which will benefit all. With this knowledge base, schools can provide a relationally focused, emotionally connected and trauma-informed approach to supporting and educating the adolescents in their care. This is a slowing down in the approach to education, but the students will get much further, much faster, as a consequence. They will become adult citizens able to emotionally relate and socially connect so that they can achieve in careers, relationships and their future families.

CHAPTER 10

Achieving Partnership with Parents and the Professional Network

Children spend most of their time at home with family, followed by their time in school. While peer relationships become increasingly important throughout childhood, parents and educators will remain the most influential figures in children's lives at least until adolescence.

Children can also display different parts of themselves at home and at school. This can be especially marked when vulnerable pupils are trying to adapt to feel safe. Pupils may be well behaved and compliant at school while being oppositional, challenging and angry at home. Conversely, some pupils appear well regulated and secure at home while the challenges of school tip them into high arousal and dysregulated behaviours. The process of compartmentalizing parts of the self, alongside the need to hide and express different needs, explored earlier in this book, can present a confusing picture to the adults in the child's life. Compartmentalization is part of the survival strategies children adopt when growing up in frightening worlds. Each adult gets a view of the child, often unaware of what is being hidden from view. To truly understand the child and the struggles the child is having, parents and the team supporting her need to share their viewpoints. Parents and educators need to work together, understanding each other's experiences of the pupil and planning together how to support the pupil to get the best from school.

Alongside this compartmentalizing within the pupil, a process called 'splitting' can also occur when a vulnerable pupil is being supported. This can impact on the teams supporting the pupil, the parents and the whole network. This arises out of a tendency for us to view the world as black and white when we are finding the complexity too difficult. It is a defence against overwhelming anxiety which makes it difficult to acknowledge that oneself and other people are a mixture of good and bad. Instead, good is attributed to some parts and bad to other parts of the network. A parent is viewed as good, an educator bad. A social care team is seen as bad, while school is viewed as good. This splitting process can be highly destructive, causing all members of the network to move into defensive positions. When social engagement is lost, then trauma is organizing the relationships. Chaos, rigidity and hostility follow as these defensive positions become entrenched. If networks can hold on to the DDP principles, they will be guided back to open and engaged states. Holding an attitude of PACE will help these defensive processes to reduce and good working together to follow.

This chapter will explore the importance of parents, school and whole networks working together in order to help the vulnerable pupil thrive in school and benefit from education.

Working with parents

For teams supporting the pupils and parents, working together begins with a sharing of stories. Staff members become more aware of the pupil's previous experience and the journey the family have made. This might be a birth family's journey of recovery, finding health and developing resilience. It might be a story of a family's continuing struggles to overcome earlier diversity. It might be a foster or adoptive family's journey of bringing a child into the family. Parents, in turn, become more aware of the staff members' experience of the pupil within school and within the individual class. They also understand more the constraints and complexities of supporting a vulnerable pupil alongside many other pupils.

As stories are shared, understanding increases and working together will improve. This working together can become reflective rather than reactive. As the adults remain curious, they become more understanding of the various stresses the other is facing. Empathy and acceptance follow. They are also more likely to find opportunities for playfulness, finding a lighter moment together in what can be challenging times. PACE is high when working together is going well.

This does not mean disagreements won't happen. Parents and the team supporting the pupil can feel strongly about what the pupil needs in school, and their views are not always the same. If each holds on to curiosity, seeking genuine understanding of the other's beliefs, anxieties and worries, then co-operation and finding a solution that works for both are more likely to occur.

Open and engaged working together also reduces the experience of being judged and blamed. Without understanding, it is easy to fall into a pattern of mutual blame and recriminations. Each party can move out of this unhealthy dynamic. Putting your own concerns to one side while taking time to understand the perspective of the other is a slower route to working things out together, but it can lead to solutions that are more likely to work, resting as they do on solid understanding and co-operation.

Pupils will experience more safety when being supported by parents and educators who are working well together. Vulnerable pupils are vigilant to what is going on around them. They pay close attention to the relationships in their life, including how these people are relating to each other. When they pick up hostility between home and school, they will feel less safe. This will increase their hypervigilance towards these relationships as well as increasing any conflicts of loyalty they might be experiencing between parent and educator. 'Who shall I keep on side?' and 'How shall I do this?' are big questions for pupils trying to attend to their own safety.

Peter at age 13 had just moved to a new school given some incidents of bullying at his previous school. His foster parents had been strong advocates for Peter and had met with his teacher and management to ensure that there would be safety for Peter. Peter had made the transition well and had formed a close relationship with his classroom teacher, Mr Perry. One morning Mr Perry was away, and the class had a substitute teacher. Often for children with developmental trauma, a new teacher increases their hypervigilance, and behaviour reflects the increased arousal. For Peter, his worry translated into a high level of distractibility. He couldn't stay seated and was pacing around the room distracting others, many of whom were glad for the distraction. Any directive from the teacher was ignored. Finally, the teacher became angry and told the class that all of them would be staying in over break to complete their work. A few of the boys were angry at Peter, blaming him for the consequence. Peter burst into tears and ran out of the room.

The next morning, Peter and his foster parents came for a meeting with the principal and Mr Perry. They were angry and accused both of not doing enough to keep Peter safe. Mr Perry started to argue that he hadn't been there that day but then noticed Peter's discomfort. He took a deep breath and said, 'You are right! I really should have known that a new teacher that Peter didn't know would have been scary for him and that the new teacher could have used some help knowing how Peter learns and manages the best.' Mr Perry turned to look at Peter: 'I am sorry Peter that I didn't think more about how me being away might have been for you. I didn't think far enough.' Peter's body language changed immediately, and he looked relieved. Mr Perry continued: 'Your parents are right to stick up for you! I'm glad that you have such good advocates. I think your parents and I are going to get along great because we all know what a terrific kid you are! We don't have to disagree on that one, do we?' Mr Perry had recognized that Peter would have been in a bind with one set of adults being mad at the other. His use of PACE had helped Peter's foster parents feel supported and he had communicated a joint intent to keep Peter safe.

When they receive messages that parents and the team supporting them have confidence in each other, these pupils can relax. Hypervigilance reduces and safety increases. The pupils can now put anxieties and worries to one side, confident in the parents and team to work things out. They can focus on learning.

Close working together will also ensure that potential triggers within the curriculum are spotted and considered. Pupils not living with birth families, or who have abuse and neglect in their background, can be very vulnerable to triggers, reminders of past and present distress. Anxiety increases as school topics touch on sensitive issues. Thinking about themselves as a baby, writing about 'my family' and studying a book with themes of abuse, separation and loss are all potential landmines in the pupil's school day. When the team supporting the pupil and parents are talking regularly, these potential triggers are likely to be spotted. They can plan together how to support the pupil. The parent will be able to prepare the pupil for what is to come and to support him during the topic. The teacher will be able to get advice from the parent on what the pupil might be thinking or feeling and to plan the best way to help him with the topic work. The support staff can think about the additional support that the pupil might need alongside this topic work. This can become a positive experience instead of a distressing one. Pupils can write about their experience of moving from a family very eloquently when well supported. The school topic might give them a first opportunity to talk with parents about previous experience. Importantly, the parent and team working together will foster an environment of trust and support. The pupil is then more likely to seek support from these adults, rather than to try and deal with a worrying topic alone.

Managing safeguarding concerns

Pupils will often disclose experience with parents to members of their support team. These may be the first relationships outside the home where they have felt safe. This may be the first time the pupil has felt confident to tell someone else what is happening. Sometimes the pupil's disclosures are benign, even amusing. Parents and educators can smile together at the pupil's disclosure that Daddy ate two whole pizzas on Friday night. At other times, the disclosures may be more worrying.

The team supporting the pupil will have safeguarding procedures that they need to follow. This will give them the confidence to manage these difficult experiences. When there is a good working relationship between parents and the team, these procedures are more likely to be followed without blame and judgement. The team will be more aware of the stresses on the family, and the context within which events have happened. Reporting a concern with this understanding can increase empathy within the whole network for pupil and parent. Parents who feel supported are much more likely to seek help and to tell people about what has happened. This increases safety for everyone. As parents are supported, stress within the family can reduce and parenting practices can become positive again.

Being part of the network around a vulnerable pupil

Educators have an important role to play within the networks that develop around vulnerable pupils. These networks can be complex, often involving multiple agencies. The potential for confusion and misunderstanding about each other's roles is large. When networks become unthinking, they contribute to the trauma and lack of safety around the pupil. Each member will struggle to acknowledge limitations of their own agency, they will defend their involvement with the pupil and family to protect their reputation and they will be unable to think about the pupil and family's needs (Stott, 2006). When individual network members can remain open and engaged, with an attitude of PACE and a willingness to listen to and understand the different stories and perspectives of each other, the network can contribute to the pupil's recovery from trauma.

Members of the teams supporting the pupils can feel like small cogs in a large wheel, but attending network meetings is an important part of supporting the pupil in school. If they can contribute to the good functioning of a network, safety for the pupil will increase, and this will be felt within the school environment. Staff members can attend these meetings in a spirit of open engagement. They can use and model PACE; they can provide some slowing down to allow thinking to occur. These staff members will be playing their part in facilitating good network working. Defensiveness can breed defensiveness in network meetings, but if one or two of the individuals within the network can remain open and engaged, the whole network is likely to be drawn into this more positive state.

Being part of a network provides an opportunity for network members to get to know and understand each other. Again, this will be felt by the pupil, further adding to feelings of safety. For example, a looked-after pupil may have been challenging all day, knowing that a birth family contact is happening after school. The teacher knows from the social worker that the birth mum does not always turn up and will therefore have some understanding about what might be troubling the pupil. His support to the pupil can help to reduce the stress the pupil is experiencing. When the social worker arrives at school to collect the pupil, the teacher can let her know of the pupil's increasing anxiety. The social worker is now better able to support the pupil to manage the contact experience. Additionally, the pupil is witness to the good networking between social worker and teacher, increasing a sense of safety and support.

Good partnership working between school and family can also contribute to good network support for the family (Bombèr, 2016, book five). The understanding that can develop between the team supporting the pupil and parents can allow the team members to be advocates for the family, speaking for the parents in their absence and supporting them when they are unable to attend the network meetings. Again, this habitual practice of open, engaged responding to each other can be infectious within the network, allowing an open and engaged meeting as a consequence.

Conclusion

Partnership working is an essential part of supporting vulnerable pupils. Educators and parents working together can gain understanding of each other's perspectives, challenges and worries. Co-operation instead of antagonism can emerge, and safety for the pupil is increased. This spirit of working together can also contribute to the networking around pupil and family, allowing social engagement, understanding and joint solutions to problems.

Hayden was struggling with school. At 11 years of age he still struggled to organize himself and so the move to secondary school had been especially difficult. His more mature peers were drawing away from him, and the change of teachers for each lesson was taxing his already weak regulation abilities. His dysregulated behaviours were further alienating him from his peers.

The team supporting Hayden were keen to help him but were out of ideas. They decided to hold a meeting and extended an invitation to Hayden's adoptive parents. They suggested that they also invite the therapist who was working with them as a family. As the meeting began, the team were eager to find solutions, suggesting some different possibilities. The therapist paused them. She suggested that they begin by revisiting Hayden's early history and sharing stories with each other of how he was doing at home and school. Although this took time, by the end of the meeting they all understood Hayden and why he was struggling much better. Ideas for helping him were then easier to find and much more likely to be successful.

Slowing the network down, finding time to share stories and insights and increasing understanding for each other's roles and perspectives can all contribute to safe, thinking networks which have the pupil and family's needs at the centre.

CHAPTER 11

Understanding Attachment History

We are now going to move from exploring the educational support of the pupil to a focus on how educators can look after themselves. Much as aeroplane procedures always suggest, helping yourself before helping others is an essential part of supporting vulnerable pupils. As we have explored, these pupils have a range of emotional and neurodevelopmental difficulties that make parenting, educating and supporting them challenging. The combination of emotional and neurodevelopmental difficulties can be an especially difficult pairing, with each contributing to the difficulty presented by the other. Such pupils find it very difficult to let adults help them. The sum of this is that the pupils will develop security only slowly.

Being responsible for the education, behaviour and emotional well-being of pupils is particularly challenging when their, or our, well-being is low, behaviour is challenging, and safety is hard to find. Further challenge comes when the pupils are reluctant to accept support. Educators are vulnerable to running out of emotional energy. Staying strong and resilient is an essential part of successfully supporting the vulnerable child through the school year. This emerges out of good self-care coupled with a high level of social support. Good self-understanding is an important addition to this mix. This is where this chapter begins. Understanding relationship history can open the door to understanding the impact that supporting a pupil is having on the educator.

Exploring our own past relationship history

Our own relationship history can have a big impact on the way we relate to a child. Imagine a teacher who grew up in a home where there was a high level of conflict. This teacher may have chosen relationships around herself within which conflict is unlikely. Her choice of partner and her parenting of her own children may be a reaction to this early history. When this teacher has a pupil in her class who brings chaos and conflict in his wake, she is going to be ill-equipped to manage. Her anxiety will increase as the pupil provides her with an echo of her own earlier experience. She may not recognize this link, but her emotional response will be there all the same. Without support and understanding, she may find herself becoming defensive in response to this pupil. Her usual calm teaching style might desert her, and she may find herself behaving in ways that she does not recognize.

This becomes even trickier if a pupil reminds the teacher in some way of a past relationship. Maybe the pupil reminds her of herself as a teenager when things came to a head between her and her parents. This was a time when she became rebellious and engaged in activities she would prefer to stay forgotten. The teacher might find that the shame she feels about her own past is activated and she may express more urgency, worry or control in her attempts to influence the pupil and prevent her from 'going off the rails'. Anxiety for this pupil becomes mixed up with her feelings about her past self, adding to the already complex dynamic between her and the pupil. Without good self-awareness and understanding, the teacher is vulnerable to being invaded by her own past experience, reducing her ability to be open to the pupil's unique experiences.

Memories of any past relationships can be triggered by an educator–pupil relationship, whether it is parents, siblings, extended family, work colleagues or romantic relationships. For example, an educator may have a relationship with a sibling which has always been bullying. If the pupil starts to become demanding or threatening, this past relationship may come back into the present and the educator experiences fear or anger towards the pupil that actually belongs in the past with these historic relationships.

This unconscious response to past relationships, impacting on current ones, is linked to the educator's attachment state of mind. Earlier in this book we explored the attachment patterns of relating that children develop to adapt to the environments they are being raised in. These patterns represent models of relating that are used to guide later relationships that the children encounter. Children will have multiple models based on the range of relationships they have experienced; parents, grandparents, childminders all can exert an influence on the patterns of attachment that the child develops and can draw on in different situations. As the children reach adolescence and beyond, these multiple models become cumbersome for the more sophisticated relationships the young person is now managing. A task at this developmental stage is to form a single but more complex model of relating that can be taken forward into adulthood. A simple model such as 'I am lovable, and you will support me' will become more sophisticated: 'I am lovable to some people but less so to others; I can expect support from people I experience closeness with, but this is less likely from people I find less easy to get along with.' The educator above, for example, may have a model which reminds her that she is a good person who is good at developing close relationships with others. The same model cautions that conflict-ridden people are best avoided and reminds her that she is not comfortable when others are arguing.

Attachment states of mind

As attachment states of mind are influenced by multiple models in childhood, they can be a complex mix of experience. However, it is usual for this to be dominated by one particular style of attachment relating with others.

Thus, if a child has most experience of attachment security, but with some experience of loss that is well supported, it is likely that as an adult her attachment state of mind will be predominantly secure, usually described as autonomous. She might remain vulnerable to further experience of loss, but she is also likely to be confident to seek support for this should it arise. For a person who experienced a father who valued independence, that person may have a generally autonomous state of mind but lean towards some self-reliance in situations that remind him of his father.

Attachment states of mind are therefore a reflection of the complex range of experiences each of us encounters while growing up. Bearing in mind this complexity, we will describe the different attachment states of mind as they are described when thinking about adult attachment.

Autonomous

As mentioned above, the secure attachment pattern of childhood becomes an autonomous attachment state of mind. These adults have a balanced view of their childhood. They recognize and value the strengths it has given them but can also acknowledge any difficulties they encountered. They are aware of how this experience has made them the adult they are today. These experiences mean that as educators they can cope well with their pupil's negative as well as positive emotional states. This makes them sensitive and responsive educators able to stay regulated when a pupil expresses distress or dysregulation.

Preoccupied

An ambivalent attachment pattern in childhood becomes a preoccupied attachment state of mind. When teaching a pupil triggers this state of mind, educators become absorbed or preoccupied with past relationships. They find it hard to distance themselves from this childhood experience. It is as if they are back there again, and this can result in a high level of emotion, including anger. The feelings they have towards the person in the past become enacted in their relationship with the pupil. This preoccupation is generally unconscious; the educators experience themselves as responding to the pupil and not to the left-over feelings from their past. Being unaware of this influence, the educators will struggle to alter or adapt their responses to be attuned to the pupil's needs.

Mr Smart could see Philip and Carlos whispering to each other. It really wound him up and he didn't know why. He could feel himself getting increasingly dysregulated. He had noticed that this happened whenever pupils whispered while he was teaching. He had become quite angry in front of them as a result and later would regret his actions, feeling embarrassed. They were only whispering, he thought. Why did he get so upset? Thankfully he talked about it with a therapist, who was curious with him about this, and it soon became clear that this dynamic was triggering memories of having been overlooked as a child. Happily married and with a successful senior leadership post in school, he hadn't realized how powerful unresolved loss could be, having suppressed this memory for years. It made a huge difference, knowing what this upset was really all about. Mr Smart then knew to breathe his way through dynamics such as these and to remember that this was completely different from what he lived through as a child. He reported that this took the pressure off.

Dismissive

An avoidant attachment pattern in childhood becomes a dismissing attachment state of mind. As adults, memories of childhood can be idealized as the memory of negative experience is blocked, or as they deny that this has been of any significance. This is most noticeable when talking about negative experiences. These adults can talk in a matter of fact way about very difficult experiences, appearing to be emotionally unaffected by these memories. They especially value self-reliance and rather frown on people who appear dependent. When teaching a pupil triggers this state of mind, the educators tend to withdraw from the emotional experience that the pupil is triggering within them. This is most likely to occur when the pupil is expressing emotional distress. This distress is minimized as the educator encourages the pupil to suppress it. Their own emotional avoidance means that these educators are less aware of how the pupil is currently feeling. This is because they are unconsciously trying to remain unaware of how they felt at the time of their own past experience. These educators will be more comfortable with self-reliance in the pupils as they are more likely to be responsive to them when they are emotionally self-sufficient. They may convey their disapproval of a pupil expressing some emotional neediness and will find it hard to keep in mind an overly self-reliant pupil's need to feel safe by being dependent.

Unresolved

Most difficulty is posed when educators have unresolved relationship trauma in their past. These traumas can lie buried inside, ready to be triggered at unpredictable times. Once these are triggered, the educators can become absorbed with the fear or grief associated with this trauma. If the pupil unwittingly acts as such a trigger, then the educator will not be able to protect or reassure the pupil. For the pupil, it will be as if the educator isn't emotionally there, as her unavailability becomes apparent. Distress in the pupil can trigger a dysregulated or a dissociated response in the educator as memory of the trauma surfaces. An educator might, for example, become rigidly focused on the teaching task, not seeing the pupil's need for regulation at that time. She might become uncharacteristically angry when the pupil does not co-operate. The educator is feeling anxious or distressed, and this overwhelming emotional experience reduces her availability towards the pupil.

Often the memory triggering these responses is implicit; the educator is not consciously aware of it. The educator can become frightened as she fears what the pupil triggers within her or the loss of control that this can lead to. The unresolved attachment traumas from the past therefore prevent the educator perceiving and meeting the pupil's need for safety and comfort. This is frightening for the pupil, and thus traumas are perpetuated.

Lena was a lovely warm teaching assistant who started to become very tearful in class. This really impacted on her support to the pupils. Her usual nurturing approach had started to be replaced with an increasing impatience. She was increasingly unhappy at work and she began talking about leaving to find another job. When she was given the space to reflect with a trusted other in school, it became clear that the dynamic going on in the classroom was triggering a memory of a traumatic and painful loss a long time ago. The school staff were able to give her a lot of support, including some counselling, to help disentangle what was her unresolved trauma and loss and what was the child's difficulties. With this help, she recovered her emotional balance and started to enjoy work again.

Knowing your own attachment state of mind

Educators can use their attachment history exploration to notice if they tend to try and avoid feeling things, preferring to rationalize and intellectualize as in the dismissing attachment state of mind. Alternatively, they may find that they are easily overwhelmed by emotional experience without being able to reflect on this experience, as in the preoccupied attachment state of mind. In either case, the educator will benefit from correcting the balance. Supportive relationships can help her to do this. The dismissing staff member can learn to become more open to her emotional experience, while the preoccupied staff member can learn to reflect on this experience from a distance, so that she is less caught up in her immediate emotions.

Figure 11.1, together with Table 11.1 at the end of this chapter, can help you to reflect on your own attachment history. You can mark on the line where you think you fit in relationship to the descriptions of the different attachment states of mind. Remember that this can be different for different relationships. Don't assume that if you had a difficult childhood experience you will automatically have difficulties in your attachment state of mind. It is possible to gain security after childhood, especially if you have experienced healthier relationships later in life. Notice how you are in current relationships to help you understand your attachment state of mind. If you do feel you are being affected by attachment experience, there is literature that can help you (e.g. Dent, 2018). Therapy can also be helpful to recover from the impact of past difficulties.

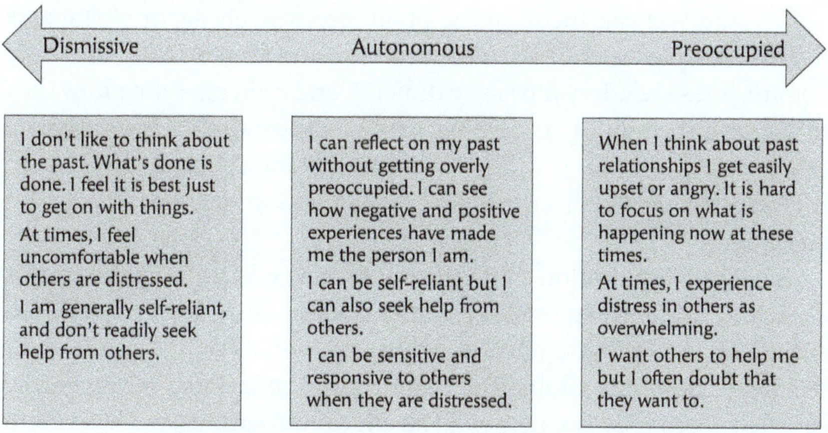

Figure 11.1: Attachment state of mind continuum

The importance of self-exploration as part of self-care

From these descriptions you may notice that when attachment experience is negatively influencing you it often happens outside your consciousness. You may know that you are struggling with a pupil, but not be able to associate this with your own past experience. The pattern you fall into is often an unconscious one as adaptations or responses you developed in the past are re-enacted in the present.

Things that are unconscious do not need to stay unconscious. The best way of not being hijacked by your own attachment history is to be able to reflect on it and understand it. When we can make the unconscious conscious, it no longer has the power to control us and we can behave more flexibly and mindfully as a result. For educators, exploration of past relationship history, including early attachment experience, is therefore an important part of understanding current challenges with pupils in the classroom. This can be an emotional experience, and for some educators it might leave them feeling vulnerable as a consequence. It is important to consider therapy or counselling as a way of getting support when self-exploration is difficult. In the UK, education staff are offered six free sessions, usually by the council, which can be extended if needed.

When it is understood, the past becomes a road map for understanding present triggers and obstacles. Knowing that you are feeling angry with a pupil because he is reminding you of your father can help you to regulate the angry feelings. Those feelings can then reduce and you can focus on the pupil responsively again. Being able to reflect on past relationships with compassion for yourself is therefore helpful. These relationships were difficult, and understanding how they influenced the adult you have become is important. As you integrate this past experience, it will help you to distance yourself from it. In this way, current experience does not keep taking you back to your old struggles.

Such self-exploration can be useful for any educator. However, it is especially useful when teaching vulnerable pupils. As we have explored earlier, these pupils are often searching for predictability, and ways to feel in charge of the adults. Their controlling behaviours are especially satisfied when they can discover the educators' buttons; pushing them leads to a predictable response which helps the pupils to feel safer because it is within their control. Anticipating that an educator is going to be angry with you is hard to live with, but knowing that you can make the educator angry feels a whole lot safer if only because it is predictable.

Educators will not get very far if they fall into control battles with the pupils; these pupils are generally the masters of control, and usually win! Being able to step aside from the battle by being in control of your own responses can, however, be helpful. Understanding your own triggers is therefore an important part of supporting pupils who feel a need to control.

Moving from defensive to open and engaged

Understanding yourself better helps you to understand the way a particular pupil impacts on you. Not all pupils will impact on you in the same way.

As staff members notice how their responses to the pupils are linked to their responses to previous relationships, they will be able to consciously change the way they are responding in the present. They will be able to remain open and engaged to the pupils rather than becoming defensive with them. Self-reflection does not stop the triggers; they may always be there. After all, your history is yours and cannot be re-written. There is a difference, however, between unconscious triggers that are in charge, making life uncomfortable for you, and conscious triggers that allow you to be flexible in the present. When we are aware of what is happening, it puts us back in charge. We can notice and choose not to engage with the trigger. We stay open to the pupil, letting the impact this is having on us move to the background.

Noticing in the moment but choosing not to be controlled by a trigger can feel very freeing. It is, however, an act of repression, pushing away the feelings and thoughts that have arisen. Although repression is the best solution for that moment and interaction, later reflection will be important. Remember that reflecting with a trusted other can be especially helpful to increase your self-understanding. This processing of your experience can increase your resilience to similar, future moments within your teaching career.

Alternatively, you might recognize that you are struggling because of a trigger and choose to move away from the pupil for a while. Handing over to another adult with that pupil can allow you to take care of yourself and then return to the pupil in a more open state. The members of the team supporting the pupil can work together to support each other at these difficult moments.

The following example illustrates how an educator became aware that her behaviour signalled something about her own life. She was able to repress her anger, move away from the student in the moment and ask for help from a colleague.

Mrs Abassi started to become aware that she was increasingly irritated with Amara, a student who had moved to the UK from Somalia three years previously. Amara had settled in well during the first year of school and was popular with a wide group of friends. She was a solid student and worked hard to learn. When Amara first came to the school, Mrs Abassi had taken her under her wing and spent extra time helping her develop her English and making sure she understood school routines. She and Amara had developed a close relationship. As Amara had settled in, there was less need to spend time together, but Mrs Abassi had been proud of Amara's ability to make the transition so smoothly.

At the start of the new school year, Mrs Abassi started to notice that Amara was spending less and less time paying attention to work, and more and more time engaged in social interactions. Mrs Abassi started to correct Amara harshly for minor transgressions when she saw her in the hallway and to be rigid in her expectations for behaviour. Amara was initially surprised by her teacher's change in demeanour and was polite in response. One day, however, she didn't respond, and as Mrs Abassi walked away, Amara and her friends started laughing. Mrs Abassi was furious and wanted to spin around and single Amara out and shout at her. She felt that she was losing authority in front of a group of senior students and felt a simultaneous desire to shout at the group and run quickly out of the school.

Luckily, Mrs Abassi knew that neither option would be good for anyone and she sought out the head of the department, Mrs Kent. Mrs Kent immediately recognized her distress and plugged in the kettle.

Mrs Kent: 'What's up? I can see you are really upset.'

Mrs Abassi: 'Amara is ruining her life!'

Mrs Kent: 'Wow! That sounds like a big worry. I can see why you would be upset if you thought that a child is in that much trouble. What makes you think Amara is ruining her life? I thought she was doing well at school both academically and socially.'

Mrs Abassi: 'She is!'

Mrs Kent: (feeling puzzled) 'So help me understand your upset.'

Mrs Abassi: (with a big sigh) 'I don't know why I am so mad! I just am.'

Mrs Kent: 'There is obviously something about this that is really troubling you. I know you care deeply about this girl and have invested a lot of time and energy into helping her succeed. Do you think that you are perhaps upset because she doesn't need you so much any more?'

Mrs Abassi: 'No, I don't think that's what it is.'

Mrs Kent: 'Okay.'

The two sat sipping tea quietly.

Mrs Abassi: 'I think I am envious of her.'

Mrs Kent: 'Oh?'

Mrs Abassi: 'Yes, now that I am thinking about it with you, I realize that I didn't have it as easy when I moved to the UK as a teenager. I had to work hard at school and at home. I wasn't allowed to have friends. My parents had given up everything for me and my sister, so I didn't argue. I just worked hard. I was very lonely in secondary school. I was away from my country and everything that I knew. I couldn't talk to my parents and I didn't have friends to talk to. I was pretty unhappy.'

Mrs Kent: (with empathy) 'That would have been a very difficult time for you.'

Mrs Abassi: 'Yes, and I realize that I have been punishing Amara for having what I never had. How selfish of me!'

Mrs Kent: 'You are hard on yourself. I am pretty impressed that you have figured this out. What are you going to do with this?'

Mrs Abassi: 'Tomorrow after I have had a good sleep I am going to apologize to Amara and tell her why I have been so harsh with her lately. I hope she will forgive me.'

Mrs Kent: 'Let me know if you need another cup of tea afterwards!'

Sometimes a staff member can't physically take a break from a pupil because there is no one else to help. It is possible, however, to take a break from dealing with the issue at hand. It is easy to feel that if we are not dealing with a behaviour immediately we are somehow failing. Apart from very young children who live in a more immediate world, pupils will cope with a delay. Acknowledge that you are upset right now, and let the pupil know that while you are not happy with what he has done you do still want to support him. You need time to think about this so that you can help him to make amends for his actions while getting your support for him right. In this way, the pupil is left in no doubt that while he has done something wrong, he is still cared about. You may need to stay with him to ensure safety, but you do not need to worry about discipline right away.

This might be a time to do something regulating if the pupil is open to this. You could let the pupil have some space while keeping a distant but watchful eye on him. When you can become open and engaged again and if the pupil is sufficiently regulated, it can be helpful to reflect together on what happened. Remember to begin with the pupil's experience and only later expect him to think about the impact on you or anyone else involved, as in the 'Practising in the Moment' sequence.

There may be occasions when you have reacted to something from the pupil which, on reflection, does not need discipline. Perhaps the pupil was stressed and dysregulated; he shouted at you and it was this shouting that triggered you to provide a consequence when he needed regulation. You may want to give yourself some space to regulate before you can provide regulatory support for the pupil. Again, this is difficult for a younger child who will need immediate co-regulation to help him. If it is safe, an older child can be left for a short period while you take care of yourself. Again, leave the pupil in no doubt about what is happening: 'I am feeling upset right now. I want to help you but just need a moment to calm myself down.'

Managing these moments when the past meets the present can be some of the trickiest times in working with pupils. It is so easy to get caught up in your own reactions and not notice what is going on. Before you know it, you are engaged in a control battle with a pupil and the relationship is suffering. Be compassionate to yourself, know that teaching is a hard job and supporting this pupil has its challenges. You will repair the relationship later, and the pupil will discover that even when things go wrong it is recoverable.

Conclusion

This chapter introduced reflections on self-care with an exploration of attachment and past relationship history. In considering how educators can take care of themselves we stressed the importance of self-understanding. This is because unconscious knowledge is a dangerous thing; it has unlooked- for impacts when we least expect it. This can have an effect both on the relationship with the pupil and on how educators feel about themselves. Sometimes this can impact on performance in a way that impacts negatively on the pupil, jeopardizing the pupil's emotional well-being and the teacher's career. Louise knows of a teacher who had had a very unhappy childhood, constantly being belittled when she was a child by her parents. When Nia came along, a very traumatized pupil, the teacher would actively provoke her and occasionally humiliate her. For example, Nia couldn't sit still in assembly, and the teacher would point her out in front of everyone. Sometimes she would make her stand; sometimes she would get her to move about. Louise described feeling so uncomfortable that she had to report this member of staff to her seniors. It became clear that she wasn't even aware of what she was doing or of the connection between her past and what was being played out in the present. Fortunately, this teacher was open to support, which reduced the impact of her past on her teaching.

Feelings of failure, despair and hopelessness, and a sense that you don't think you can continue, often have some of their roots in the attempt to manage the impact of a past relationship while struggling to manage a current one. Understanding your own history and the impact it has on you, together with your own supportive relationships, can help you to avoid falling into a state of blocked care. This will be the subject of the next chapter.

Table 11.1: Exploring attachment history

Attachment state of mind	Reflection on childhood experience	Impact on current relationships
Autonomous *Balanced and valuing* You experienced a secure attachment history or have resolved a difficult attachment experience through reflection and understanding, leading to earned security.	You are likely to talk about childhood realistically. You will be able to give a coherent account of a difficult experience or loss. You will be aware of the influence of your past on your present.	You are able to regulate, reflect and have empathy for self and others. This makes it relatively easy to be sensitive and responsive towards other people. You are likely to be able to provide comfort. You are likely to remain regulated and be open and engaged when others display distress and need comfort, however this is displayed. If you do become defensive, you will be able to be compassionate towards yourself and move back to being open and engaged.
Dismissing *Minimizing* You experienced an avoidant attachment history which has led to a tendency to distrust emotional expression and to value self-reliance. This has stemmed from experience of not being connected with or soothed when distressed early in life.	When talking about your childhood you are likely to focus on positives rather than negatives, but may struggle to remember actual experiences. You are likely to feel that negative experiences have not made any difference to you. You are likely to value self-reliance and devalue dependence. You are less likely to look to others for support when distressed.	You are likely to find it more difficult to recognize or respond to emotional expression in others and will feel uncomfortable when others are distressed. You can feel disconnected from others and from your own emotions and needs. You will value self-reliance and independence in others. You are more likely to become defensive as you minimize emotional distress in others, encouraging them to get over it and moving quickly to problem solving.

Attachment state of mind	Reflection on childhood experience	Impact on current relationships
Preoccupied *Maximizing* You experienced an ambivalent-resistant attachment history which has led to a tendency to use emotional expression to keep others engaged with you. This has stemmed from an unpredictable experience of feeling safe, soothed and seen by parents, and the experience of being flooded with their anxieties and fears.	When talking about your childhood you are likely to be preoccupied with this experience. It will be harder for you to feel distanced from these past events. You may find yourself feeling easily angry and emotional within current relationships. You may often expect to be let down and you work hard to try and prevent this.	You may get overwhelmed by the needs of others, as you experience anxiety about your ability to comfort them. You try hard to be a good teacher, parent, friend and colleague who is valued by others, but self-doubts make it hard to focus on the needs of others. You are likely to experience others as not as interested in you, and this can lead to you working harder to get their interest. When others are distressed, this can overwhelm you. This leads to defensive responding as you experience anger or frustration. This emotional experience makes it hard to be open and engaged.
Unresolved *For past loss or trauma* You had a frightening experience with parents. This might have included difficult losses or separations. Fear of a parent triggers incompatible needs to move away (flight) and towards (comfort seeking) the parent at the same time.	You are likely to still experience a lot of grief related to past relationship experience. You may find it hard to talk about traumatic events, leading to incoherence when talking about these. It is difficult to balance emotions, have good relationships and think clearly under stress.	You are likely to find that the distress of others can trigger fear and be emotionally overwhelming. Defensiveness will come either from the experience of fear of others, or the fear of loss of control with others.

CHAPTER 12

Self-Care, Other Care and Blocked Care

This chapter will explore blocked care. This is a state that educators can enter when supporting a pupil is very stressful, sometimes alongside other stresses in life. In blocked care, educators struggle to approach or enjoy their time with the pupils. Sometimes they may struggle with one pupil, while continuing as normal with the other pupils. When experiencing blocked care, educators are more likely to be defensive than open and engaged. An important protection from and aid for recovery from blocked care is how well educators look after themselves. It is this need for care, from self and others, that will begin this chapter.

Self-care

Self-care, ensuring that educators look after themselves, is a critical part of supporting vulnerable pupils. Staying open and engaged with someone who is behaving defensively begins here. It is only through self-care that educators can build emotional resilience and enhance their ability to move out of defensive responding.

Self-care involves several things, all of which are important to help the educators remain open and resilient towards the teaching and support tasks ahead of them. These include physical, emotional and spiritual care. Educators need opportunities to build their emotional reserves. If they don't have time and space to recharge their emotional batteries, then they are likely to run out of resilience more quickly. It can be difficult to find time for this. The demands of the pupils, teaching the curriculum, additional paperwork and networking, as well as working as part of a team, can fill up more than the available time. There is also a home life to manage and perhaps the educator's own parenting demands and need to support others. Time for self can feel like a luxury, but it is a necessity. Only with time for self will educators find the energy to have enough resources to help pupils.

Other care

We all need others to take care of us at times, although the most self-reliant of us might struggle to admit this. The ability to turn to others for support, and the social relationships that surround us, are an important part of how we take care of ourselves.

This is especially so when educators are supporting children who have experienced developmental trauma. As we have previously explored, staff members are vulnerable to the emotional impact of these children and the trauma that they bring into the school with them. It is important that education staff monitor their reactions to the pupils, knowing when they need to take care of themselves so that they can stay open to the pupil. This is when it can be helpful to have a small team working together to support a pupil. The team work closely together, and all know the pupil and each other well. When a member of the team is getting stressed, it is helpful, if possible, for the staff member to 'swap in' with another member of 'Team Pupil' for a while (Bombèr, 2016).

Educators need a good level of emotional support – people around them who are not judging them or anxious to fix things. Offering solutions to someone who is sharing difficulties can be frustrating, leaving the staff member feeling misunderstood and with a deeper sense of failure. After all, if it was that easy to fix, it is likely that the staff member would have done this by now. The staff member often needs a listening ear, without his difficulties being minimized or his practice being criticized. As he experiences this emotional support, he might then want to think about what he could do differently. Now some joint problem solving might be helpful but led by the staff member.

With time for self and good social support, educators will find that they are less emotionally overwhelmed by the pupils and the demands of teaching and supporting them. This also provides valuable protection from and opportunities to recover from blocked care. This will be explored later in this chapter.

Looking after yourself and emotional well-being

Dan Siegel and his colleague suggest a 'healthy mind platter' for self-care (Rock and Siegel, 2011). They suggest that we attend to a range of things that will improve our state of emotional well-being:

- *Physical health:* aerobic exercise that increases heart rate and improves physical health. Opportunities for exercise can also sustain emotional well-being.
- *Focus:* periods of focusing on one thing at a time. With so many demands on educators, it is rare that only one thing is being attended to. Without making a special effort, the educator can become worn down by giving multiple attention to multiple tasks. A conscious decision to attend to one thing for a period can help the educator feel a greater sense of control over all the things requiring his time.
- *Down time:* allowing time in the day when nothing needs to be attended to. This is perhaps the hardest thing to allow yourself to do. It can feel far too indulgent to do nothing when there are so many things demanding attention. A period of doing nothing can, however, be restorative, and when tasks are returned to, the educator can be more efficient because of this period of rest.
- *Connecting:* time to connect with others and receive social support. We have already considered the importance of social support. Understanding from others around us is an important part of maintaining well-being.
- *Sleep:* getting enough good quality sleep. We all know how restorative a good night's sleep is. We have also all experienced the frustration of not getting this sleep. Aiming for good sleep, alongside good sleep hygiene, is therefore important. Equally, accepting periods where sleep does not come easily can reduce the stress of these times.
- *Play:* time to be spontaneous and have fun. It is surprising how easy it is to forget about worries when focused on enjoyable activities and having fun. The problems don't go away, but time away from these can be very helpful. Problems can feel smaller when the educator has been able to have some time away from them.

- *Time in:* reflecting on the inner world. The final item on the platter is part of developing yourself as a reflective, mind-minded educator. If educators are going to be able to notice and understand the internal world of the children, then they need to be in touch with their own internal experience. Understanding and accepting this allows educators to develop compassion for themselves – an important part of keeping themselves healthy.

It can feel quite daunting when this list is reviewed. It seems a big ask to fit all these things into the days and weeks, with work and home life being already all-consuming. However, attention to this can improve mental health and emotional well-being, allowing more time and energy for all the tasks of work and home. When educators are spending less time combating stress, it is surprising how much more time they have for themselves and their teaching.

What is blocked care?

Continually offering a relationship without this being reciprocated can have a profound impact on educators. Dan Hughes and Jon Baylin have written about 'blocked care' to describe the difficulties parents can experience when they are not getting enough back from their child (Hughes and Baylin, 2012). Blocked care is equally likely to be experienced by educators supporting vulnerable pupils, because these children find reciprocity difficult. Educators, like parents, can find themselves giving without receiving back (Bombèr and Hughes, 2013).

Blocked care is closely related to blocked trust in the child. When in a state of 'blocked trust' children tend to withdraw from a relationship rather than approaching it. They fear relationships and do not experience security in the support they receive.

Educators who are used to pupils trusting them and feel confident in their abilities to offer a safe classroom and relationship to the pupil can have the rug pulled from under them when trying to teach a pupil with blocked trust. The pupil resists a relationship with the educator and rejects the safe and supportive experience the adult is trying to provide. The pupil either disengages in learning or tries to manage learning on her own. The adult is left feeling ineffectual and unable to reach the pupil. Baylin and Hughes (2016) describe how a parent can be blindsided by intense negative reactions to their offers of love and care. Educators can also find their offers of support and care rejected by a pupil. This rejection can be intensely painful – a pain which the adult will reasonably, and often unconsciously, try to protect himself from. The pupil's habitual defence against anyone trying to relate to her can feel very personal when the adult becomes the target. The relationship can become lost when both staff member and child have retreated behind walls of blocked care and blocked trust.

Understanding the biology of blocked care

Knowing that blocked care is rooted in biology is a mixed blessing. On the one hand, understanding that this is a biological process can reduce feelings of shame and the sense of failure that educators can experience with pupils. On the other hand, this does mean that it can't be overcome through will power alone. Grit and determination to feel less blocked with a pupil simply doesn't work if the environment around the educator isn't conducive to aiding recovery from blocked care. Educators need social support from colleagues, helpful management support, supervision and good self-care if the biological systems are to switch on again.

Dan Hughes provides a biological understanding of blocked care (Hughes, in Alper and Howe, 2015). He describes the caregiving systems that need to be active for a person to provide the caregiving experiences that the child needs. This includes soothing and regulating a distressed pupil, engaging a switched-off pupil and calming a pupil in a fear state. When the pupil consistently fails to respond with appropriate attachment responses – to be soothed, regulated, engaged and calmed – then this is experienced by the educator as rejecting of him. This is stressful, and the staff member's own caregiving systems become weak or unstable. Over time and with the educator getting little back from the pupil, the functioning of the caregiving systems in the brain is suppressed. This moves the staff member into defensive responding and impairs his ability to attune to and connect with the pupil who is resisting him.

There are five caregiving systems functioning within the brain which allow educators, like parents, to care sensitively and responsively for the pupils. We will briefly describe these here, but to explore this more deeply see Hughes and Baylin (2012).

- *Approach.* The hormone oxytocin is released in parents to prime them for caring for their children. This will also be released in educators who have the care of the children for the school day. This facilitates them to stay open and engaged with the pupils instead of becoming defensive. The drive to approach and support the pupil is activated, while the drive to avoid is de-activated. When supporting a pupil who consistently rejects our care, less oxytocin is released and the drive to avoid is more likely to be activated.
- *Reward.* Social engagement with a child leads to the release of dopamine. This sustains the caring process by helping the educator enjoy interacting with and supporting the pupil. This is a reciprocal process as each enjoys and has pleasure being with the other. When this reciprocal process does not happen, there is less dopamine and thus no feelings of pleasure. This leads to disengagement.
- *Child reading.* The attuned relationship with a child facilitates the educator's deep interest in the child, and a desire to make sense of her experience. The education staff can use their empathy and mind-minded abilities to understand the pupil's feelings and needs. When the attuned relationship fails, this empathy and mind-mindedness declines. The staff member becomes defensive and thus not open and engaged to the pupil's experience. High levels of stress can reduce reflective functioning, impairing the ability to be mind-minded towards all pupils. This impacts on the ability to make sense of the pupil's experience. Teaching can become narrowly focused on trying to change behaviour or get pupils to complete tasks, while empathy and compassion are reduced.
- *Meaning making.* We are drawn to make meaning of our experience with children. At its best, educators construct positive narratives (stories) about the pupils and about themselves as members of the teams supporting the pupils. The stories we tell are linked to our own attachment histories. Even when we are lucky enough to have a secure attachment, without reciprocity we tend to make negative meanings about ourselves or our pupils. Staff members start to see themselves as bad or ineffective or

pupils as lazy, manipulative or deliberately defiant. More negative attributions lead to more defensiveness.

- *Executive system.* This is the integrative centre of the brain that co-ordinates the functioning of the brain, bringing together all its parts so it can act as a whole. The executive functions allow for integrated brain functioning so that cognitive and emotional parts of the brain work well together. These processes are responsible for guiding, directing and managing cognitive (thinking), emotional and behavioural tasks. Executive functioning allows purposeful, goal-directed and problem-solving behaviours. In this state, educators can regulate their emotions and maintain a caring and supportive state of mind towards the pupils.

  This functioning is less dependent on the pupil's influence on the staff member. Executive functioning will reduce under stress, but if the education staff have reasonable executive function, they will be able to support the pupil safely. However, without the other caregiving systems working well, the joy in teaching is lost. The educators do the job but experience no pleasure in this.

  If educators have weaker executive functioning, perhaps because of their own attachment history, this will be more of a struggle. Defensive responding towards pupils can escalate into interactions that are more frightening and harmful. Highly punitive sanctions or neglect of needs might occur as the staff members respond to their dysregulated emotional experience and their fears and beliefs about the pupil's wrongdoing and/or their own failure. Despite the best of intentions towards the pupils, the staff members can behave in a way that is emotionally harmful. This is not a time for judgement or for giving advice. This will add further stress to an already over-stressed executive functioning system. The staff member needs support and understanding to help him recover a more moderate and healthy approach towards the pupil. As his stress reduces, his executive function will recover and he will become more open to advice and guidance.

When not in a state of blocked care, educators can stay open and engaged to the pupils. Inevitably there will be times where they become defensive, but they do not get trapped here. Shifting between open and engaged and defensive responses is a normal part of relationships, depicting the usual give and take of relationships. Blocked care, however, represents the staff member being unable to shift out of a negative state of mind towards a pupil. The staff member remains defensive towards this pupil as a protection against the pain of rejection that he is experiencing (Baylin and Hughes, 2016). As blocked trust suppresses the pain of loss, neglect and abuse a child has experienced or anticipates experiencing from parents and other adults, so blocked care suppresses the pain of rejection a staff member is experiencing from a pupil.

How does blocked care develop?

Blocked care can develop in a range of ways, as a more generalized influence on the educator or in specific response to a pupil or current circumstance. Four types of blocked care have been described by Dan Hughes and Jon Baylin (2012). These will be briefly summarized.

Chronic blocked care

This can occur when an educator has experienced very high levels of stress beginning early in life. In this case, the ongoing stress means that the care system and the self-regulation system are poorly developed. Thus, the caregiving process is difficult to activate, and this, combined with an underdeveloped executive system, makes attuning to the pupil's needs very difficult. The educator might be very good at teaching the curriculum, but the more relationship-focused aspects of teaching might be much harder for him. Educators are likely to need a high level of support and therapy to help develop these weaker functioning systems.

Acute blocked care

This can occur when the educator experiences a period of more acute stress which he is finding difficult to cope with. This overwhelms the educator's ability to cope, and caregiving is suppressed. Again, it is the more relationship-focused aspects of teaching that can suffer. Support at this time is essential so that this temporary state of blocked care does not become more enduring.

Child-specific blocked care

This can occur when a pupil has his own attachment difficulties. The pupil does not respond in the way the educator is expecting or is used to with the other pupils she has taught. In particular, the pupil does not respond in a positive, reciprocal way to the educator's support. This violation of expectations leads to more defensive responding from the educator as she feels rejected by and/or angry towards the pupil. This results in blocked care. Educators can be especially sensitive to this reaction to a pupil if that pupil reminds them of someone in their past with whom they had a difficult relationship.

Stage-specific blocked care

Pupils can go through stages of being more argumentative and less open to relationships with their educators. Some educators do well when the pupil is engaged and receptive to them but really struggle during these stages of more challenging behaviours, especially when they experience this as rejection from the pupil.

Additionally, some stages of a pupil's development might be more sensitive for an educator, perhaps because of the experiences she had at the same stage of development. For example, if a teacher experienced the separation of her parents at the age of ten while making the transition to secondary school, this teacher might be especially vulnerable while preparing her own pupils for this transition.

Protection or recovery from blocked care

As explored at the beginning of this chapter, self-care is an essential part of being a successful educator. Teaching, alongside all the other demands of work and home life, is draining of time and resources. Just coping with the day-to-day demands can be enough, and finding time for a social life, recreation and relaxation can feel impossible. Yet without these things emotional resilience will drain away. Stress tends to fill us up until it overflows, impacting on how we feel and how we behave. Self-care builds a valve which we can use to safely release this stress. This increases our emotional resilience, improving our capacity to stay open and engaged to others and reducing the descent into blocked care.

Increasing your emotional health through good self-care will provide some protection from blocked care. Recovery from blocked care might need more intensive support from others. Many of the things that we have already considered within this book can also be helpful. Here are a few ideas for further increasing your self-care, developing protection from blocked care and recovering from blocked care if you find yourself in that state. It is worth emphasizing that support from understanding others is probably the most central part of this self-help.

Know yourself

As we explored in the last chapter, knowing yourself and especially the impact that past relationship experiences have had on you can be an important part of supporting vulnerable pupils. Reflecting on relational history, in particular early attachment experience, can increase self-understanding and make reactions in the present much more understandable. This understanding can help you to strengthen parts of yourself. For example, developing your need for connection if you tend to distance yourself emotionally; developing your capacity to soothe yourself when others make you anxious.

Develop your capacity for reflection and regulation

Knowing yourself and the impact of your history is a starting point for improving your ability to reflect and regulate, especially at times of stress when these are threatened. It is also helpful to be open to noticing and understanding day-to-day internal experience – your own thoughts and feelings, which are neither right nor wrong. As with the children, this experience just is. Knowing these with compassion and without judgement can have a big impact on how far you are able to emotionally regulate when you are threatened by overwhelming emotion. This means being open to and reflecting on this emotional experience, developing the capacity for being mind-minded. Being open to noticing and understanding your own internal experience can increase your empathy and compassion for yourself. This can reduce feelings of failure and hopelessness, allowing you to stay in touch with the internal experience of the pupils you are teaching. When emotion and reflection work well together the brain is strengthened, allowing more resilience to stress. As we will explore later, regular mindfulness practice has also been shown to be useful for restoring balance in the brain and strengthening healthy reflection and regulation.

Practise the use of PACE

The attitude of PACE allows the caregiving systems to work well, strengthening these and improving integration between them. At times of stress, if you can maintain an attitude of PACE towards yourself, you will be able to avoid, or at least minimize, the harsh inner critic that tells you that you are inadequate, useless, unlikeable and so on. When we can be compassionate to ourselves, we can mitigate the falling into shame and be open to more positive self-thinking, more open to others helping us and more open to relationships where we are in the caregiving role. As we stay more open and engaged, the pupil will also become less defensive, which is easier for both adult and child, and the relationship can build. Understanding, connecting and being compassionate towards your own internal experience will build resilience, and help you to stay open and engaged to others even when experiencing stress.

This use of PACE requires educators to embrace the mistrust the pupil is presenting them with. This has been variously described as hugging a porcupine or a cactus (Baylin and Hughes, 2016, pp.90–91). As these authors note:

> We believe that the most powerful intervention for helping mistrusting children learn to trust trustworthy caregivers is to help caregivers embrace the child's mistrust. Rather than trying to redirect the child and eliminate the mistrust, the caregiver who can approach and welcome the child's mistrustfulness, greeting this part of the child with empathy and compassion, can create a window of new learning for the child, an opportunity to experience the crucial difference between past experiences with caregivers and the experience of being with a truly safe caregiver.

Understanding, connecting and being compassionate towards your own internal experience will build resilience, and help you to stay open and engaged to others even when experiencing stress.

Good social support

A range of relationships around you can increase resilience and emotional health. It is well known that social isolation is associated with people who are experiencing depression. As social creatures, we need people; biologically our brains are designed to link with others. Social relationships are fuel for our brains.

Social relationships can serve a range of functions. They can offer practical support, helping out with tasks and giving practical help in the classroom. They can also offer emotional support – having people you can turn to, and talk openly and honestly with, is important for emotional well-being. Some people are better at helping practically, while others provide a good shoulder to lean on. We need relationships in and outside school. We feel loved by some people, while others are great for getting out and having fun with. Different people will provide different things, and we need a varied social group around us. Intersubjective relationships with trusted others can be very protective. These are the people who understand what you are feeling and thinking without judgement or evaluation. They can offer support but won't be too quick to give advice, and they offer you moments of fun and laughter. With people like this around, you will be able to withstand the stress of teaching a challenging pupil and be able to stay with your own use of PACE towards that pupil. These are the people who can provide protection against blocked care and can help you to recover from this when it does arise.

There are people to avoid as well, especially if you are feeling vulnerable. Try to keep away from people who are critical or judgemental of you, or if you need to spend time with such people, make sure that you balance this with more people who can offer you unconditional support. The more people you know who have an attitude of PACE towards you, the better.

Therapy

Therapy can also provide support for educators in or at risk of developing blocked care. Therapeutic support offers a non-judgemental, intersubjective relationship with the opportunity to experience PACE from another. This can strengthen emotional regulation while providing you with support to reflect on current and past experience and to make sense of how you are responding to this.

Mindfulness

One of the most promising interventions for helping parents and educators is mindfulness. Jon Kabat-Zinn has explored how mindfulness practice can help people with a range of difficulties, from depression to living with chronic pain (see Kabat-Zinn, 1990). In a study by Harnett and Dawe (2012, cited in Alper and Howe, 2015), it was found that using mindfulness helped parents to reduce the stress they experienced when parenting their children. Hughes and Baylin (2012) describe how the practice of mindfulness can increase sensitive, attuned parenting. Mindful attention helps children to feel cared about and deeply connected with and therefore can improve the relationship between educator and pupil.

Despite the increasing popularity of mindfulness, which can lead to scepticism and concerns that its claims are too good to be true, mindfulness is something to take seriously in our quest to find ways of successfully supporting vulnerable pupils. Dan Siegel has demonstrated that mindfulness can improve the capacity for compassion and intersubjectivity. This improvement is seen both interpersonally with others and intrapersonally for ourselves (Siegel, 2010). This fits well with the DDP-informed approach which promotes the intersubjective relationship and the use of empathy and compassion for ourselves and others.

Mindfulness is the ability to deliberately focus attention on feelings, thoughts and experiences in the present moment and in a non-judgemental and accepting way (Kabat-Zinn, 2004). The mindfulness practitioner notices his here-and-now experience without evaluation or efforts to change it. It therefore has a strong resonance with PACE, which helps the educator to notice and understand the pupil's emotional experience without judgement, evaluation or attempts to change it and to convey this understanding to the pupil through the intersubjective relationship. PACE therefore facilitates a mindful approach.

Building a daily practice of mindfulness into a busy schedule does not have to be as hard as it sounds. When Kim had a particularly stressful time in her life, she found that it was not easy to ensure she had 20 minutes available each day to do a mindfulness practice, even though she knew it would be beneficial. However, she noticed how much of her daily dog walk she spent worrying and reflecting on what happened the day before or what might be ahead for her on that day. She was so busy living in the past and future that she had no time to appreciate the present. She decided to approach her regular dog walking mindfully and a whole world opened up to her that she had been ignoring. This simple change to her lifestyle helped reduce the stress she was experiencing.

If you prefer a more structured approach to this, there are mindfulness practitioners who can guide you to learn simple practices. Alternatively, there are a range of resources on the internet, such as Dan Siegel's wheel of awareness practice.[1]

Conclusion

Vulnerable pupils have huge struggles to feel safe and secure. Without this they will grow up into adults with continuing difficulties with relationships. It takes a lot of strength, resilience and perseverance for educators, alongside parents, to take these pupils gently by the hand and to guide them back into the world of relationships, to help them to discover that safety and security can be found there. There are risks along the way. Blocked care is something that any of us can succumb to, and there is an extra risk associated with supporting vulnerable pupils. This is a biological process that responds to the pain of offering a relationship that is not reciprocated. In this chapter, we explored how to understand blocked care and the prevention and recovery from this. This has brought us up close to the importance of self-care and other care.

Throughout this book, we have met a number of children, teachers and support staff, fictional composites of children and staff we have worked with. These examples illustrate the range of challenges facing the teams supporting these children.

The pupils, who display their difficulties through angry and oppositional behaviour, are emotionally and physically challenging. The teachers and support staff working with pupils like Cole (Chapter 1), Noah and Brandon (Chapter 2), Ahmed (Chapter 6) and Benjamin (Chapter 1) will need a high level of support. Equally difficult are those pupils, like Lee (Chapter 3) and Liam (Chapter 4), whose developmental immaturity and poor regulation can lead to disruption that the support team have to manage. The compliant but quietly resistant children, like Nadia (Chapter 1), or the children who refuse connection and support, like Ben (Chapter 1), Grace (Chapter 3) and Siobhan (Chapter 4), are just as difficult emotionally, although their needs may be less obvious. It is an additional burden for the team when children like Catherine

---

1 www.drdansiegel.com/resources/wheel_of_awareness

(Chapter 6) struggle with peers or Ellen (Chapter 3) with managing a visitor in the classroom.

Alongside supporting the behaviours and emotional needs of these children, the teachers and support staff are also managing the impact on themselves. Children with experience of developmental trauma can be highly controlling, and teachers like those of Noah (Chapter 2) and Natalie (Chapter 3) will describe feeling 'emotionally blackmailed' by these pupils. Feelings of failure can run high, and this is made more difficult when pupils like Adnan (Chapter 2) struggle with any correction, however gently given, or when teachers have a pupil like Jack (Chapter 3), whose performance is variable, changing from day to day.

All these children illustrate the large range of challenges that can be presented to the staff who are having to manage a high level of emotional need presented by children who have experienced developmental trauma – all this and teaching the curriculum too!

When supporting children with these types of struggles, difficult memories from the staff member's past can be triggered. Mrs Kay (Chapter 9) experienced this with Lucy, and we also met Mr Smart, Lena and Mrs Abassi (Chapter 11) with their own individual stories about this. These educators were each surprised by the intrusion of their own attachment history, leading to difficulties in the present. Without sensitive support and opportunities for reflection, this could potentially threaten their careers.

Reviewing this list of examples, it is clear that attention to your support and self-care needs as educators is essential. By prioritizing your own needs, you are putting the pupils first. We can give these pupils back their futures, but only if we ensure we get the support and care we need. Only then can we have the resilience to go some of the way on the long journey that the pupils are making as they manage the impact of developmental trauma during their progress through school.

APPENDIX 1

A Guide to DDP Principles and their Application in an Educational Setting

In this appendix, we provide an overview of the principles within the DDP model and how these can be applied when supporting developmentally traumatized pupils in education settings. These principles guide how to help vulnerable pupils to form and maintain emotionally healthy relationships. These can then act as a secure base to facilitate exploration and learning. All pupils are likely to benefit from an education setting that is informed by an understanding of trauma. The DDP framework with its attention to building safety and security and its valuing of emotional connection can benefit everyone. This includes staff to pupil, colleague to colleague, manager to employee, and supervisor to supervisee. When the principles are held throughout an organization, and are modelled from the top, everyone will feel supported and the vulnerable pupils will get the help they need.

Supporting healthy relationships

Intersubjective relationships

Pupils who have experienced developmental trauma often develop controlling patterns of behaviour in order to avoid or take charge of relationships. They fear intersubjective experiences because these have been a source of terror in the past. Emotional connection within relationships is necessary for health and emotional growth. It is therefore helpful if intersubjectivity and its importance for emotional well-being is understood by all staff. A school atmosphere that supports everyone to be interested in and attentive to the emotional experience of each other ensures an emotionally healthy organization. A staff member in school is then well supported to develop, over time, a secure relationship with the pupil who has experienced developmental trauma, offering opportunities for intersubjective experiences and helping the pupil to experience safe connection.

The attachment relationship

Pupils with reasonably secure attachment experience will come into school with age-appropriate capacities for dependence and independence. They will be appropriately self-reliant, while also being able to seek support when needed. They will be confident of the secure base at home, making it easier to manage transitions to and from school and to cope with the school day away from their attachment figures. Educators can facilitate a school environment within which safety and security is prioritized for staff and pupils. Within this, pupils are supported to have their dependency needs met while being encouraged to develop independence at their own pace. When pupils have experienced frightening or unavailable attachment relationships, their development is impacted and they will bring disorganizing and controlling patterns of relating into school. This will impact on relationships with staff and with their peers. They may also experience considerable separation anxiety, making transitions to and from school difficult. These pupils will need more attachment support in school than the more secure pupils. This includes identifying a secure base for them in school and a key adult who can act as an attachment figure during the school day. For very troubled pupils, key adults can work together to offer this security. In this way, the main attachment figure will have a back-up attachment figure to hand over to when needed.

Staff members with secure attachment experience will also have capacities for independence and dependence. They need support to be self-reliant and competent in developing creative, innovative means of meeting the needs of their individual pupils. At the same time, they need to be encouraged (without shame) to accept assistance when needed from senior educators and mentors as well as specialist support staff.

Staff members with insecure attachment experience will need help to reflect on this experience and become more aware of the vulnerabilities that they have developed stemming from it. Staff members with a tendency towards dismissing emotional neediness, arising from early avoidant attachment experience, will need support to recognize and support the emotionally needy pupils. They will also need to be aware of their own tendency towards self-reliance, which can get in the way of seeking support when needed. Staff members with a preoccupation with their own needs, arising from early ambivalent attachment experience, will need support to provide consistent and predictable support for their pupils. They also need to be aware of their own tendency to rely on others at the expense of developing independence.

PACE

PACE is a way of being in relationships that facilitates connection. PACE is an attitude focused around attending to and being interested in the inner life of the other. Curiosity represents a slowing down within the relationship, taking the time to discover what the other person thinks and feels, and communicating this understanding with acceptance and empathy. Curiosity and acceptance demonstrate that the other person will not be judged for how they think or what they feel. Empathy demonstrates a willingness to be with the other, supporting them through difficult experiences. Playfulness brings fun and joy into the relationship, providing different and more hopeful relationship experiences.

School environments can be very fast paced, with pressures both externally and internally to get things sorted. Educators need to get on with the lesson, and support staff have multiple demands on their time. Everyone is governed by the school bell and what needs to be achieved before it rings. Stopping to be curious can feel like a luxury. However, this fast pace is at odds with being a reflective educator. The more the adults can slow things down, the more reflective they can become. This is what precipitates change. Reacting rather than reflecting may lead to compliance from the child, but this will be at the cost of increasing security (Bombèr and Hughes, 2013). In slowing down, you will get there quicker, facilitating increased security within the pupils and lasting change. PACE will help you to slow down, stop reacting and instead use reflection to guide your responses.

Within school settings, having PACE as a way of being within all relationships will mean that staff members feel supported and have resilience to the many challenges they can meet. They in turn will more easily hold the attitude of PACE with the pupils, even when those pupils are particularly challenging.

PACE communicates to the pupil that the staff member is interested in them and not just their behaviour or what they are learning. Curiosity and reflection help the pupil to feel understood and accepted. Even when guidance is needed with behaviour, the pupil discovers that his inner experience, which has triggered the behaviour, is not judged. Instead, the staff member provides empathy and support for complex emotional experiences. When educators can remain curious, they are open to the pupil, wanting to understand why he is struggling. This understanding will inform helpful ways of supporting the pupil with these difficulties. This represents a valuing of the relationship even when things are difficult. The aim is to remain emotionally connected to the pupil at the difficult times as well as when it is easier. With a deepening of these connections, the pupils experience increased trust and safety. They can then engage with education in a way that they couldn't while experiencing mistrust and fear.

Open and engaged

It is only when a staff member is in an open and engaged state with a pupil that she will be able to respond with PACE and connect intersubjectively. It can be difficult to maintain this state when the pupil is closed, and defensive. Biological states match between individuals, so it is easy to be pulled into the defensive state of the other. On these occasions, PACE is lost, replaced by an evaluative or judgemental attitude. This shuts down intersubjective connections, closing down the relationships. When a member of the teaching team can maintain the open and engaged state, avoiding the pull into defence, the pupil will then move to an open and engaged state also. This enhances the connection between them, and the pupil becomes open to support and learning. Of course, staff members will at times move into defensive responding. They, supported by colleagues, need to notice when this happens. If the staff member takes care of herself, she can then return to an open and engaged state with the pupil.

Adult-to-adult relationships also need to be attentive to remaining open and engaged at times of stress or difficulty, and to supporting each other when defensive responding does occur. This will be easier when the school ethos values and places importance on self-care for all. The school can then become a comprehensively open and engaged organization.

Supporting the pupil with experience of developmental trauma

When educators are open and engaged towards their pupils, and each other, opportunities for healthy connections arise. PACE promotes healthy intersubjective and attachment experiences. This strengthens the relationships. The school environment is then better equipped to support vulnerable pupils. The pupils will experience the following effects:

- *Increased safety and security.* When pupils are in a state of fear in school, they will often be hypervigilant, aroused and reactive. Some pupils may be more withdrawn, appearing shut down. These pupils are mistrustful, assuming the worst about the educator's intentions and having little confidence that the educator wants what is best for them. Through connection within relationships, fear can subside and vigilance is reduced. The pupil becomes calmer, more engaged and more open to exploration and learning. Vulnerable pupils need the educator to notice their verbal and non-verbal communications, giving clues to the pupils' current state of safety or danger. Safety is increased by the staff member acknowledging and accepting the pupil's experience with PACE. She can then allow the pupil to take a break, move to a place of safety and/or engage in activities that provide regulatory support.
- *Co-regulation of affect.* Developmental trauma reduces emotional growth and slows down development. Pupils are left emotionally immature, with difficulties regulating their emotions. They experience the emotion, expressing this through their affect, but do not know how to manage this experience. They are left disadvantaged among their peers, isolating themselves or trying to control these relationships. In this way, they try to manage the emotional arousal of not quite fitting in or being able to meet the expectations of others. As with younger children, they need more adult support. They are helped through a process of co-regulation. The staff members match the vitality, intensity and

rhythm of the affect the pupil is displaying without getting caught up in the emotion themselves; for example, not becoming angry but supporting the pupil with his anger. In staying regulated themselves they soothe the heightened arousal of the reactive pupil or increase low arousal of the shut-down pupil. This helps the pupil move into affective balance.

- *Co-creation of narrative (developing understanding of experience).* The lack of healthy relationship experience early in children's lives leads to difficulties in reflecting on experiences. Children live in the here and now, driven by their emotion. Their narratives about what is and has happened to them are often incoherent and fragmented. As children start to trust in relationships and can allow these adults to help them to regulate, there are opportunities to help them figure out what they are experiencing. As staff members tentatively put words to experiences, the pupils can gradually identify and more fully express their inner life. Their reflective capacity develops and they become more able to reflect on experience, giving them more flexibility in responding.

DDP-informed communication

Building relationships and helping pupils develop safety and trust are helped when adults apply the following strategies:

- *Use a storytelling tone of voice to communicate with the pupils.* To help pupils to feel safe and to develop trust they need educators who can talk to them in ways that hold their attention and maintain an open and engaged state. Much of the time in school, pupils are hearing lectures and reasons why they should or shouldn't do things. This aims to change the pupil. To build trust, pupils need educators who are genuinely interested in understanding their experience. This interest can be conveyed with the storytelling tone of voice and rhythm. As the pupils feel understood, they will be in a better state to figure out, with adult support, what to do. They will also be more open to learning and exploration.
- *Use affective-reflective dialogue.* As the staff member talks with the pupil, reflecting on a situation or experience, she also

communicates affectively (attending to emotional experience verbally and non-verbally). This affective-reflective stance allows the story of the situation or experience to emerge. For example, a staff member might be talking with a pupil about how angry he was feeling when he was verbally abusive to a peer. The staff member makes sense of these reflections; there is an emerging story – you were hurt by something your peer did, this made you angry, you shouted and swore at your peer. Alongside this, the staff member empathizes with the affective experience, conveying understanding that the pupil was feeling so hurt by his peer, then he got angry, so much so that he couldn't calm down. Discovering narratives of experience requires adult and child to figure out the story together. Good stories attend to content and affective experience – without both of these the story becomes difficult to engage with. As staff member and pupil engage in figuring out the pupil's experience, the affective-reflective dialogue builds a connection between them that feels safe. This allows the pupil to feel confident that the staff member is interested in him and has good intentions towards him.

- *Follow-lead-follow.* Pupils need educators who are sensitive and responsive to their wishes as well as their initiatives. They need us to follow where they lead. They also need our help and guidance to find new ways of understanding and new ways of being. They need us to lead so that they can follow. Follow-lead-follow describes a process of being with pupils based on reciprocity and co-operation. We follow and we lead, responding to the responses of the pupils to these initiatives. This becomes integrated into successful interactions.

  This approach is helpful when we engage pupils in dialogues to help them make sense of what they are experiencing. Pupils are not helped when they are told what to think or feel. This can feel very invalidating. However, pupils with a history of developmental trauma are poor at knowing this for themselves. They need help to discover the meaning of their inner world. The educator needs to start where the pupil is, listening to the pupil's communication through words and behaviour. This gives the adult clues as to what the pupil is experiencing. She accepts this fledgling narrative and wonders about it. The pupil experiences being understood. The staff member then leads the pupil into a deeper understanding. The pupil will respond to this and the staff member follows again.

- *Talk with, about and for.* Talking with pupils in a way that helps them to feel emotionally connected and understood can be alarming for children who have learned not to trust others. They need the educators to gently lead them into these connections, helping them to tolerate them without becoming overwhelmed. This can involve not always talking directly to the pupil. 'Talking about' can be done by wondering out loud or talking to another person while the pupil listens. This 'talking about' is not critical of the pupil or designed to teach him. Rather, it conveys interest in the pupil and his experience, helping him to feel understood. It can be very helpful for a pupil to experience a staff member as getting them without judgement. 'Talking for' is another way of communicating that deepens the experience of being understood for the pupil. The adult gives the pupil a voice by talking for him, allowing him to have words for his experience when he cannot find the words himself.

- *Attend to verbal and non-verbal communications.* We all communicate both verbally and non-verbally. A staff member can get important clues about the pupil's experience by attending to both. It is especially helpful to notice when there are discrepancies between what is being communicated verbally and non-verbally. Noticing and reflecting on this can deepen understanding.

Maintaining connections while also supporting behaviour

- *Relationship repair.* Attend to ruptures in the relationship and to repairing these. Relationship ruptures are a normal part of human interactions. In healthy relationships, these ruptures are repaired, strengthening the connection between them. In adult–pupil relationships it is the adult who needs to ensure that this repair happens. She notices a misattunement perhaps because of a misunderstanding or because one or both has become defensive. She acknowledges the difficulty that has arisen and communicates that she is committed to the relationship. The repair focuses on bringing the relationship back into attunement again. The pupil feels supported, and shame is regulated. The pupil is then able to reflect on his own part in the experience and can let the staff member help him to make his own repairs as appropriate. Adult-led repair allows experiences to be managed while preserving the relationship. The pupil will experience this support and reach his own need to put things right. If instead the staff member demands an apology from the pupil, the responsibility for repair is being put on him. This reduces security.

- *Connection with behavioural support.* Emotional connection is an important part of helping a vulnerable pupil to feel safe and supported at school. As school is experienced as a secure base, and relationships are trusted, the pupil can move out of a fear state and become open to learning. Alongside this, the pupil will be encountering challenges and difficulties. He may have anxieties connected with academic work, managing peer relationships or because of problems being experienced at home. These stresses can reveal themselves in challenging behaviour. The pupil will need support with behaviours, but as much as possible he needs educators who can stay emotionally connected throughout this support. Connection before behaviour challenges builds trust and relationship. Connection during behaviour challenges maintains the trust and helps the pupil to use the support to calm arousal and to manage any natural consequences that occur because of the behaviour. This includes letting the staff member support him to repair relationships that have been impacted by the behaviour. Connection afterwards allows the pupil to experience difficulties being surmountable and to discover that relationships can remain strong.

APPENDIX 2

Understanding the Theory Informing DDP Interventions

KIM S. GOLDING

This appendix provides a brief overview of the body of theory that has guided the development of DDP and with which practitioners of DDP need to be familiar.

1. Developmental trauma

Complex trauma involves multiple or chronic exposure to adverse experiences (Cook *et al.*, 2005). The term developmental trauma is used to describe the experience of complex trauma from within the family early in life. This experience has a profound impact on the child's development, influencing multiple areas of functioning (van der Kolk, 2005). As the trauma arises from within close relationships, it has also been called relational trauma. The child is left with difficulties in self-regulation and interpersonal relationships. The child can neither manage overwhelming emotion nor can he turn to potentially supportive relationships for help via co-regulation.

Children who have experienced developmental trauma experience a profound lack of safety. They need parents to provide them with safety, but the parents are the cause of the trauma. This impacts on their attachment experience, leading to disorganized controlling attachment patterns, and on their capacity to enter reciprocal relationships offering intersubjective experiences. These two relationship experiences, which provide the foundation for children's development, are now greatly impaired. It is therefore not surprising that children who have experienced developmental trauma have biological, social, emotional, cognitive and behavioural difficulties alongside fragmented and negative self-identities (Cook *et al.*, 2005).

In order to cope with lack of safety, developmentally traumatized children establish defensive patterns of relating which impact on future relationships. They do not trust others, including new parents, to keep them safe. Their behaviour is based on expectations derived from past experiences. This highly controlling behaviour leaves little room to discover that their expectations are no longer valid. The children continue to defend against a threat that is part of their past.

Living with a constant sense of threat and in a defensive biological state means that emotional growth is hampered. The children's developmental age is therefore much younger than their chronological age. A sense of identity begins to develop early in life, at the same time as developmental trauma is experienced. This leads to a negative sense of self. Children believe that they are unlovable and that others will hurt or abandon them. They live with chronic feelings of shame, which further reinforces defensive responding to current experiences. The children display highly controlling, rejecting and hurtful behaviours which impact on the parents' resilience to remain open and available to the child. When the parents become defensive in turn, the child's negative sense of self is confirmed.

Within DDP, the child is supported to heal from this early traumatic experience through the current relationships they are experiencing, including the relationship with the therapist. Through different, healthier relationship experience, defensive ways of responding can relax and the child can become open to new experiences in the world. Emotional growth can increase as the child learns new ways of being within close relationships – ways of being that help them to seek comfort when needed and enable them to join in the joy of being in a relationship. As defences reduce, curiosity grows, and the child becomes open to exploration and learning. Terror and shame reduce as the child experiences a new, more regulating relationship. While the lessons of early childhood are not forgotten, these can now sit alongside learning that relationships can also be nurturing and supportive. The child develops a revised sense of identity, one within which the possibility of being lovable opens. The child experiences different, more responsive and sensitive relationships, revising both sense of self and expectation of others.

2. Relationships

Infants are born needing relationships. The importance of this is revealed when we observe that the immature infant has such mature capacities for engaging with others. Much infant research helps us to understand how well equipped infants are for relationships (Field, 2007). For example, very young infants will show preferences for looking at faces rather than objects. Early visual development encourages this as infants focus at about the distance of their parent's face when being held. Infants recognize their mother's voice from birth and have preference for this over a stranger's voice. All parents will know about their infants' conversational skills. They take turns, the parent talks and the infant 'talks' back; similarly, they will imitate the parent's behaviour, sticking out a tongue in response to a parent poking his tongue out, for example.

As the infant matures and becomes more mobile, he can use an intersubjective experience known as social referencing. The child looks to the parents for clues about what he should do. For example, the visual cliff experiment demonstrates that infants will crawl over a transparent floor, stopping when the ground appears to drop away (the cliff). They will, however, continue to crawl when encouraged by a parent. Infants therefore use their early abilities to interact with parents, experiencing a contingent, reciprocal relationship. They thrive when parents respond to them in ways which are linked to the infant's behaviours – the infant calls and the parent responds. Parents and infants are mutually responsive to each other, and research has shown that they are in synchrony with matching affective, behavioural and physiological states. These states become disturbed in the infants when the parents offer a still face. Thus, an infant will become visibly distressed during the still face experiment when the still face, representing a non-contingent response, appears. While these infants quickly recover as the parent repairs the rupture in the relationship, the memory can remain. Toddlers have been shown to react negatively to strangers who they received a still face from once as an infant (Field, 2007).

All of this research demonstrates how well equipped infants are for relationship from birth. This is no accident of evolution. Infants need relationships in order to survive. There are two aspects to this relationship experience that are essential for children to thrive:

- *Attachment* (Bowlby, 1988/1989). Safety and security arise because infants and young children can turn to the parent for support when experiencing distress. Notice that this is a one-way relationship. The child seeks security, the parent offers it. Thus, an infant will cry to call a parent to her for soothing. With maturity, the developing child can also seek proximity to the parents at these times. The parent is an attachment figure, a secure base to turn to for nurture and comfort when emotionally unsettled. This early attachment experience will then impact on the child's continuing and later relationships through the development of patterns of attachment. This will be explored further below.

- *Intersubjectivity* (Trevarthen, 2001). A central goal of the attachment system is to ensure that infants and children can attain and maintain a sense of safety. This safety is a necessary condition to allow another system to operate, the exploratory system. These two systems work in complementary fashion; when unsettled, the attachment system is activated and the child seeks comfort, but once soothed, the exploratory system can come into its own as the child turns to explore the world, beginning with the social-emotional world of relationships. The parents support their infants and children in this exploration through a sharing of the child's experiences, described as intersubjectivity. Note that this aspect of relationship experience is two-way or reciprocal. The parent is open to the child's influence, leading the parent into exploration; the child is open to the parent's influence, learning through this mutual exploration. Intersubjectivity will be explored further below.

The attachment relationship

Secure attachment develops out of a relationship that offers emotional and physical safety, soothing a child when safety is lost, and helping him to return to feeling safe again. This is done through the process of recognizing the child's needs, accepting these needs as reflecting the child's current state, and acting to meet these needs. This is described as sensitive parenting. Secure attachment provides the optimum conditions for a child, allowing him to develop successful early and later relationships. Through a process of co-regulation with the attachment figures, the child builds emotional understanding and regulation. Allan Schore describes attachment as a regulatory system that prevents us from becoming overwhelmed by the stresses of life (Schore and Schore, 2014). Similarly, the attachment figures help the child to co-construct his understanding of the social world.

Developing social cognition allows the child to be supported to develop an understanding about other people and themselves in relation to others. Through this development, supported by close adults, the child can achieve a positive sense of self (Thompson, 2016). This in turn provides a pathway to becoming a young person with good reflective functioning, the ability to understand why things happen and why people behave as they do. This occurs alongside the development of mentalization abilities, being able to understand, and take into account, the mental state of another person, that is, what they are thinking and feeling (Fonagy *et al.*, 2016). Through the experience of secure attachment children develop an internal working model of self as lovable and successful and of others as loving them and able to meet their needs. This model acts as a template for developing future relationships (Bowlby, 1988/1989). A positive internal working model allows children to grow into adults who are independent but also able to seek help from others when needed. This allows them to manage stress and to develop resilience.

All parents will be insensitive to their children some of the time, causing micro-ruptures to the relationship. The sensitive parent will notice the ruptures and seek to repair them. This experience of relationship rupture (stress) and repair (resolution of stress) builds stress regulation and resilience (Tronick and DiCorcia, 2015).

Attachment insecurity develops out of relationships with parents that are largely insensitive and within which the repair is rarely initiated. The insensitive parent does not attend to the signals that the child gives or does not accept that the child has the needs being signalled (misattunement). This means that they do not meet the need, causing relationship rupture, neither do they attend to the relationship, repairing it to re-establish a state of attunement. From a young age, children learn to adapt to this relationship experience by learning patterns of behaviour that reduce the stress of this misattunement. These are called insecure attachment patterns. Thus, in an avoidant attachment, children learn to minimize their attachment needs because their parents are least available or most misattuned when their child is emotionally needy of them. They develop patterns of emotional self-reliance and compliance to maintain some sense of safety at times of greatest need when parental availability is most threatened.

In an ambivalent attachment, children have discovered that their parents are unpredictable in whether they will meet their needs. They therefore use the opposite strategy of maximizing their attachment needs (whether or not they are experiencing distress) in order to maintain the attention of the parents. Once this is gained, they also do not let this attention go easily, demonstrated through a resistance to being soothed. Unlike the self-reliance of the avoidant strategy, these are coercive, attention-needing strategies.

Within both the avoidant and ambivalent patterns, children have learned to miscue their attachment needs based on their expectations of parents, rather than their internal state of comfort or discomfort. Mary Dozier (2003) describes this as a pattern of hidden and expressed needs, whereby only attending to the expressed needs leaves the child in a state of emotional distress and reinforces the learned attachment pattern. Children who move into foster or adoptive homes draw their new parents into patterns of responding that are reminiscent of their early attachment experiences. Only when the parent can meet both expressed and hidden needs can the child discover that this relationship might be different to what he has previously experienced.

For children who have experienced developmental trauma, the parenting they have lived with is not just insensitive but also highly frightening and/or neglectful. Children's instinctive needs to seek security and protection from parents when feeling threatened is overridden because the source of threat is coming from these same parents. This experience is highly disorganizing emotionally, cognitively and behaviourally, hence the term disorganized attachment. Children learn to survive by developing controlling strategies of relating. Their behaviour is organized around this need to control, which is achieved through extreme use of the avoidant, self-reliant and ambivalent attention-needing strategies. These strategies are taken with the child when they move into new homes. The child expresses a need for control and hides a need for relationship. This is experienced as highly rejecting by the new parents, who can withdraw from or become equally controlling of the relationship because of the hurt they are experiencing. The child is left in a state of fear.

DDP brings the attachment figures into the work with the children. The parents are supported to provide the child with sensitive but also gently challenging parenting, which can demonstrate the difference from previous relationships. The parents learn to read the miscuing from the child so that they can attend to the hidden needs as well as expressed needs. As the children experience the availability of the parent and therapist, they learn to rely on them to regulate the emotional states that are related to current stress as well as those that are a hangover from their past relational experiences. This is a process of co-regulation of emotion. Instead of working hard not to feel the need for comfort, the children become more confident to turn to the parents to meet this need. As emotional needs are met, the children can experience a different relationship, allowing moments of joy instead of always guarding against anticipated terror. This in turn opens curiosity and the children learn that their current and past experience makes sense. Therapist and parents work together to discover and make sense of the children's stories of terror and shame, developing a coherent narrative of this experience. They help the children to discover new stories of hope and belonging.

The intersubjective relationship

As social mammals, human infants are born ready for relationships and for the intersubjective experience that guides them in understanding these relationships as well as themselves. Trevarthen (2001) describes intersubjectivity as a process within which experiences are shared, and each person influences the other in making sense of these experiences. This therefore describes a reciprocal influence as each is open to the influence of the other. We learn about ourselves from these shared experiences (primary intersubjectivity). For example, a child who experiences a loving, absorbed relationship with a parent comes to experience herself as lovable and of interest to others because of the intersubjective connection between them. We also learn about others and the world around us (secondary intersubjectivity). A parent arrives home stressed from work. The child experiences her mother as abrupt and misattuned. The child is left feeling unsettled and worried. The other parent maintains an intersubjective relationship with the child, and through this connection the parent can soothe the child and help her to understand that Mummy is cross with work and it is not the child's fault. Intersubjectively, the child is helped to make sense of the experience, and in the process is soothed and comforted, which also strengthens the attachment system.

It can be helpful to explore this last example a little further. The first parent could not enter an intersubjective relationship with her child at that time as she was preoccupied with her day. She needed to take care of herself first. Her affect, the bodily experience of her emotional state, is influenced by her difficult day and she is tired and irritable. The child is not soothed by this as her mother's affect does not match her own experience of being worried. Similarly, the mother's attention is still on the events of the day. She cannot share the child's attention, which is a vigilance to her mother's mood and checking out whether this is safe. At this point, each has a different, non-complementary intention. The mother's intention is to absorb the stresses of the day, the child to monitor safety. The lack of matched affect, shared attention or complementary intention means that for the time being they are not intersubjectively connected. The other parent, in a more relaxed state herself, notices the child's discomfort. She can match affect, not feeling worried herself, but getting in tune with the vitality and intensity of the child's worry. They are both attending to the same thing with a complementary intention of helping soothe the worry on the part of the parent and becoming soothed on the part of the child. The child experiences safety as her emotion is regulated, and she can make sense of the experience. A joint narrative about Mummy going to work, having some worries at work and arriving home stressed is created between them. This narrative helps the child understand the experience without developing any associated shame that can come from a misattunement with the parent. To complete the story, Mummy was able to take care of herself, and later attended to her relationship with her daughter, repairing the rupture that had inadvertently been caused by her bad mood. The child goes to bed feeling safe and loved, knowing that things can go wrong and be put right again, and it is not her fault.

Through these intersubjective connections negative emotions are soothed and calmed. A child is frightened by a loud noise; the parent soothes the child, accepting the child's fear, and holding it with her. The potency of the loud noise reduces as the child feels comforted. In a similar way, positive emotions are amplified. Imagine a parent and child jumping in puddles together; there is more laughter and fun than either of them would experience if they were doing this alone.

Children who have experienced developmental trauma will have experienced parenting environments where they receive no intersubjective experiences or where these experiences are filled with fear and terror. They are likely to have a very different relationship with their parent compared with the securely attached child. These children are often anxious and vigilant, continuously monitoring the environment for signs of threat. This does not allow them to enter the open and engaged state of deep interest and curiosity about the world of the non-traumatized child.

Returning to the example above, let's imagine it a bit differently. A parent arrives home from work stressed and angry. This is taken out on both the other parent and the child. The parent is hit because dinner is not on the table. The child is shouted at for staring and being in the way. The parents' attention is on each other, one in order to vent frustration and the other to placate in order to try to keep herself and her child safe. Neither of them can be intersubjectively present for the child, who is left in a stressed state. The misattunement between them all is experienced by the child as shame, an inner sense that somehow this is all her fault. The shame is left unregulated and the child is left with a narrative of fear and terror, with a sense of being to blame. Many experiences like this become built into the child's identity of being not good enough.

While as infants these children are born to be open to intersubjective connection, this openness is quickly lost as the children withdraw from reciprocal, mutually influencing interactions. The children most typically take charge of their own safety by developing non-reciprocal, controlling relationships. Within these they reject the influence of the parent, holding on to their influence only. The early experience of intersubjective relationships, together with the lack of attachment safety, leads to a child who feels safer controlling than interacting in reciprocal relationships. These patterns of relating generalize to future relationships with alternative parents, educators and peers. Children who have experienced developmental trauma find it difficult to believe that anything is different when they move into healthier parenting environments. They frequently hold on to their controlling patterns of behaviour, being reluctant to test out whether things are different now. Parents experience that their nurture and intersubjective presence are rejected by the child. This can be a deeply painful experience, and these parents may eventually withdraw from the reciprocal aspects of the relationship as well, leading to a condition described as blocked care by Hughes and Baylin (2012).

Within DDP, offering intersubjective experiences is a central part of the therapeutic stance that the therapist takes. The therapist strives to get into a connection with the child, allowing a rhythm to develop between them as he becomes interested in what the child is interested in. His deep interest in the child is expressed through a storytelling tone of voice, PACE attitude and attention to the relationship. At times, the child might offer a theme to the therapist, something of significance that is occupying her attention at that time. The therapist will follow this theme, maintaining the same intersubjective stance and storytelling attitude. The child continues to experience herself as of interest to the therapist, and the safety that this establishes can allow her to be led into a deeper exploration of the theme. If the child begins to struggle with this, or her attention moves elsewhere, the therapist again follows the child, maintaining the intersubjective connection and gently leading the child back to the theme when she is ready to attend to it again.

This relational approach represents a slowing down in therapy, allowing attention to the relationship at all moments. Initially the parent is largely witness to this process, offering insights when these are perceived as likely to be helpful. Later the therapist invites the parent into the process, often by talking about the child, and the story they have been discovering together, or helping the child to tell this story to the parent in her own words. If a child struggles to find the words, the therapist might 'talk for her', always checking that the words the therapist chooses resonates with the child and fits with her sense of the story. The parent, helped by the therapist, responds with PACE, and the intersubjective relationship becomes shared between all present. The child is helped to experience safe intersubjective connections which are very different from what they have experienced in the past and what they expect in the present.

3. Shame and the development of identity

Experiences of shame and guilt are important stages in a child's development (Tangney and Dearing, 2012). Shame develops first as part of the socialization process. Shame arises out of experiences where the attunement with the parent has been broken. A child is singing nursery rhymes with a parent (attunement). The child notices a cat across the road and runs out to see it. The parent angrily pulls the child back out of the road, remonstrating with him for doing something so dangerous (break). The child cries, unsettled by the temporary loss of the intersubjective relationship with the parent. This experience is tolerable for the child because the parent completes the cycle with relationship repair. She comforts the child, letting him know that while his behaviour (running into the road) was wrong, this has not stopped her loving him. Shame reduces, and parent and child return to a state of attunement.

As the child matures, the lessons from these experiences of shame are learned and the child internalizes the rules and values of the parents (do not run into the road, be gentle when stroking the dog, share nicely with your sister, etc.). Transgression of these rules leads to feelings of guilt. The child pulls the dog's ear, then feels bad because she knows this is wrong (guilt). In response to this feeling of guilt she experiences remorse, feeling empathy for the dog. She now strokes the dog nicely (makes amends).

We all feel times of shame. These are the times when we have transgressed important values we hold. We feel exposed in our sense of low worth and want to hide from others, especially the ones we have transgressed against. Shame makes us feel bad about ourselves and makes it hard to attend to the feelings of others. Fortunately, if we have had good early socialization with parents who are able to repair ruptures, we will experience more guilt than shame. We regret our actions and feel empathy for those hurt by them. Feelings of remorse allow us to focus on the other and seek to make amends.

When children have experienced developmental trauma, they have not had healthy socialization experience. Times of attunement with parents are scarce, and breaks too many. In addition, the parental repair which allows shame to be regulated doesn't happen. These children have had too many shaming experiences with no support to regulate the intense emotion generated. They are left with toxic levels of shame and the development of guilt is disrupted.

These experiences of shame and guilt influence the development of self-identity. Well-regulated shame experiences and the healthy development of guilt lead to the development of a sense of self as good. The child understands that she is a good person who sometimes makes mistakes that can be repaired. Unregulated shame and weak development of guilt lead to the development of a sense of self as bad. The child believes that she is no good, unlovable and unworthy of the attention of others. She expects to hurt others but finds it hard to focus on this, consumed as she is with her own sense of failure.

Recognizing children in shame is relatively easy. These are children who avoid connection with us. They cannot look at us and often they will hide. As well as physically hiding they have learned to hide behind a shield (Golding and Hughes, 2012). This consists of characteristic behaviours developed to reduce the intense feelings associated with unregulated shame. The child will lie, blame others and minimize their actions to defend themselves from an overwhelming sense of badness. When these fail, the children collapse into intense rages directed at others or themselves.

Now is not the time for recriminations, for consequences or for trying to make sense of what has happened. Within the DDP model, a child in shame needs co-regulation, as with other negative emotions. DDP-informed interventions regulate shame by offering the child intersubjective relationships. The adult encourages the child to trust him to support her through the stress of the moment. The child's feelings of shame are accepted, and this is conveyed through the tone of voice and storytelling rhythm that the adult is using to talk with the child. The adult uses his presence to demonstrate that he cares enough to support the child even at these most difficult times. There will be time later to explore what happened, to help the child to repair the damage done. For now, it is enough to demonstrate that the adult is there, supporting the child even at the darkest of moments.

This helps the child to make sense of her behaviours differently. She recognizes that she is not bad but had some strong feelings which led to behaviours that were not helpful. As the child develops a less shame-based sense of self she will be able to experience remorse and seek to make amends, supported by the relationship with the adult that she has learned to trust.

Within therapy, the therapist is alert to signs of shame in the child. He slows down the conversation so that he and the parent can provide co-regulation for the child. As the shame is regulated, the adults can help the child make sense of her experience. Narratives of pain and shame become narratives of strength and resilience within the intersubjective connections provided by the therapy (Hughes *et al.*, 2019).

4. Neuroscience

As the field of neuroscience has grown, we are understanding much more about the functioning of the brain and nervous system. What is being discovered resonates with many of the findings of research into attachment, intersubjectivity and the impact of trauma (Hughes *et al.*, 2019). In particular, the human nervous system has evolved to be interpersonal, designed to thrive within relationships and to function optimally in conditions of safety. At times of increased stress or threat the nervous system can also draw on more primitive defences – this represents a vigilant state – with increased alertness to signs of physical or interpersonal danger. This can quickly trigger the child into states of fight, flight or freeze, which are designed to support survival and in the short term can be very helpful. However, when threat is chronic, or is perceived to be ever present, the child experiences little sense of safety. The defensive system then becomes habitual. The child moves into a state of perpetual vigilance, ignoring signs of safety and withdrawing from curious exploration or learning. Survival becomes the driving force.

In developmental trauma, where much of the threat is interpersonal, a state of blocked trust develops (Baylin and Hughes, 2016). The brain's monitoring system becomes biased to respond to relationship experiences as if they are unsafe, leading to activation of the defensive nervous system. This is facilitated by a suppression of the social engagement system. The child feels safer withdrawing from the relationship or coercively controlling it. There is also an inhibition of the social pain system. When a person experiences social pain they have an innate instinct to seek social support. By inhibiting social pain, the child can maintain a non-interpersonal stance to the world. Unfortunately, this also means that the support of healthy adults is lost. When nervous systems are interrelated the child can use the adult's more mature nervous system, especially the higher cognitive function located in the cortex, to provide regulation, thus restoring equilibrium. The child's immature brain 'borrows' the adult's brain to provide the physiological support needed – a process described as social, or parental, buffering (Gunnar *et al.*, 2015). Without this, the child is left in a defensive state, relying on an immature nervous system with well-developed defensive structures but with a less well-developed cortex. Rather like driving a car with an accelerator but no brake, the child is left responding to threat with no means of calming and soothing the threat system when the danger is past or has been misperceived.

Stephen Porges (2017) has been researching the role of the vagal system in understanding social defence and social engagement. This involves neurobiological systems within the brain and extending throughout the body. Porges's polyvagal theory explores how the autonomic nervous system operates under conditions of threat and safety, based on a process of neuroception. This is a process of detecting safety, danger or life threat that is outside conscious awareness, triggering different physiological states. When safety is detected, the ventral vagal social engagement system activates, and we can relax (immobilize) and engage with others (mobilize). When a threat is detected, the sympathetic nervous system provides physiological responses, readying the body for mobilization via fight and flight responses. In situations of life threat, the parasympathetic nervous system has an immobilizing function allowing shutdown, analogous to the 'playing dead' which is seen when a predator is at the point of catching prey. Only when the social engagement system is active can the autonomic nervous system support health, growth and restoration. In other states, the autonomic nervous system is supporting defence (Porges, 2018).

This is important for the practice of DDP, which aims to move children out of defensive states and into socially engaged states, allowing them to heal and grow. Differing states tend to synchronize when individuals interact, as two people in a social interaction cannot stay in opposing states of defence and engagement. Commonly, because priority is given to safety, when one person is defensive it evokes an analogous defensive response in the other. If, however, one of the dyad can remain open and engaged, it will eventually lead to the other person moving into this state also. Children who have experienced developmental trauma are frequently in a defensive state, evoking defensiveness in the parents and therapists they are relating to. Within DDP, therapists and parents strive to maintain an open and engaged state, or to move back to this state when noticing that they are becoming defensive. This allows the child to become more open and engaged, at least for a time. With repeated experience of relationships supporting the child to move out of defensive states, the child begins to feel safer and the bias to danger built into their nervous systems can start to change. Noticing a tendency to become defensive, learning to inhibit this and maintaining an open and engaged state are therefore crucial aspects of DDP practice, for therapists, parents and anyone supporting children who have experienced developmental trauma.

Glossary

Abandonment: Children who do not receive the physical or emotional care that they need experience this as abandonment by their parents. Abandonment can be psychological rather than physical. The parent is present but not emotionally available. Physical and psychological abandonment leads to continuing fears that abandonment will be repeated in the future by significant people in their lives.

Arousal state: Our arousal state describes how physiologically alert we are. As arousal increases, a person moves from calm and reflective to increasingly reactive.

Attachment theory: Psychiatrist John Bowlby developed attachment theory to describe the bond that develops between a child and parent. This bond is a response to the degree to which a parent helps a child to feel safe and secure. Attachment is dependent on an *attachment behavioural system.* Children have an innate predisposition to display attachment behaviours when they are feeling insecure or distressed in some way. The attachment behavioural system is activated, leading to the child seeking proximity to the attachment figure, protesting separation from that person and therefore seeking to use the caregiver as a secure base. This behavioural system works together with the *exploratory behavioural system.* This is also an innate predisposition, this time to seek novelty and new experience. It focuses attention on exploration and learning. These two behavioural systems are complementary – as one is activated, the other de-activates dependent on current circumstances.

The way that parents respond to the cues or signals that children give about their need to attach or explore represents the degree to which they are sensitive or insensitive to these signals. From this experience, the children develop attachment patterns:

- *Secure:* The attachment that children develop when a parent is experienced as sensitive and responsive to their emotional needs. The child learns trust in others and appropriate self-reliance.

- *Ambivalent-resistant:* Also called anxious attachment. This develops when attachment needs are triggered but the child has experienced the parent as inconsistent and unpredictable. The child maximizes the expression of attachment need in order to maintain the availability of the parent.
- *Avoidant:* This develops when attachment needs are triggered but the child has experienced the parent as rejecting. The child minimizes the expression of attachment need in order to maintain the availability of the parent.
- *Disorganized-controlling:* This develops when attachment needs are triggered but the child has experienced the parent as frightened or frightening. The child has trouble organizing his behaviour at times of stress. As they grow older, children with these patterns of relating under stress learn to control relationships to force predictability. Controlling relationships develop instead of reciprocal relationships.

Within the insecure patterns, children develop ways of hiding and expressing needs in line with their expectations of their parents.

This attachment experience leads to the development of an *internal working model*, a cognitive model of the relationship (i.e. a memory or template) that the child has experienced. This model influences how the child will respond to future relationships, including how he relates to adults and peers in school.

Children develop multiple models of attachment influenced by the range of relationships that they have experienced. The model guides the behaviour that they will display within the different relationships that they go on to encounter.

Through adolescence and into adulthood, these attachment patterns based on multiple models transform into an attachment state of mind based on the way the multiple models combine to give the adult a single more complex model to guide behaviour. Four states of mind are described which can be linked to the childhood patterns:

- *Autonomous attachment state of mind* emerges from secure patterns. The individual with this model is likely to have experienced a secure attachment relationship or to have resolved difficult experience with attachment figures. This experience will help the individual to be a sensitive and responsive parent.
- *Dismissing attachment state of mind* emerges from avoidant patterns. This individual is likely to have learned to distrust emotional expression and to value self-reliance. As a parent, this experience will make it harder for the individual to recognize the

child's attachment needs, will increase discomfort with the child's distress and will lead to a valuing of independence in the child.

- *Preoccupied attachment state of mind* emerges from ambivalent patterns. This individual is likely to have learned to coercively use expression of emotion to keep others engaged. As a parent, this individual is likely to find the child's needs to be overwhelming and will quickly feel emotional and angry towards the child.

- *Unresolved attachment state of mind* emerges from disorganized-controlling patterns. Past loss and frightening experiences remain a source of trauma. As a parent, the child's distress can trigger memories of this early trauma, meaning that the parent is unavailable to the child when needed most.

Attunement: An emotional connection between two people in which one person mirrors or matches the rhythm, vitality and affect (externally displayed mood) of the other.

Authoritative parenting: Parenting that provides children with a high degree of warmth and nurture alongside clear and appropriate boundaries. The children are enabled to develop autonomy (independence) in line with the developmental stage they are at. Educators can also be authoritative in the approach they take with the pupils in school.

Autonomy: The degree of personal independence an individual possesses.

Behaviour management: Sometimes called behaviour modification, this provides a set of strategies for parents and educators to use with the focus on changing the behaviour of the child. The aim is to reduce challenging behaviour and to increase prosocial behaviour – the behaviours we want to see children using. This is achieved through the use of consequences, sanctions, praise and rewards. In this book, we use the term *behaviour support* to describe an approach which has a focus on relationship, building connection and helping regulation. The support for the behaviour is then provided in the context of this relationship. This is captured in the expression '*Connection with Teaching*' (see also *Social learning theory*).

Blocked care: In a healthy parent–child relationship, caregiving in the adult synchronizes with care-seeking in the child. This is supported by five regions in the brain which when working well will help the adult to be a caregiver:

1. *Approach:* the parent seeks connection with the child.

2. *Pleasure:* reciprocal process as each enjoys being with the other.

3. *Child reading:* the parent wants to make sense of the child.

4. *Meaning making:* the parent seeks to understand the child. This links with past experience of attachment and relationships. Parents make meaning through the lens of past relationships.

5. *Executive system:* this integrative centre of the brain makes all of this work but is less dependent on the child's influence.

A state of blocked care can result when the child is unable to engage in a reciprocal relationship with the parent. The brain regions (1–4) de-activate, leaving only the executive system working. Educators who are providing a high level of care for children can also succumb to blocked care when supporting children who struggle with reciprocal relationships.

Blocked trust: A failure in social relatedness. It develops as a response to frightening and painful relationship experiences with caregivers. The innate need for comfort and companionship is suppressed, leading to chronic defensiveness and a lack of social engagement. The child strives to be self-sufficient, keeping the caregiver at a distance through controlling rather than reciprocal relationships. This adaptation means that the child is not getting the social buffering needed to manage stress and alarm in the world.

In blocked trust, five systems in the brain have adapted to living in a harsh social world:

1. The *stress system* is chronically activated, easily triggered and hard to switch off.

2. The *social switching system* does not move easily between social engagement and self-defence as appraisal of threat and danger during interactions is set very high.

3. The *social engagement system* is suppressed.

4. The *self-defence system* is activated.

5. The experience of *social pain* is blocked.

This state of blocked trust comes with the child into worlds outside the home, such as school. Children will experience blocked trust in educators, as they have with parents.

Consequences: Any piece of behaviour is followed by consequences. These consequences will to some extent determine what we do in the future. Consequences therefore can be used to help someone to behave differently. In this book, we have called this use of consequences *coercive consequences*, as they are used in an effort to change the behaviour of the other. When the pupil is supported in a relationship, she comes to understand her behaviour and the impact it has had on another. This can lead to feelings of remorse and a desire to make amends. The pupil seeks a consequence which can help her to repair. The educator can support her with this, and thus the consequence becomes part of a collaborative process of planning for and making this repair. In this book, we have called these *collaborative consequences*.

Controlling behaviours: These represent a need to feel in charge within the relationship. This is generally because the person fears a relationship which is reciprocal. She feels vulnerable being open to the influence of the other, so she seeks to coercively influence instead.

Defensive: When we experience physical or psychological threat, we instinctively move to defend ourselves through a range of fight and flight behaviours. If these options are not available to us, we will move into shut-down responses (dissociation) as a means of survival. These defensive reactions are governed by the nervous system, which can be sensitized to react more quickly in individuals whose earliest experience has been frightening.

Discipline: The giving to another of skills and knowledge through teaching. In childhood, parents and educators use discipline to teach children about their expectations of them and to give them guidelines and principles they can use to live their lives. These are based on the adults' morals and values.

Dissociation: The process by which a person defends against overwhelming stress by cutting off from conscious awareness what is being sensed or felt. At its extreme, the person cuts off from contact with others or the world, becoming numb, unfeeling or unaware. Dissociation reduces the ability to make sense of self or others.

Dyadic Developmental Psychotherapy (DDP): This was originally developed by Dan Hughes as a therapeutic intervention for families who were fostering or had adopted children with significant developmental trauma and insecurity of attachment. The model has also been applied to birth families with parents who want to learn to parent in a different way and to support their child in recovering from trauma. The therapist facilitates the child's relationship with his parents through the development and maintenance of an affective-reflective dialogue which explores all aspects of the child's life: safe and traumatic, present and past. The therapist and parents' intersubjective experience of the child provides the child with new meanings which can become integrated into his autobiographical narrative, which in turn becomes more coherent. In this way, the child experiences healing of past trauma and achieves safety within current relationships. The conversations and interactions (verbal and non-verbal) within the therapy room are all based on PACE and have a quality of storytelling.

DDP therefore is an approach within which the child and parents work together with the therapist. The child gains relationship experience which helps him to grow and heal emotionally as family members develop healthy patterns of relating and communicating.

DDP has a broader application as Dyadic Developmental Practice (see Figure I.1). This provides a set of principles that can support networks, inform and enrich parenting, and can support the child outside the home, for example in residential settings and at school.

DDP is theoretically based on the models of attachment theory and intersubjectivity and is consistent with the needs of children and young people who have experienced developmental trauma.

Executive function: The executive functions allow for integrated brain functioning so that cognitive and emotional parts of the brain work well together. These processes are responsible for guiding, directing and managing cognitive (thinking), emotional and behavioural tasks. Executive functioning allows purposeful, goal-directed and problem-solving behaviours. When this brain functioning is compromised, it is sometimes described as executive dysfunction.

Intersubjectivity: This describes the relationship that first develops between infant and parent. The infant has an innate ability to co-ordinate her actions with those of her parent so that they are both synchronized. This is a necessary experience for social interactions, enabling children to emotionally connect with others. Their responses are contingent on the response of the other. This is a bit like a game of tennis, when a ball is hit backwards and forwards between two players. Each player is influenced by the other.

Mentalization: The ability to predict responses based on an understanding of the inner experience of others – for example, an understanding that someone is upset by an event might lead to an expectation that the other person will cry. This is dependent on the ability to take the perspective of the other person (*perspective taking*). Mentalizing and perspective taking rest on the ability to think about our own mind and the mind of others – to have *theory of mind*. This in turn leads to a capacity for *reflective function*, which is the ability to understand why things happen and why people behave as they do.

Mentalization involves one person holding the other's mind within their own mind and helping the other to experience this mind within their own.

One aspect of mentalization is the ability to be *mind-minded* – to be able to understand and take into account the mental state of another person, what the person might be thinking, feeling, wishing, believing, desiring and so on. When an educator can understand the internal experience of the child, it is easier for her to emotionally connect with him.

Mindfulness: The process of bringing attention to experiences occurring in the present moment. Attention can be directed to internal experience; for example, our internal world of thinking and feeling. Alternatively, it can be directed to external experience; for example, directed to what we are seeing, hearing, smelling, tasting or sensing. When we are mindful, we are living fully in the present. It is therefore difficult to be mindful when feeling depressed, as this tends to take our attention to the past, or when anxious, as this tends to focus attention on to the future. Regular practice of mindfulness has been found to improve mental health.

Narrative: A cohesive story of real or imaginary events. The narrative is at the heart of storytelling. Discovering the story is an important part of DDP, as we make sense of the experience of the other.

PACE: The therapeutic attitude that is used within the DDP model to facilitate emotional connection. The attitude of PACE offers an unconditional relationship expressed through playfulness, acceptance, curiosity and empathy.

Regulation: An individual's ability to control and modulate her level of emotional arousal. This ability to regulate is influenced by the experience of emotional co-regulation. This is the experience children need when parents or educators help them to manage their emotional arousal. Emotional dysregulation represents a lack of regulatory ability. This occurs when an individual fails to control and modulate her level of emotional arousal. The emotional experience overwhelms the individual.

Relationship repair: A psychological term used to describe the process whereby one person in a relationship repairs a rupture that has occurred within the relationship. Staff members re-establish a positive emotional connection between themselves and a pupil (attunement) following a time when the relationship has been ruptured. The rupture can occur either because of the behaviour of the child or of the staff member. This does not mean that the educator has done something wrong. Simply giving attention to another child can cause a rupture in a relationship with an emotionally needy child. The repair is about demonstrating the importance of the relationship, not apologizing for mistakes.

Self-esteem: This describes how people perceive themselves and their abilities. It represents their sense of their own worth. High self-esteem suggests that an individual perceives himself positively, while low self-esteem represents a low opinion of self and worth to others.

Shame: A complex emotional state within which a person experiences negative feelings about himself; a feeling of inferiority, not feeling good enough.

Social engagement: The capacity to engage in social relationships; being open to responding to as well as influencing others in the relationship. Biologically we are innately prepared to engage with others, but when we experience fear and trauma such engagement reduces. Within the DDP model the phrase '*open and engaged*' is used to describe a relationship where partners within the relationship are open to social engagement with each other. This is the opposite state to *social defensiveness*, when social engagement is reduced.

Socialization: A developmental process of helping children to acquire the skills that they will need to engage in social relationships. This includes learning cultural norms and values so that the children are equipped to live within their own communities. This socialization process goes on through childhood and into adulthood, influencing behaviour, beliefs and the way that people make relationships.

Social learning theory: This stems from a branch of psychology called behavioural psychology. Within social learning theory there is a focus on how behaviour is reinforced. The term reinforcement refers to the consequence to behaviour. This consequence can be a *negative reinforcer*. This is experienced as unpleasant. The person behaves in a certain way in order to avoid the negative consequence; for example, a parent buys a child some sweets to stop him crying – the sweet-buying behaviour in the parent has been negatively reinforced. Alternatively, it can be a *positive reinforcer*. This refers to a consequence to a behaviour that is experienced as pleasant and thus rewarding. The person behaves in a certain way in order to gain the pleasant consequence; for example, the child cries because the crying has been rewarded by sweets – the child's crying behaviour has been positively reinforced.

Reinforcement, which is strengthening of behaviour, can be contrasted with *punishment*, which is weakening of behaviour. In behavioural psychology, punishment refers to a consequence to a behaviour that is experienced as unpleasant. The person stops behaving in order to avoid the unpleasant consequence; for example, if a child was smacked when crying for sweets, the child's crying behaviour would be punished, leading to the child stopping crying. As punishment also leads to shame and feelings of low self-worth and doesn't teach the child what behaviour is acceptable, it is generally considered to be a poor technique. Parents and educators are advised to reward good behaviour rather than punish bad behaviour. Social learning theory has less focus on relationship and emotional connection and therefore is not attachment focused.

Teams supporting the pupil (Team Pupil): Within the school, a small number of staff can be brought together with the purpose of providing additional support to an individual pupil. These staff work closely together to understand the pupil and her unique needs and support each other to meet these needs. The pupil knows these staff well and understands that they are her team to support her. Louise calls these teams 'Team Pupil' in recognition of their unique role for the individual pupil (Bombèr, 2016).

Theraplay: This is a relational therapy for children and their parents. The therapist supports the parent and child relationship by encouraging patterns of playful, healthy interactions within four dimensions:

- *Structure* – the parent is encouraged to help the child to feel secure by offering predictability and support. This helps the child to develop control over his body.
- *Engagement* – the parent is encouraged to engage the child in play, which helps them both to experience joy in the relationship.
- *Nurture* – the parent is encouraged to offer a warm, nurturing relationship, which helps the child to trust that comfort will be offered when needed and helps him to feel loved and valued.
- *Challenge* – the parent is encouraged to help the child to try new things by offering the right level of support to help him to succeed.

Theraplay sessions aim to enhance attachment, build self-esteem, allow trust in others and, above all, experience joyful engagement.

Trauma: In this context, we are reflecting on psychological trauma rather than a physical trauma, such as a break to a bone, although both can overlap. Trauma is an experience of an event (or events) that involves actual or threatened death or serious injury to self, or witnessing such an event happening to another person. Learning about unexpected or violent death, serious harm or threat of death or injury to family or friends can also represent a trauma. For the event to be traumatizing, the response by the individual is of intense fear, helplessness or horror. In other words, it is the experience of the event that determines whether it is a trauma for the individual. An event is traumatic if it is extremely upsetting and at least temporarily overwhelms an individual's internal resources. Such traumas can include extreme emotional abuse, major losses or separations, degradation and humiliation.

Complex trauma occurs when an individual is exposed to multiple traumatic events with an impact on immediate and long-term outcomes (e.g. war, ethnic cleansing). When complex trauma occurs through childhood with early onset, is chronic and prolonged, occurs from within the family and impacts on development, it is described by some researchers as *developmental trauma*. This is a useful description for the experience of children who develop attachment difficulties, blocked trust and fear of relationship. The children can become *trauma-organized* in a pattern of highly controlling behaviours. When educators are *trauma-informed*, they can help the children to discover other ways of being.

Unconditional support: Support which will be given 'no matter what'. When support is only given if certain circumstances exist, it is described as conditional: 'I will support you only if…', instead of 'no matter what'.

Verbal and non-verbal: Verbal represents the use of words to communicate, whereas non-verbal is the way we communicate without words. Communication is generally a mixture of verbal and non-verbal behaviours.

Zone of Proximal Development: Russian psychologist Lev Vygotsky suggested the Zone of Proximal Development (ZPD) to describe how children can achieve more when the adults or older peers provide them with support to do this (see Figure 7.2). He describes the ZPD as 'the distance between the actual developmental level as determined by independent problem solving and the level of potential development as determined through problem solving under adult guidance, or in collaboration with more capable peers' (Vygotsky, 1978, p.86). In this book, we use this idea as a helpful way for thinking about the structure and supervision that pupils need to support their emotional development as well as their cognitive development. Expecting too much of pupils is outside their ZPD, while expecting too little means that the pupil is not in the zone and doesn't make progress. If the team supporting the pupil provide support within the zone, the pupil is likely to make educational and emotional progress.

References

Alper, J. and Howe, D. (2015) *Assessing Adoptive and Foster Parents: Improving Analyses and Understanding of Parenting Capacity*. London: Jessica Kingsley Publishers.

Baumrind, D. (1978) 'Parental disciplinary patterns and social competence in children.' *Youth and Society*, 9, 238–276.

Baylin, J. (2016) *Mistrust to Trust: The Neurobiology of Attachment-Focused Therapy*. Conference presentation. DDP conference, Glasgow.

Baylin, J. and Hughes, D.A. (2016) *The Neurobiology of Attachment-Focused Therapy: Enhancing Connection and Trust in the Treatment of Children and Adolescents (Norton Series on Interpersonal Neurobiology)*. New York, NY: W.W. Norton.

Bloom, S.L. (2013, first published 1997) *Creating Sanctuary: Toward the Evolution of Sane Societies*. New York, NY: Routledge.

Bombèr, L.M. (2007) *Inside I'm Hurting: Practical Strategies for Supporting Children with Attachment Difficulties in Schools*. London: Worth Publishing.

Bombèr, L.M. (2011) *What About Me? Inclusive Strategies to Support Pupils with Attachment Difficulties Make it Through the School Day*. London: Worth Publishing.

Bombèr, L.M. (2016) *Attachment Aware School Series. Bridging the Gap for Troubled Pupils. Book 1: The Key Adult in School; Book 2: The Senior Manager in School; Book 3: The Key Educators in School; Book 4: The Team Pupil in School; Book 5: The Parent and Carer in School*. London: Worth Publishing.

Bombèr, L.M. (2020) *Know Me to Teach Me. Differentiated Discipline for Those Recovering from Adverse Childhood Experiences: The Latest Neuroscience Applied and Made Practical*. London: Worth Publishing.

Bombèr, L.M. and Hughes, D.A. (2013) *Settling to Learn. Settling Troubled Pupils to Learn: Why Relationships Matter in School*. London: Worth Publishing.

Bowlby, J. (1988/1998) *A Secure Base: Clinical Applications of Attachment Theory*. London: Routledge.

Cook, A., Spinazzola, J., Ford, J., Lanktree, C., Blaustein, M., Cloitre, M. and van der Kolk, B. (2005) 'Complex trauma in children and adolescents.' *Psychiatric Annals*, 35, 390–395.

Dent, H. (2018) *Why Don't I Feel Good Enough? Using Attachment Theory to Find a Solution*. London: Routledge.

Dozier, M. (2003) 'Attachment-based treatment for vulnerable children.' *Attachment and Human Development*, 5, 3, 253–257.

Field, T. (2007) *The Amazing Infant*. Oxford: Blackwell Publishing.

Fonagy, P., Gergely, G., Jurist, E.L. and Target, M. (2002) *Affect Regulation, Mentalization, and the Development of the Self*. New York, NY: Other Press.

Fonagy, P., Luyten, P., Allison, E. and Campbell, C. (2016) 'Reconciling Psychoanalytic Ideas with Attachment Theory.' In J. Cassidy and P.R. Shaver (eds), *Handbook of Attachment* (third edition). New York, NY: Guilford Press.

Forbes, H.T. (2012) *Help for Billy: A Beyond Consequences Approach to Helping Challenging Children in the Classroom*. Boulder, CO: Beyond Consequences Institute.

Geddes, H. (2006) *Attachment in the Classroom: The Links Between Children's Early Experience, Emotional Well-Being and Performance in School*. London: Worth Publishing.

Golding, K.S. (2017) *Everyday Parenting with Security and Love: Using PACE to Provide Foundations for Attachment*. London: Jessica Kingsley Publishers.

Golding, K.S. and Hughes, D.A. (2012) *Creating Loving Attachments: Parenting with PACE to Nurture Confidence and Security in the Troubled Child*. London: Jessica Kingsley Publishers.

Golding, K.S., Fain, J., Frost, A., Mills, C. *et al.* (2013) *Observing Children with Attachment Difficulties in School: A Tool for Identifying and Supporting Emotional and Social Difficulties*. London: Jessica Kingsley Publishers.

Golding, K.S. Worrall, H., Turner, M. T., Roberts, J. and Cadman, A.E.(2016) *Observing Adolescents with Attachment Difficulties in Educational Settings: A Tool for Identifying and Supporting Emotional and Social Difficulties*. London: Jessica Kingsley Publishers.

Gott, S. (1999) *Teach to Inspire Better Behaviour: Coping with Aggressive, Disruptive and Unpredictable Behaviours*. London: Optimus Education.

Gunnar, M.R., Hostinar, C.E., Sanchez, M.M., Tottenham, N. and Sullivan, R.S. (2015) 'Parental buffering of fear and stress neurobiology: Reviewing parallels across rodent, monkey, and human models.' *Social Neuroscience*, 10, 5, 474–478. doi:10.1 080/17470919.2015.1070198.

Harnett, P.H. and Dawe, S. (2012) 'The contribution of mindfulness-based therapies for children and families and proposed conceptual integration.' *Child and Adolescent Mental Health*, 17, 195–208.

Howard, J.A. (2013) *Distressed or Deliberately Defiant? Managing Challenging Student Behaviour Due to Trauma and Disorganized Attachment*. Toowong, Queensland: Australian Academic Press.

Hughes, D.A. (2007) *Attachment-Focused Family Therapy*. New York, NY: W.W. Norton.

Hughes, D.A. (2009) *Attachment Focused Parenting*. New York, NY: W.W. Norton.

Hughes, D.A. (2011) *Attachment Focused Family Therapy: The Workbook*. New York, NY: W.W. Norton.

Hughes, D.A. and Baylin, J. (2012) *Brain-Based Parenting: The Neuroscience of Caregiving for Healthy Attachment*. New York, NY: W.W. Norton.

Hughes, D.A., Golding, K.S. and Hudson, J. (2019) *Healing Relational Trauma with Attachment-Focused Interventions: Dyadic Developmental Psychotherapy with Children and Families*. New York, NY: W.W. Norton.

Jennings, P. (2018) *The Trauma-Sensitive Classroom: Building Resilience with Compassionate Teaching*. New York, NY: W.W. Norton.

Kabat-Zinn, J. (1990) *Full Catastrophe Living: Using the Wisdom of Your Body and Mind to Face Stress, Pain and Illness*. New York, NY: Delacourt.

Kabat-Zinn, J. (2004) *Wherever You Go, There You Are: Mindfulness Meditation for Everyday Life*. London: Piatkus.

Meins, E. (1997) *Security of Attachment and the Social Development of Cognition*. Hove: Psychology Press.

Perry, A. (2009) *Teenagers and Attachment: Helping Adolescents Engage with Life and Learning*. London: Worth Publishing.

Perry, B.D. (2006) 'Applying Principles of Neurodevelopment to Clinical Work with Maltreated and Traumatized Children: The Neurosequential Model of Therapeutics.' In N. Boyd Webb (ed.), *Working with Traumatized Youth in Child Welfare*. New York, NY: Guilford Press.

Phillips, S., Melim, D. and Hughes, D.A. (2020) *Belonging: A Relationship-Based Approach to Trauma-Informed Education*. San Francisco, CA: Rowman and Littlefield.

Pollak, S.D. (2003) 'Experience-dependent affective learning and risk for psychopathology in children.' *Annals of the New York Academy of Sciences*, 1008, 102–111.

Porges, S.W. (2017) *The Pocket Guide to the Polyvagal Theory: The Transformative Power of Feeling Safe*. New York, NY: W.W. Norton.

Porges, S.W. (2018) 'Polyvagal Theory: A Primer.' In S.W. Porges and D. Dana (eds), *Clinical Applications of the Polyvagal Theory: The Emergence of Polyvagal-Informed Therapies*. New York, NY: W.W. Norton.

Rock, D. and Siegel, D.J. (2011) *The Healthy Mind Platter*. Available at www.drdansiegel.com/resources/healthy_mind_platter.

Schore, A.N. (2012) *The Science and Art of Psychotherapy*. New York, NY: W.W. Norton.

Schore, J.R. and Schore, A.N. (2014) 'Regulation theory and affect regulation psychotherapy: A clinical primer.' *Smith College Studies in Social Work*, 84, 2–3, 178–195.

Siegel, D.J. (1999) *The Developing Mind*. New York, NY: Guilford Press.

Siegel, D.J. (2010) *The Mindful Therapist: A Clinician's Guide to Mindsight and Neural Integration*. New York, NY: W.W. Norton.

Siegel, D.J. (2014) *Brainstorm: The Power and Purpose of the Teenage Brain*. Melbourne/London: Scribe.

Staff, R. (2016) *Parenting Adopted Teenagers: Advice for the Adolescent Years*. London: Jessica Kingsley Publishers.

Stern, D. (2000) *The Interpersonal World of the Infant*. New York, NY: Basic Books.

Stott, L. (2006) 'Holding it all Together: Creating Thinking Networks.' In K.S. Golding, H.R. Dent, R. Nissim and E. Stott (eds), *Thinking Psychologically about Children who are Looked After and Adopted: Space for Reflection*. Chichester: John Wiley and Sons.

Sunderland, M. (2008) *The Science of Parenting*. London: Dorling Kindersley.

Tangney, J. and Dearing, R. (2002) *Shame and Guilt*. New York, NY: Guilford Press.

Thompson, R.A. (2016) 'Early Attachment and Later Development: Reframing the Questions.' In J. Cassidy and P.R. Shaver (eds), *Handbook of Attachment* (third edition). New York, NY: Guilford Press.

Tranter, D., Carson, L. and Boland, T. (2018) *The Third Path: A Relationship-Based Approach to Student Well-Being and Achievement*. Toronto, ON: Nelson.

Trevarthen, C. (2001) 'Intrinsic motives for companionship in understanding: Their origin, development, and significance for infant mental health.' *Infant Mental Health Journal*, 22, 95–131.

Tronick, E. (2007) *The Neurobehavioral and Social-Emotional Development of Infants and Children*. New York, NY: W.W. Norton.

Tronick, E. and DiCorcia, J. (2015) 'The everyday stress resilience hypothesis: A reparatory sensitivity and the development of coping and resilience.' *Children Australia*, 40, 2, 124–138. doi:10.1017/cha.2015.11.

Turner-Halliday, F., Watson, N., Boyer, N.R.S., Boyd, K.A. and Minnis, H. (2014) 'The feasibility of a randomised controlled trial of dyadic developmental psychotherapy.' *BMC Psychiatry*, 14, 347.

van der Kolk, B. (2005) 'Developmental trauma disorder: Towards a rational diagnosis for children with complex trauma histories.' *Psychiatric Annals*, 5, 401–440.

Vygotsky, L.S. (1978) *Mind in Society: The Development of Higher Psychological Processes*. Cambridge, MA: Harvard University Press.

Subject Index

Author Index